100 YEARS OF

FLAT TRACK RACING

THE BARBARA
FRITCHIE CLASSIC

FREDERICK
MARYLAND

Ted Ellis

FREDERICK
FAIRGROUNDS
½ MILE TRACK

MOTORCYCLE

PURSE OF
$3,000.00

RACES

SATURDAY, JULY 4

Races Start 2:30 P.M. - Time Trials 1 P.M.
Admission to Grounds & Grandstand
ADMISSION INCLUDES PROGRAM
Adults $7 Advance $8 At Gate
Children Under 12 Years $2.00
FREE PARKING RAIN DATE JULY 5
Promoted For Charity By
FREDERICK LIONS CLUB

1982 Poster courtesy of Dick Basford

iv

Introduction

There are instantly recognized names in the motorsport world. Isle of Mann, Le Mans, Indianapolis, Daytona, Pike's Peak, Ulster, Macau, Bonneville… Not so recognizable is Frederick. The Barbara Fritchie Classic, The Fritchie, the BFC, Frederick Maryland, or as one young rider was over-heard describing it, *"We're going to some big race on the 4th of July in Maryland."*

Regardless what you call it, it is an event you should know more about. It is an event with a history that will surprise most. It is a race that has quietly gone on, decade after decade with little notice. The history of flat track motorcycle racing, as I have discovered while researching this book, is itself largely neglected. There is little writing that goes into much detail about the general racing during the earliest days of the sport. Most which do exist are more about a specific person or event. In dozens of websites headlined *"Motorcycle racing history,"* there is precious little *"history"* for flat track prior to World War II.

By that time, motorcycle racing was already in its second or third generation and nearing half a century in age, Yet, there is little information on how it got there. In North America at least, the history of dirt track racing is the history of motorcycle racing, almost until the 21st century.

Board track racing has been the recipient of considerable interest in recent years and every bit of it is warranted. However, most of those fascinated by motordrome and (wooden) speedway racing overlook that throughout the same period, the same men, often on the same machines, were racing on much more numerous dirt tracks throughout this country.

At any one time there were only about 20 board tracks operating, but almost every county fairground in America had a half-mile or longer dirt track. Today the board tracks are all gone but we are still racing on dirt tracks. In Frederick, we're still racing on *the same dirt track* where the lords of the boards raced during the roaring 20's. While there were older races, this one is still running without appreciable interruption on the very same track where the pioneers of the sport raced over one-hundred years ago.

I have been a fan of this race and dirt track racing in general for close to 50-years. Yet, what I uncovered surprised me. The race's history has just been quietly lying there. Patiently waiting. Frederick Maryland, rather than being a part of the evolution of the sport, has been almost frozen in time. A living fossil. A surviving example of what this sport came from. What it was through the years.

In racing circles, few places on earth can compare to the timelessness of the Frederick ½ mile. The sport today is quite different from its origins in various ways. While we cannot relive the past, ignoring it is a disservice to all those who brought us to where we are today.

Motorcycle racing in Frederick began before motorcycle racing became a sport. The first racing at Frederick, just as at a thousand other cities around the world, began as an impromptu exhibition. A presentation of an odd, new, previously unseen machine, and a *"demonstration of its lightning speed"* to quote The Frederick News report in July 1900.

This is how it began. This is how it progressed. It is a story repeated at tracks across the country. The archival news stories from Frederick are essentially repeated in papers from New York to Tampa, Boston to Kansas City, Chicago to Los Angeles. Frederick Maryland may not be where it *first* began, but it is arguably the last place where it is *still* being done ever since that beginning.

The Fritchie is more than a race. On July 5, 1919 it served as the city's official welcome home celebration for World War-I veterans. For decades, the privately sponsored race was the community's *only* Independence Day celebration. It filled the void while city finances during and after the great depression could not support public festivities. One of the largest Barbara Fritchie crowds drawing over 7,500 fans, was the first post-WW-II race in 1947. The Fritchie was the largest individual fundraiser for Frederick charities for half a century. This race fed the unprecedented popularity of motorcycling from the 1960's through the 1990's as the largest American born generation in history lived out their youth.

This is more than a motorcycle race, this is history. Racing history, Frederick history and *American history*. It is a story that deserves to be known and told and here, in Frederick, unlike most of the places where the same events unfolded, it has miraculously survived to be told. More correctly, more amazingly, you can still experience it in Frederick.

One of the more difficult challenges I faced was the wealth of material that had to be left out. I wish I could have included every photo and every word of every story. All the information about what happened at every race. All the things that have been impacted and influenced by this race and those involved with it over more than 100 years. Especially, I wish I could list every name. This easily overlooked regional race has a reach far beyond the realization of even those of us who thought we knew about it.

Some sources left me in awe, like holding a 1990 photo in my hand that I knew almost nothing about while reading Geo Roeder's emailed description of that very scene in clear detail. It was George's first Fritchie and he described the general setting of the scene and everyone in it… without knowing I had a photo of what he was telling me about. George's recollections and the picture had both amazingly come into my possession by email *from different people* on the same day.

Or there is R.L. Lyons, rattling off numbers and names of riders and anecdotal stories about events in 1947, 1950 or 1996 as if it were yesterday. I have a photo of the BFC crowd taken 45 years ago with my best friend and I among those leaning on the fence that summer before our senior year at high school. I randomly discovered that photo on the web eight years ago but knew no more about it…until discovering that one of the people I was interviewing was the photographer who captured that scene in 1975. I have not sought out the story of this race. It has sought me.

I have done my best to preserve this history with as few blank spaces as possible. The photos are small and fuzzy, and all converted to B&W to keep this book affordable. It is the photos that make it real. I am convinced that with a few minutes of adjustment, if any of those racers or fans from the beginning years magically appeared at the track today, they would fit right in. From 1919 rider Bruce Shafer to 2019 rider Grant Shafer, racers come, and racers go, but for as long as there are motorcycles, *motorcycle racing* will exist.

The act of *operating* a motorcycle is a simple mechanical skill. Anyone can learn to do it. The *attraction* of riding a motorcycle is emotional though. It is nothing like driving a car. It is more than simple transportation. The world is viewed differently. You see *yourself* differently. You are exposed and vulnerable. A motorcycle either reinforces self-confidence, or it confirms a lack of it. The following excerpt will resonate with anyone who has ever had the motorcycle bug. For those who have not, it may serve to confirm your suspicions that we are truly insane.

"THEN THERE WERE MOTORCYCLES. I LEARNED TO RIDE ONE IN TALLAHASSEE WHEN I WAS ABOUT 14 OR 15. ... TALLAHASSEE WAS FULL OF HILLS, AND I LOVED RACING UP AND DOWN 'EM, SOMETIMES TRAILING MY FRIEND OR RIDING NEXT TO HIM, SO I COULD HEAR THE SOUND OF THE EXHAUST AND MAKE SURE TO FOLLOW CLOSELY AND YET NOT TOO CLOSELY. I KNOW IT SOUNDS STRANGE — *A BLIND TEENAGER BUZZIN' ROUND ON A MOTORCYCLE* — BUT I LIKED THAT; THAT WAS ME. I HAD ALWAYS BEEN NERVY, AND I ALWAYS HAD A LOT OF FAITH IN MY ABILITY NOT TO BREAK MY NECK." – Ray Charles, from "Brother Ray: Ray Charles' Own Story"

Contents

PROFESSIONAL
MOTORCYCLE RACES

FREDERICK FAIRGROUNDS

MONDAY, JULY 4

Time Trials Begin 12:15   Races 2:00 P. M.

DELPHEY BROS. PROMOTERS   A.M.A. SANCTION

REPRODUCTION POSTER, 1939

x

Gratitude

Every racer who has ever stood on the winner's podium and rattled off the names of his or her sponsors knows this expression of thanks is not to be taken lightly.

This is my thank you to those who have made this project possible. These are _my_ sponsors. Those who have given something money cannot buy. Their knowledge. Their confidence. Their friendship. They have welcomed me into their homes, businesses, and pits. They have endured my emails and phone calls. They have given freely of their time and shared private memories. They have provided irreplaceable photos, records, and memorabilia to be copied and shared with you the reader. These are the people who truly wrote this book. I just put the bits and pieces in one place. Every memory, every photo, every word, whether included or not has contributed to this book. My only regret is that I could not share them all. Thank you, every single person who has contributed to this journey.

Richard Lyons attended this race during many of its milestones since 1947. He provided firsthand insight. The incredible connection between the past and the present is epitomized by Richard who amazingly, has witnessed much of it firsthand. He is a master link that holds both ends of the history chain together and I am indebted to his willingness to help.

First and foremost, I thank my wife and family for putting up with me throughout this process. Thank you to; Frederick News-Post who has helped on so many levels of this journey, Richard, Sharon, Ian and the entire Riley family, Maryland Asst. Climatologist Phil Stratton who confirmed historical rain outs, Heritage Frederick and Anita Hoffman and Larry Moore, Bill Jackson and the Harley-Davidson archives, David Sites, Bert Sumner, Bob Herrick, Richard Lyons, Betsie Handley, The Stockton Sentinel, Mike Sponseller, Dick Basford, John Cannon, Craig Shipp, Google Maps, Curtis Fisk, Bill Snyder, Royal Sherbet, Ryan Stewart, R.C Jones, Howie Zechner, all the riders and stakeholders who selflessly gave their time and memories and to so many, many more who assisted in and supported this project. Thank you, one and all.

This book is dedicated to the memory and accomplishments of J. Paul Delphey, his brothers and all their descendants.

J. Paul and Clarence Delphey outside the shop with their dogs after a successful raccoon hunting season.

The author does not warrant any records in this book as a legal declaration.

BFC posters after 2007 are all the creations of *Access Media Lab*, Middletown, Maryland and reproduced by permission for this book. Further use requires the permission of Access Media Lab.

The author is not legally nor financially associated with, nor has he been compensated or directed by, the Barbara Fritchie Classic, or Frederick Fairgrounds. All opinions stated, are solely those of the author.

Most of the photos appearing herein are either my own or reproduced with permission of the owner. Some are in the public domain.

I have not been able to identify the source of some archival illustrations whose value in explaining the history was deemed necessary for inclusion. All have been obtained from public sources where proper citation was lacking and while sought out, the owner could not be ascertained. Where identification could not be made, the illustration has been manipulated (usually tightly cropped) to avoid impacting the original.

Despite any minor commercial value it may attain, this book was conceived for and is being offered, primarily for its informative, educational, and historical significance to the Frederick Maryland *and* Motorcycle Racing communities.

Barbara Fritchie Classic July 4th, 1920's, 1970's & 2020's

Barbara Fritchie

The name of the Barbara Fritchie Classic motorcycle race is a mystery to most. Who was Barbara Fritchie and why is the race named for her?

Barb was not associated with motorcycles at all. In fact, a motorcycle roaring around the fairground track in her hometown of Frederick Maryland would have been as foreign and frightening to Barbara Fritchie as a UFO descending from the heavens, and Barb didn't scare easily!

Barbara Hauer was born in Lancaster county Pennsylvania ten years before the declaration of independence was written. Her family, like many from that area, migrated to Maryland and in 1806, when Barb was 39-years old, she married John Fritchie, a glove maker in Frederick.

The Fritchie's lived in a modest, but typical for the period house on West Patrick street next to the bridge over Carroll Creek, which meanders through the city from west to east. The Fritchie's had no children and John died in 1849 leaving then 83-year-old Barbara to live alone in the little house beside the creek. As a well-known and highly respected citizen of Frederick, Barbara Fritchie lived a long and fruitful life. Mrs. Fritchie's national fame would come for a storied event in September 1862, only three months before her passing, while the American Civil War raged on in her beloved country.

Maryland was considered a southern state. Slavery was legal and many Marylanders held southern sympathies. President Lincoln suspended the state's legislature – to prevent them from voting to secede – and placed the state under martial law. There were violent riots in Baltimore by confederate sympathizers and the union army massed in and around Washington city to protect the president, congress and the nation's capital.

It was this situation that led confederate General Robert Lee to invade the state just west of Washington in September 1862. Several small-scale skirmishes took place, but most of the union army remained ensconced around Washington, preparing defenses for an attack while Lee's confederate army spread out to occupy most of the western half of the state.

Expecting a citizenry that would welcome them as liberators, here in *western* Maryland, Lee instead encountered small farmers and rural villagers who overwhelmingly retained allegiance to the federal government. Countless residents, like Barbara Fritchie, were descendants of German immigrants. They were independent, self-reliant and deeply religious. While not fervent abolitionists like many of those farther north, for the most part, these Marylanders did not engage in slavery. Certainly not on the scale of their eastern Maryland counterparts. The confederate occupation was relatively peaceful, but certainly not very well received.

So it was that on a late summer day as a column of the confederate army was moving west through Frederick, they were confronted by a frail but feisty 96-year-old lady holding an American flag and hurling insults at the southern soldiers.

That old lady of course, was Barbara Fritchie. Or at least, that's the story behind the legend.

Source: Woman's Work in the Civil War: a Record of Heroism, Patriotism and Patience (1867) page 10.

More than a year later, in October 1863 "The Atlantic Monthly" magazine published a poem named Barbara Frietchie written by John Greenleaf Whittier and the story has been a proud part of Frederick lore ever since.

Barbara Frietchie

BY JOHN GREENLEAF WHITTIER

Up from the meadows rich with corn,

Clear in the cool September morn,

The clustered spires of Frederick stand

Green-walled by the hills of Maryland.

Round about them orchards sweep,

Apple- and peach-tree fruited deep,

Fair as a garden of the Lord

To the eyes of the famished rebel horde,

On that pleasant morn of the early fall

When Lee marched over the mountain wall, —

Over the mountains winding down,

Horse and foot, into Frederick town.

Forty flags with their silver stars,

FORTY FLAGS WITH THEIR CRIMSON BARS,

FLAPPED IN THE MORNING WIND: THE SUN
OF NOON LOOKED DOWN AND SAW NOT ONE.
UP ROSE OLD BARBARA FRIETCHIE THEN,
BOWED WITH HER FOURSCORE YEARS AND TEN;

BRAVEST OF ALL IN FREDERICK TOWN,
SHE TOOK UP THE FLAG THE MEN HAULED DOWN;

IN HER ATTIC WINDOW THE STAFF SHE SET,
TO SHOW THAT ONE HEART WAS LOYAL YET.

UP THE STREET CAME THE REBEL TREAD,
STONEWALL JACKSON RIDING AHEAD.

UNDER HIS SLOUCHED HAT LEFT AND RIGHT
HE GLANCED: THE OLD FLAG MET HIS SIGHT.

"HALT!"— THE DUST-BROWN RANKS STOOD FAST.
"FIRE!"— OUT BLAZED THE RIFLE-BLAST.

IT SHIVERED THE WINDOW, PANE AND SASH;
IT RENT THE BANNER WITH SEAM AND GASH.
QUICK, AS IT FELL, FROM THE BROKEN STAFF
DAME BARBARA SNATCHED THE SILKEN SCARF;

She leaned far out on the windowsill,

And shook it forth with a royal will.

"Shoot, if you must, this old gray head,

But spare your country's flag," she said.

A shade of sadness, a blush of shame,

Over the face of the leader came;

The nobler nature within him stirred

To life at that woman's deed and word:

"Who touches a hair of yon gray head

Dies like a dog! March on!" he said.

All day long through Frederick street

Sounded the tread of marching feet:

All day long that free flag tost

Over the heads of the rebel host.

Ever its torn folds rose and fell

On the loyal winds that loved it well;

And through the hill-gaps sunset light

Shone over it with a warm good night.

BARBARA FRIETCHIE'S WORK IS O'ER,

AND THE REBEL RIDES ON HIS RAIDS NO MORE.

HONOR TO HER! AND LET A TEAR

FALL, FOR HER SAKE, ON STONEWALL'S BIER.

OVER BARBARA FRIETCHIE'S GRAVE

FLAG OF FREEDOM AND UNION, WAVE!

PEACE AND ORDER AND BEAUTY DRAW

ROUND THY SYMBOL OF LIGHT AND LAW;

AND EVER THE STARS ABOVE LOOK DOWN

ON THY STARS BELOW IN FREDERICK TOWN!

So now you know who Barbara Fritchie was and why this race, synonymous with Barbara's beloved hometown, is named forever in her honor. The race is held on July 4th Independence Day, to honor her devotion to country and it provides men and women the chance to demonstrate their bravery for all to see as they challenge each other, and the fairground track. Each one of them seeking to become like Barbara, "*stars of Fredericktown!*"

Barbara Fritchie never saw a motorcycle, but I like to think she'd be honored by the symbolism.

8

How

Competition pre-dates history. We are told that originally it was just the struggle to survive. Man, challenging nature to acquire enough food and shelter for him and his loved ones. Then, more than 300,000 years ago, tool making emerged. The use and improvement of those tools equated to being even better able to survive. Making the coolest spear or being the best spear thrower in the valley won things a lot more important than a trophy and a tee shirt!

This tendency to improve and be the best would evolve along with mankind. At some point it transformed from a question of survival to the less critical relevance of sport. Horse racing, sometimes called "*the sport of kings*" was the sport of the wealthy and famous from early in our history but held the attention of everyone when races were staged.

Bicycles and bicycle racing were wildly popular at the turn of the 20th century. So much so that an article in The Frederick News on July 1, 1897 tells that even the paper had become so caught up in the fad that *The News* offices had become a bicycle shop. "*Call at The News office and be equipped with a wheel... or with anything you need in the way of bicycle supplies.*" Bicycle races, bicycle parades and bicycle tours were being held regularly by the time motorcycles came onto the scene. As we will see later, it was from bicycle racing that motorcycle racing first emerged in Frederick.

Some of the earliest bicycle and motorcycle races were held on public roads but that quickly proved troublesome while the roads were still being used by the public. A scathing letter published in *The News* in 1898 denounced such (bicycle) road races as dangerous and bothersome. Few roads could be closed for sport, but when the races were moved to the local horse racing track, not only was it safer for both public and racers, but easier for the promoter to control access and collect entry fees! The attraction of track racing was simple convenience. Spectators as well as judges could witness the entire race from one convenient location. Essentially every county seat town in America had a fairground and almost every one of them included a racetrack.

Racing and all competition are still evolving today, but like that cool spear 300,000 years-ago, it is still all about being better than everyone else. Having an edge, whether it is an equipment advantage or superior personal abilities. It is still all about being the best.

Bicycle Repairing.

I have added to my Gunsmith business a Bicycle Repair Shop, where only the best material will be used, the charges moderate and best of workmanship. Bicycles Beautifully Enameled (baked enamel) and Ornamented. Call and see samples of Vulcanizing, Bronzing, &c. Nothing but the best of work will be done at my shop. Bicycle Sundries of all kinds always on hand. Repairing of Guns, and Door Locks. New Key and Bell Work in all its branches. Fire-proof Safe Work a specialty.

I ask a share of your patronage.

FRANK F. TYERYAR,

Practical Gunsmith,

11 EAST FOURTH STREET, FREDERICK

Telephone No. 265.

P. S.—Call up Phone 265 and I will send a trusty hand for your wheel, and after it is repaired I will return it to your home.

apl.14-'99-tf.

Oct. 6, 1899, The Frederick Citizen

In 1897 Harry Franklin Shipley and his partner, George Bopst opened what proved to be a very popular store in downtown Frederick. In 1909, Harry bought out his partner and Shipley & Bopst simply became H.F. Shipley. In 1915 Shipley opened a new, larger, more modern department store at 103-107 N. Market street.

It was in 1909, the same year Shipley bought out his partner that Harley-Davidson motor company first began to seek independent dealers for their motorcycles. It is thought that year, or soon afterward, may also be when the Shipley store became the Harley-Davidson motor company's Frederick outlet. Shipley is documented selling motorcycles by at least 1911 and Harleys by 1912. It would be three brothers from another Frederick family though who established the racing tradition that has spanned more than a century.

Reading Standard Company
306-340 Water Street, Reading, Pa.

H. F. Shipley Agent
105 N. Market St. - Frederick

A very dapper "Great Gatsby era" Harry Franklin Shipley

H. EBERT & SONS.

The Delphey brothers are purported to have begun buying repairing and reselling used motorcycles in 1914. They first opened shop in a now lost space on Chapel Alley between East 2nd and 3rd streets. Soon afterward they would move to the old Ebert's Carriage factory warehouse at 140 West Patrick street where they would remain in business until 1998. Some have claimed it was in 1918 that J. Paul Delphey took over Harry Shipley's Harley-Davidson franchise. The Harley-Davidson company records list the Delphey dealership, H-D #1810, as beginning on April 4, 1919. Histories often credit "*horseless carriages*" with displacing buggies, but at the old Ebert's shop it was *horseless horses* that took over.

```
Delphey's Sport Store            1810
140 West Patrick St.               3 5
Frederick, Maryland  21701          4
                          M

         J. Paul Delphey, Prop.
         4/4/19
         301 662 0071
```

Delphey dealership rolodex card from Harley-Davidson archives

WANTED
Any amount of second-hand Harley-Davidson motorcycles. Any model. Will pay highest cash price.
J. Paul Delphey

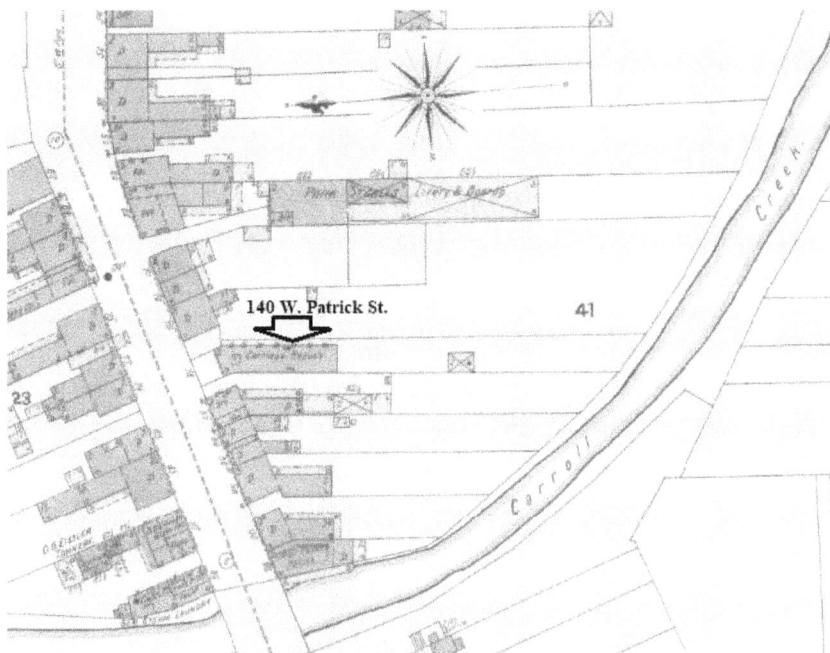

1904 Sanborn map showing (future) Delphey shop location.

There were three Delphey brothers, (involved in the business) The oldest was Joseph Paul, known to everyone as "J. Paul" or simply "Paul." Two years his younger was Clarence and five years younger than Clarence was the daring and dashing Chester. According to Chester's daughter, the boys began refurbishing and selling second-hand motorcycles in 1914.

Courtesy of Heritage Frederick

15

The preceding photo is dated 1919. It obviously shows numerous people with motorcycles. One of those machines has an odd, completely enclosed sidecar with a "TAXI" sign in the front. A notation on the photo claims it is *Frederick's first taxi, owned and operated by Clarence Delphey.* It is unknown if this was the first taxi. Advertisements in the Frederick papers before and after 1919 document several taxi operators in the city but do not mention what type vehicles they use. Judging from the picket fence and linier building (stables?) in the background, the photo appears to be at the fairgrounds. Perhaps on race day, Oct. 21, 1919.

Chester Delphey, and 63 other young Frederick men, were drafted on July 6, 1918 for service in the U.S. Army during World War-I. Chester, not surprisingly, was assigned as a motorcycle messenger attached to the 33rd heavy field artillery.

It was a duty that greatly improved military communication in the days before radios or other wireless communication. Near the front lines though, it could be an extremely dangerous assignment. When arriving at his duty station, Chester was warned by an experienced French Colonel that on the western front, motorcycle messengers were lost at a rate of one per day.

The motorcycle market back in The States had until now been crowded with dozens of brands and Harry Shipley's department store down the street from the Delphey home sold Harley-Davidson's and Reading Standards. The market as a whole was suffering a slump during and immediately after the war and whether Shipley planned to get out of the motorcycle business completely, or just picked the wrong brand to drop, Mr. Shipley's Harley-Davidson franchise had passed to Paul Delphey by the time the youngest Delphey brothers got home from the war.

Unknown U.S. Army dispatch rider in France, 1918. Courtesy Nat'l Archives

While all three were fervent motorcycle enthusiasts, Paul was the consummate businessman. Clarence was a top-notch mechanic. Chester, still stirred by youth and the excitement from the war, became an accomplished racer. It was a perfect combination for the period when a major newspaper once described motorcycle riders as, "*half daredevil, half mechanical genius.*" The business prospered following the end of the war. Chester won the ten-mile mid-Atlantic open championship at Baltimore in 1921 but later that year he had a bad crash receiving injuries to both ankles that ended his racing career. In 1925, Chester moved to Hagerstown, 25 miles west and opened a Harley shop there.

In the early 20th century hunting and fishing were probably engaged in by more American men than any other leisure activities. The Harley-Davidson brand embraced the outdoor sports and regularly used hunting and fishing motifs in their advertising. The Delphey's were passionate sportsmen and this rugged aspect of the Harley image was a natural for them. I still remember visits to the Delphey stores as a young boy. The many stuffed mountain goats, sheep, elk, deer, and moose heads and of course the giant grizzly bear. One of the brother's more interesting ventures was *The Harley-Davidson Racoon Hunting Club*" headquartered in the Delphey motorcycle shop on W. Patrick Street in Frederick.

1922 Delphey Ad

Racing though, had become a mainstay in the motorcycle industry from the very beginning. With close to 100 manufacturers just in the United States in 1920, the brand competition was intense. The motorcycle dealer's cliché of *"win on Saturday, sell on Monday"* was just as pertinent in the 1920's as at any other time in history.

J. Paul could easily show his customers how his motorcycles could enhance their hunting and fishing trips by providing almost horse-like access to those wild places where game and fish are found, but there remained a segment of the market he wanted to draw in… and Chester knew just where to do it.

The Great Frederick Fair was begun by the Frederick County Agricultural Society in 1853. It was originally held on the grounds of the Frederick (militia) Barracks on S. Market Street, now home to the Maryland School for the Deaf. Following the civil war in 1867, the Agricultural Society built a new fairground on East Patrick street in 1867. Originally the fairground had shooting galleries, bowling alleys facilities for bands and dancing, baseball fields and from the very beginning, a racetrack. The first horse races were held during the 1868 fair and were viewed by United States President, Ulysses S. Grant who had traveled from Washington to enjoy a day at the fair.

Period harness racing

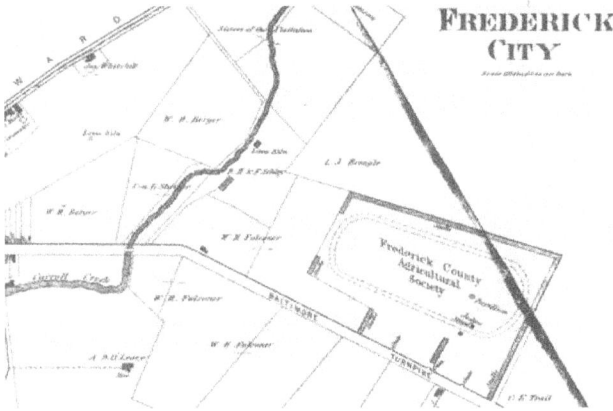

1873 Titus atlas map of Frederick, Maryland

The roads to the Frederick Fair will be lined with local motorcycle race enthusiasts today when one of the biggest race meets ever held in the state will be staged... The Indian Motorcycle Company has decided to send three of its best riders to compete. Among them will be Gene Walker, "Hard Luck" [Fred] Nixon... and Bill Dreyer.

Frederick News, October 21, 1919

Some of the first motorcycle races in Frederick were a feature at the annual county fair in October. In 1919 The Indian factory riders on factory works bikes were just coming off a big board track race at Sheepshead bay NY on Oct. 11. The Indian team had been

20

defeated on July 4 at Baltimore by Harley mounted Shrimp Burns and were directed to the upcoming Maryland race by their employers in Springfield. Their mid-October surprise entries came too late to arrange for the H-D team to come to Frederick and defend Maryland and no one else stood a chance against these guys and their factory bikes. As a result, the local Harley guys stayed away from the 1919 Frederick fair races rather than suffer sure defeat by the Indian pros.

There is a popular silent film of board track racing by Frantisek Marik, a Czech Indian dealer available for viewing today via the magic of the internet. Shot on Oct. 11, 1919 at Sheepshead Bay, some of those in the film would race ten days later at "*The Great Frederick Fair*." As a reminder of the eventual fate of all board tracks, the enormous two-mile speedway at Sheepshead Bay began being dismantled in November 1919, only weeks following the making of this famous film.

Screen shot from the Frantisek Marik board track racing film shot Oct. 11, 1919 at Sheepshead Bay, N.Y.

A brief news item in the Tuesday Aug. 24, 1920 Frederick News may lend some insight into how the original name of the Delphey Brother's *Classic* came into being.

"Interest in Motorcycle Classics"

" *Local motorcycle devotees are showing great interest in the big motorcycle road classics to be held in Marion, Ind., on Labor Day, Sept. 6… Mr. and Mrs. J. Paul Delphey of Frederick, will leave on Sunday for Marion…"*

An earlier article mentioned that Clarence Delphey, Marion Yinger, Lewis Hardy, Oscar Lidie, Joseph Foland and Charlie White had left on Thursday for Marion. Perhaps coincidentally – or not, just a few weeks earlier the August 1920 edition of *"the Harley-Davidson Enthusiast"* magazine contained a feature story about the Marion event including the following excerpt, *"...many of the local motorcycle riders are planning to tour over in a body to Marion on Labor Day. Perhaps right in your town, you'll find that some of the fellows are planning to do this."*

The Marion Indiana Classic, popularly known from the very beginning as *"the Cornfield Classic"* was first staged in 1919 as a road race. Following the war, it was an attempt to re-start the lagging motorcycle industry. The event was a resounding success, especially for the leading brands of Indian and Excelsior. It was neither Indian nor Excelsior that won the 1920 race though.

Kansan Ray Weishaar not only won the race on his Harley, he finished a full eighteen minutes ahead of the second-place finisher! Weishaar established Harley-Davidson history that day at Marion. While few know his name, every Harley rider and most people who have ever had a passing interest in motorcycles have seen his photo. Ray Weishaar is Harley-Davidson epitomized. It was that day, while surrounded by the cornfields of Marion Indiana that the nickname every Harley is associated with to this day was first coined.

It was the 1920 Marion Classic where Ray Weishaar shared a coke with his pet pig and took him for a victory lap, forever cementing the name *"hog"* to the Harley brand. Paul Delphey must have felt ten-feet tall witnessing the triumph. The long ride home over the rutted and potholed U.S.40 from Indianapolis to Frederick gave Paul plenty of time to think about how his own fledgling business could benefit from this accomplishment.

The Cornfield Classic was on Labor Day, the 1st Monday in September (Sept. 6th in 1920). The holiday made for good crowds. It is only speculation, but I think Paul Delphey was probably thinking through the general plans for the first Delphey Bros. Classic before he made it out of Ohio. Back home in Frederick though, riders were already preparing for the county fair races.

Ray Weishaar and the original HOG, Marion, Indiana, 1920

Used with permission of the Harley-Davidson Archives

By 1920 Motorcycle races had been a regular attraction at The Great Frederick Fair for at least a decade. A race report in the Frederick News during fair week, October 21, 1920 sheds more light on the Delphey brother's devotion to racing. This year, for unknown reasons, following the 1919 Indian domination, it appears it was the Indian riders who avoided the fair in 1920. The News gave the following results.

"In both motorcycle events the Harley-Davidson machine proved superior. The first race was a five-mile solo race and was won by Bruce Shafer of Hagerstown with Chick Gosnell, Frederick, second. Time was 6.38 seconds.

In the ten-mile side-car event, Paul Delphey and Oscar Lidie won in 13.31.   Chester Delphey and Robert Wright second, Clarence Little and Frank Smith of Hagerstown, third."

It was September 1920 that J. Paul and Chester Delphey, along with various others from the Frederick motorcycle community rode to Marion Indiana for the Cornfield Classic. It was two months later that the first (documented) involvement of the Delphey family is noted when an Armistice Day race was held at the Fairground, sponsored by Murray Brish's Indian dealership *and* Paul Delphey's Harley shop.

This joint sponsorship of the first Armistice Day race is something of a mystery. It was the only time Delphey and Brish collaborated. It remains unknown though if it was simply business, or perhaps a deliberate act to settle the apparent disagreement resulting from the Indians dominating the 1919 fair race and the Harley-Davidson's doing the same in 1920. Was the Armistice Day race a grudge match or simply a business deal that benefited both dealers by driving interest in motorcycles?

Delphey family oral history states that the Delphey's began the present race series in 1922. It has continued ever since, but that is only part of the story. I do not doubt Mr. Julian Delphey's account. However, to my knowledge, it was never recorded as *Paul, Chester or Clarence* Delphey told it.

J. Paul's son, Julian, was interviewed in the 1970's, and the story recorded for posterity, but Julian was five-years-old in 1922. His knowledge of the first race was surely provided to him by his father, J. Paul. There is no evidence whether the elder Delphey included (or neglected) some qualifying tidbit in the story explaining why 1922 was considered the first race. Other sources have put the first race as 1921. As seen above, J. Paul was involved in race promotion in 1920.

The answer is no less muddled than the question. Simply put, there is evidence to support the use of 1920, 1921 *or* 1922 as "*the first race.*" And those dates only count the involvement of the

Delphey family. If we were to age The Fritchie based on continual July 4th motorcycle racing, we could argue for at least 1919 when the WW-I veteran's welcome home race was held. Then there are the Frederick motorcycle races not related to Delphey's or July 4th or the same track, dating back to 1900!

SEE THE NEW INDIANS FOR 1915

Lightweight models   Three Speed gear   Indian Starter
Neutral Countershaft   New Magneto   Heavy Duty Clutch

SEE OUR DISPLAY AT
THE AUTO SHOW

BRISH BROS.
AGENTS

10 West Patrick Street - Frederick

Bill Harley, J. Paul Delphey and Walter Davidson on the W. Patrick St. bridge

(courtesy Frederick Magazine via Heritage Frederick)

Paul and his brothers had been so successful during the first two years of business, (allegedly selling enough motorcycles to fill a boxcar one year), that *"the silent grey fellows"* themselves stopped by one day to see what Delphey's secret was. William Harley and Walter Davidson are pictured here with J. Paul Delphey on the west Patrick Street bridge over Carrol Creek, four doors up from the shop. This honor of being personally recognized by *"**Harley**"* and *"**Davidson**"* is emphasized by the fact that in 1920 the motor company already had over 2,000 dealers in 67 countries around the world! While illegible in this photo, the octagonal sign above the front wheel of the motorcycle commemorates Barbara Fritchie, whose home was just at the end of the bridge.

MOTORCYCLE RACES
AMISTICE DAY, NOV.11, 1920
AT THE FAIR GROUNDS
2:30 O'Clock   Admission 50c

The Indian & Harley-Davidson motorcycle Dealers of Frederick are going to put on the best motorcycle races everheld on the local track. There are going to be four big events

TWO SIDECAR EVENTS and TWO SOLO EVENTS
ENTRIES OPEN TO FREDERICK AND ADJOINING COUNTIES ONLY

All entries must be made to Brish Bros. or J. Paul Delphey, both of Frederick

FALL IN LINE   EVERYBODY'S GOING

A year later, seemingly already adopting an annual race format, the very first motorcycle race solely promoted by the Delphey's was again held on Armistice Day, November 11. There is a brief article on October 30, 1921 in "The Frederick News" referring to *"up to date"* motorcycle races being held. This reference is explained by another article from race day, November 11, 1921, which notes that

26

the races being held in Frederick that day were sanctioned by the Motorcycle and Allied Trades Association, or M.&A.T.A.

Thus, while the Delphey's were clearly involved in the 1920 race and while this second Armistice Day race is clearly the "second annual" race, this 1921 event is both the first exclusive Delphey production *and* the first sanctioned race in Frederick. I believe these are the reasons J. Paul Delphey considered 1921 to be the first race.

I have not been successful in locating race results, but I did locate one news article from November 16, 1921 confirming there was a race held on November 11th.

MOTORCYCLE RACES!

TODAY
(ARMISTICE DAY)
Frederick Fair Grounds
2:45 P. M.
All Professionals
DON'T MISS IT!
Real Speed and Excitement
Over $300 in Prizes to Winners
J. Paul Delphey, Promotor

November 11, 1921

Motorcyclists Injured

While practicing to enter an event
during the motorcycle races at Frederick held Armistice Day, T.R.
Conner and Morris Fletcher, both of..

27

There were many young war veterans in the nation. It was only two years after the end of World War I, men accustomed to comradery and excitement. Undoubtedly there may have been soldiers of the Spanish American war and perhaps a few white bearded, veterans from the American Civil War in the stands that day sharing in the experience. Men such as Henry Nusbaum, a civil war vet who lived across the street from the fairgrounds in 1920. Henry was 80 years old and would continue to be active, even riding and caring for his own horse until 1925. Only a year or two before his death the octogenarian built a brick workshop himself, behind his house. As has become common to this race up to the present, Henry Nusbaum was a human link of the ages. A bridge between eras.

The Delphey brother's held races every year throughout the 1920's. The date however was not yet settled upon. As seen, they were first held on Armistice Day, November 11th. Near the end of the decade most Delphey races were on Decoration Day, May 30th. At least one race (a rain date) was held on Labor Day.

MOTORCYCLE RACES

FAIR GROUNDS

Saturday, May 30, 2:30 P.M.
Four Big Events, Including

10-MILE SIDE CAR NATIONAL CHAMPIONSHIP

WORLD'S BEST RIDERS
IN HOT COMPETITION

Auspices of Chester Delphey

BIG DAY FOR FREDERICK

Ball Game Morning;
Motorcycle Races Afternoon

July 4th was already a race day at the fairgrounds before the Delphey races began. I have not ascertained just when that race date was established, but only the inclusion of motorcycles in it. *"The Frederick Driving Club"*, the organization which held harness racing events at the fairground on Independence Day, began including

28

motorcycle races by at least 1909. The driving club gave up the July 4th date after the 1930 races and J. Paul Delphey adopted it as his race day when he resumed racing after the shock of the stock market crash in 1929. Thus, while the Delphey race did not begin until the 1920's, July 4th has been a motorcycle racing day at the Frederick fairgrounds since at least 1909 that we can be sure of. Then too, established motorcycle races were still held in Baltimore on that date, though no longer as popular thanks to Chester Delphey's 1921 results protest!

Holidays were then on (the same) specific dates annually, whenever that date fell on a Sunday, it would typically require moving the festivities to one of the other days of the week due to Maryland's blue laws. As well, there have been several rain outs, which were able to be rescheduled, so a few times through history The Fritchie has been on seemingly odd dates. An article in the June 8, 1933 Frederick News, notes that year's July fourth race as the *"second annual Independence Day"* race. That would however be the second year Delphey's race was held on Independence Day!

We learn from the same article that the race coincides with, "the three-day National Motorcycle Rally, being held in Washington, July 2 and 3." That "gypsy tour" rally was taking place at Washington from at least 1920. The mention of a three-day event, but only two of those days scheduled for Washington, means the race was an integral part of the rally in 1933 at least. In previous years there is evidence that Delphey's (particularly Chester) sponsored races later in July despite Independence Day races being held by the driving club. While no mention is made of it in period reports, we might assume these mid-July races at Frederick were in conjunction with the Washington rally. The National Rally did not survive, but the race lives on.

"…a six-mile national championship and a five-mile class A open event for the president's cup. In addition, there will be seven other events. …The motorcycle National Rally is expected to attract motorcycle enthusiasts from within a thousand miles of the nation's capital for a parade that will be reviewed by President Roosevelt from the White House on July 2. The following day will be given over to sightseeing and the celebration will culminate with the races here on July 4th.

29

WITH THE HARLEY-DAVIDSON IN WASHINGTON, D. C.

By Dick Mansfield, Staff Cartoonist Wash. Times

Reprint from October 1920 *"Harley-Davidson Enthusiast"* magazine.

Used with permission of the Harley-Davidson Archives

While motorcycle racing began decades earlier, we remember the Barbara Fritchie Classic as beginning in 1921... or was it 1922? The embarrassing truth is that we really did not know for sure. As in every family, there are stories from the Delphey kin on the race's origins, but as is also far too frequent, the story was never recorded until the originator – J. Paul Delphey had long ago passed.

An article was written in 2005 by Frederick News Post's excellent sports correspondent, John Cannon. In the article, Julien Delphey seems to give yet another beginning date – 1923! Even at much less than eighty-seven years (Julien's age at the time) such distant memories are difficult to place precisely. Missing by a year or three is acceptable. However, the question remains, was any one of these dates correct. Was one recognized over others for reasons lost to us today?

We will never know the answer to any of these questions. I believe though, I have uncovered how this race became the Barbara Fritchie Classic we know and love today. How it evolved from not only several totally unrelated annual races established long before it, but how it evolved from several *very* related, but separate races to eventually become *this* race.

The various races taking place prior to 1920 have already been established in the chronology of this event. Today, even "**Delphey's**" the business, is almost erased from Frederick's consciousness. It is difficult to envision the influence that business and *that family* once held in Frederick. This was the period before big box, one-stop stores, malls, or even shopping centers. It was the height of the era of personal service. Delphey's Sport Store was not just a motorcycle shop, it was a Frederick icon. In fact, after beginning life as a motorcycle shop, Delphey's is best remembered as an all-around sporting goods store. One of the anchor stores of the downtown Frederick shopping district. In the pre-shopping center age, Delphey's was the western end of the shopping district with satellite stores in nearby Hagerstown (1924) and Brunswick (1927).

As we have already seen, the first race any Delphey's were involved in promoting was the November 11, 1920 Indian vs. Harley race. The following Armistice Day (Nov. 11) J. Paul Delphey solely sponsored what can arguably be termed "*the second race.*" Paul Delphey took this event to the next level though by obtaining M&ATA sanctioning, encouraging riders to participate, and generally trying to make it a professionally promoted event. There were still motorcycle races being held by the county fair in October, and the Driving Club in their fourth of July races. Other organizations periodically held motorcycle races more-or-less informally and with little seeming organization or coordination.

The next summer, after the Driving Club's fourth of July races, Paul's youngest brother Chester promoted a race by himself on July 22, 1922. Chester had been competing in professional races for several years and on July 4, 1921 Chester won the five-mile Mid-Atlantic Championship (sidecar) race at Baltimore. A rowdy incident associated with the ten-mile event and Chester's performance in it, may possibly have something to do with Frederick's long enduring July 4th race date. In that 1921 Ten-mile race, Delphey grabbed the hole shot and held the lead throughout the event with Bill Minnick close behind. At the end of the race however, rather than awarding Chester the trophy, Maryland Motorcycle Club referee, Frank Boyd disqualified Chester and his hack rider, Oscar Lidie because Lidie had used what would later become *THE* tactic of racing sidecar riders up to the present. Oscar hung his body well out of the compartment to assist in balancing and counterbalancing the rig around the corners. This new tactic, while not specifically prohibited by the rules, was deemed inappropriate by Boyd.

Chester had a lot of friends in the grandstands that day. Many more had been so enthralled by Lidie's daredevil performance they joined in when Chester and his sympathizers stormed the official's stand. The Baltimore Sun newspaper, perhaps over sensationalizing it just a bit, credited several Maryland State Police motorcycle troopers as all that prevented what was described as "a mob" from bringing bodily harm to the officials in what the paper described as a full-fledged riot. The incident created so much bad publicity in Baltimore there was discussion among city leaders about banning motorcycle racing all together. One result would be the elimination of one of the two Baltimore races. First the Decoration Day race was moved to Frederick. That race, promoted by J. Paul and his brother Chester, who had caused racing to become unpopular in Baltimore, would be moved to July 4th when the Independence Day date was as well eventually abandoned by the Baltimore promoter.

Three months after Chester's Baltimore riot, on September 22, 1921, Chester Delphey and Oscar Lidie were leading another 5-mile race at Winchester, Virginia, fifty-miles south of Frederick. Lidie would lean all his weight onto the bike through the corners, which lifted the hack's wheel through the turn. As they came out of turn two Oscar's sudden return to the sidecar caused the wheel to slam onto the track and the sidecar's axel broke. The Winchester paper noted that Lidie was thrown "a considerable distance," and the motorcycle high sided and cartwheeled down the backstretch, rudely spitting Chester to the outside of the track. Racetracks were not watered in 1921. The dust was blinding for those following and Chester and Oscar were leading the race. Miraculously, nobody hit either of them. Chester suffered two very severely injured ankles, and numerous cuts, scratches, and bruises. Oscar was rushed to the Winchester hospital unconscious, with everyone fearing the worst. He had numerous bloody cuts and scratches about his face and back and severe bruises over most of his body but amazingly, neither man suffered either (obvious) broken bones or internal injuries.

TWO INJURED IN VIRGINIA RACES

Chester Delphey and Oscar Lidie make narrow escape From Death!

Sept. 23, 1921 Frederick Post headline

Chester took the 1921 Winchester crash as his cue to give up racing – as a rider. Chester was well connected in racing circles and as evidenced by the Baltimore riot, he was well thought of as well and he went full force into promoting.

Chester Delphey's July 22, 1922 race was advertised with a purse of $490 (equal to $7,500 in 2020). With other competing races still offering new tires and tubes as 2nd and 3rd place prizes, this appears to be an earnest move toward genuine professional race promotion. Chester and J. Paul's clear attempts to legitimize both motorcycle racing and motorcycle *racers*, I believe is what genuinely spawned this event we know today as the Barbara Fritchie Classic. But these guys were also part of the first efforts to take motorcycle racing from the manufacturer's sideshow it had largely become and put it on track to eventual transition into the Grand National Championship, focused on the skills of the riders and their mechanics rather than manufacturers and their deep pockets and unlimited R&D capabilities.

33

MOTORCYCLE RACES

Frederick Fair Grounds

Saturday, May 19th.

IF YOU LIKE SPEED
DON'T MISS THIS.

2.45 P. M.

1923 race ad

There was no Armistice Day race in 1922. In May 1923 we again find Chester promoting a big race on Saturday May 19. He holds another race after the driving club July 4th races, on July 12, 1923. This 1923 event is the first noted at Frederick as a *"National Championship"* race. The list of entries for the July championship race proves this event was not just some contest between local farmers and telegram curriers. "Gene Walker,

Dynamite Scott, Tom Connor, Bill Minnick, Bill Woolon…" The pre-entries included some of the top factory riders in the country on both dirt and timber.

1924 is first announced in March in a joint press release by J. Paul and Chester Delphey. All later accounts only mention Chester though. 1924 is also the year Chester moved with his family twenty miles west to Hagerstown and opened a similar, but separate store there. Perhaps in an attempt to build a customer base, Chester then begins promoting various motorcycle racing events around Hagerstown.

This situation with the popular Decoration Day date and regular National Championship sanctioning became a regular event at Frederick. Spectators numbered into the thousands annually. Everything seemed poised for success as J. Paul and Chester welcomed everyone to the 1927 race.

1927 would mark a sort-of high point in Frederick motorcycle racing with Bill Minnick setting a world record that still stands today. A very strange thing happens after that famous 1927 race though. Thoroughly searching all available records for the next several years fails to turn up any mention of motorcycle racing in Frederick. None! There is apparently something unrecorded taking place during this period as not only are the Delphey races missing, so are the always popular driving club and county Fair races. I checked the records for Frederick and those of all the surrounding areas for any mention and the record is completely blank for motorcycle racing at Frederick during these four years. There was a promoter from the Easton Pennsylvania area putting on auto and motorcycle races at the Hagerstown fairground but no mention of Frederick. And no mention of Delphey. Not J. Paul, Clarence or Chester at either city although advertisements show both stores were thriving during this period.

There are several stories about local pro racer Walter Stoddard. Stoddard, who was originally from Hagerstown, moved to Frederick to work in the Delphey shop. He became a Class A rider sponsored by Delphey's in 1929. Soon afterward, he was picked up as a Harley-Davidson factory rider. From this information we know the Delphey' still held an interest in racing. The non-resident promoters holding events at Hagerstown tells us there was still interest among the public. A brief item in the Frederick News on August 16, 1930 is the only clue. It appears in the **"do you remember?"** column. "…*when the Delphey Brothers staged motorcycle races annually at the Fairground… the races were discontinued about three years ago.*" Nothing indicates if the races were "discontinued" by the Delphey's, the fairground or perhaps the city. There is no indication

Chester caused another riot like the one that soured motorcycle racing's reputation in Baltimore.

At the very end of this mystery period, Chester begins promoting hill climbs near Hagerstown. In 1932, as though the missing years did not even exist, racing resumed at Frederick as big and popular and lavish as ever.

The 1932 Independence Day race included the previously typical National Championship events along with the extremely popular *National Champion,* Joe Petrali. A dozen or so other top pro racers joined Petrali and company and promised a great show. The race was scheduled for Saturday July 4th but was delayed by rain until Monday afternoon, July 6th. Mother nature would have something to say about that to and after conferring with the riders and the fairground officials, the Delphey's announced the race would be held the following Saturday. The day proved to be a good one, but unfortunately for the Delphey's, the crowd did not return. It was reported that the brothers lost $1,000 on the return of racing to Frederick. That is the equivalent of about $18,000 today! With spirits undampened they announced their plans for the next year's race while reporting the details of this one. Even the Great Frederick Fair races resumed in the 1930's, but the driving club would relinquish the Independence Day date they'd held for about twenty years.

Joe Petrali, 1931 H-D publicity photo

Used with permission of the Harley-Davidson Archives

This photo of Bill Minnick at the 1925 Labor Day races at the Laurel, Maryland board track is one of many early motorcycle racers pictured with an odd pet or mascot. Many have wondered about Bill Minnick's racoon for nearly a century. Where did he get it and why? One of Bill Minnick's main sponsors was J. Paul Delphey's Harley shop 35 miles from Laurel in Frederick, Maryland. While "unidentified" the man to the right of Bill Minnick in this photo bears a resemblance to Chester Delphey. One of Delphey's other projects was *"The Harley-Davidson Racoon Hunting Club."* The Delphey's kept large zoo-type cages behind the shop containing, among other animals, live racoons. Coincidence? Maybe, but we'll never know. Bill Minnick is also the guy who was awarded the win at Baltimore in 1921 causing a near riot when his friend Chester was DQ'd.

37

Motorcycle Races

(WORLD'S BEST RIDERS)

9 - BIG RACES - 9

INCLUDING

6 - MILE NATIONAL CHAMPIONSHIP

Frederick Fair Grounds

Wednesday, July 4th

ADMISSION 50c Plus Tax

FIRST RACE 2 P.M.

DELPHEY BROS., Promoters

1930's era advertising poster

PROFESSIONAL

MOTORCYCLE RACES

To avoid the rush at the gates, buy your tickets now on sale at J. Paul Delphey's, 140 West Patrick Street

FREDERICK, MD. (Fair Grounds) JULY 4th

ADMISSION $1.00

Including Grand Stand, Parking and Taxes

2:30 P. M. DELPHEY BROTHERS, PROMOTORS

1932 Ad

PROFESSIONAL

MOTORCYCLE RACES

FREDERICK FAIRGROUNDS

MONDAY, JULY 4

Time Trials Begin 12:15   Races 2:00 P. M.

DELPHEY BROS., PROMOTERS   AMA Sanction

1938 Ad

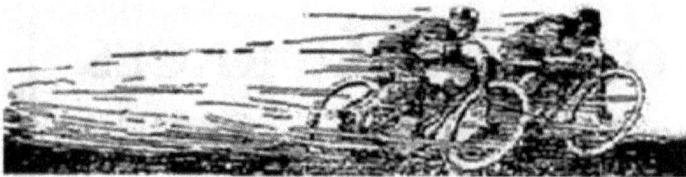

National Championship

Motorcycle

Races

Sat. Sept. 7

2:00 P. M.

FAIR GROUNDS

Frederick, Maryland

WORLD's BEST RIDERS

EXTRA ATTRACTION

**Flaming Board Wall
Crash With a Motorcycle**

<u>1935</u>

This 1935 poster for the races on Labor Day. Although originally scheduled for the fourth as usual, a week before the race it was announced the events would be pushed back to Labor Day. The flaming board wall act appears in various posters and ads all-around the area during that period. Suspected to be a local daredevil trying to make a questionable living during what would have been the depths of The Great Depression.

Motorcycle Races

FREDERICK, MD.

JULY 4 th

World's Best Riders

Time Trials 12 o'clock

Races 2:00 P. M.

10 - EVENTS - 10

Admission 50c Plus Tax

Free Parking

DELPHEY BROS.

Promotors

1940

Anyone involved with racing of any type is familiar with how the sport seems to exist in its own sometimes crazy little world. Somehow, racing had managed not only to come back and survive the Great Depression. It had arguably thrived during the 30's. The city even had to discontinue municipally sponsored celebrations for Independence Day and the Delphey Brothers motorcycle races, already being held that day, assumed the duties of Frederick's only fourth of July festivities for a decade and a half.

The news coming over the radio daily from Europe in the late thirties and early 1940's could not be ignored. So familiar had these things become to the American consciousness that an article in the local paper about Independence Day revelries in 1940 went so far as to compare the incessant crackle of fireworks and occasional louder explosions around the city to the sounds of war in Europe.

Everyone tried to go on. Racing temporarily continued despite the grim news and the bleak expectation that the States would once again, eventually be drawn into another overseas war. As 1941 turned into 1942 on the heels of the tragedy at Pearl Harbor, it became undeniably clear that the racing life would be swallowed up by world events which seemed to have spun out of control. Racing would be interrupted during the war, then it resumes, bigger, faster and more exciting than ever. Post-war racing, driven by the technological and manufacturing advances resulting from the war would launch a new era in the sport unequaled until the dawn of the computer age.

HOW IT CONTINUED

In the early 1950's, an older Paul Delphey had other interests that were taking more and more of his time and the store was turned over to his son Julian. The younger Delphey was a stalwart of the Frederick civic community, he played a leading role in the Frederick Lion's Club and suggested the club adopt the race as a fund-raising activity. Which they did. It was then that the name changed from The Delphey Brother's Classic to The Barbara Fritchie Classic. The Delphey's and their business continued to play a huge role in the annual event, but the burden of organizing and promoting the race was now on the members of the Lion's Club.

Perhaps coincidentally, the new namesake of the race, *Barbara Fritchie*, had lived 100 years earlier in a house, just a few doors away and within sight of the Delphey shop. Ironically, it is Delphey's iconic Frederick sports store that no longer exists today. The shop was razed about 2005 to make space for a public parking deck.

The Delphey's had done well in the motorcycle business, but they had diversified their company early, becoming a full-service sporting goods store. In addition to motorcycles, the ever-expanding store on West Patrick street sold guns, boats, Evinrude outboard motors, every imaginable type of hunting and fishing gear as well as equipment for team sports. Additionally, Delphey's store became the Frederick office for the Maryland Motor Vehicle Administration. It was where that thousands got their first driver's license. Chester Delphey's store in Hagerstown also served as the MVA office there.

By 1970 Julian Delphey had been elected as a popular member of the Maryland legislature. His store had more than enough to sustain it with the sporting goods business and Harley-Davidson motorcycles were experiencing somewhat of a slump. Then on October 9th, 1976, Frederick was struck with more than 7 ½ inches of rain in a 16-hour period following several weeks of wet weather. The result was a flash flood that did millions of dollars in damage to downtown Frederick. At 10:00 AM that morning, as Carrol Creek engulfed the entire downtown region, a first-floor door in the water surrounded Delphey building gave way, unleashing a forty-inch wall of water through the store. It would be several hours before the flooding abated and weeks before the mess was cleaned up. Loses far exceeded insurance coverage for most of those affected in Frederick. In the aftermath of this unexpected disaster, for the first time in fifty-eight years, the Delphey family considered the possibility of not being in the motorcycle business.

The Fritchie marched on through what many consider the golden years of flat track racing, the 1970's and 80's. The Frederick track, due to unchangeable handicaps, is slightly too narrow to qualify for a modern era Grand National Championship race, but through this period, into the early 2000's, The Fritchie was sanctioned under the AMA Hot Shoe series. The organizers tried several different surface preparations in attempts to improve the track and at one time it was graded all the way down to the clay.

While the track became *very* fast, it was too fast for the limited width. For several years, due to safety concerns, the track was restricted by AMA racing officials to bikes no more powerful than 505cc.

PULLED FROM THE BRINK - TWICE

In 2006 the workload compared to the revenue was becoming a burden to the Lions. Faced with the possibility of losing the event completely, Frederick road construction businessman Thomas Kline, at the encouragement of his grandfather, R.F. Kline, stepped in and assumed control of the race. The Lions continued to be involved and benefitted considerably, but the race was essentially under Kline's stewardship.

Thomas Kline applied his expertise in road construction aided by a cadre of Kline owned equipment and experienced operators to groom and maintain the fairgrounds track. For many years, the track prep crew were Kline employees using Kline equipment.

In the spring of 2014, it was discovered that a disconnect had taken place. Along with hundreds of others across the country, due to economic dynamics beyond anyone's control, the Kline's construction business was in trouble. There was no money to hold a race and by the time it became known, it looked like it might be too late to make it happen. It was that prospect that motivated another Frederick businessman to step up and take on the responsibilities for this race. Richard Riley called his wife Sharon at her day-job as an middle school teacher. He talked to his son's. Then he talked to his banker. So it is that Richard Riley became a reluctant and yet, very enthusiastic race promoter.

Of all those he consulted, probably the banker was the only one who thought he had lost his mind. The rest *knew* he was going to do this regardless the risks. They also knew that if anyone could make it work, Richard Riley could.

That day was May 18, 2014. It was only forty-seven days until race day. The AMA sanction had not yet been reserved. There was no working organization in place. No track equipment or operators and Richard Riley had never promoted a race himself, but like any Riley endeavor, he was not going to do it by himself. This was a family effort – the *whole* family! From Richard and Sharon down to their children *and grandchildren!* Everyone had a job… or four jobs to do.

Just like 1921, while dozens and dozens from the community make this race possible, the city's 100-year-old tradition is affectionately overseen by one civic minded Frederick motorcycle family. We've come full circle.

The Riley's are committed to seeing this race through the centennial for the sake of racing tradition. For the sake of Frederick. For the sake of all those like themselves for whom motorcycle racing is one of those emotional fascinations that you feel rather than watch or even do. It's something you flow with, rather than direct. Something that as attested to by Carl Hacker and many others, gives you the same feeling when you're 90 as it did at 20… or 10.

For many, racing – motorcycle racing - is a lot like love. For some, it is love. You need only to hear Richard Riley talking about racing, whether over the fairground's loudspeakers on race day, or just reminiscing in a corner of his shop on a slow day to know with certainty, this is *THE* man for the job.

ALL THE OTHERS…

It would be a huge disservice to hundreds of others to assume the preceding are the only people responsible for this race. There are and have been dozens and dozens of unnamed workers, most of them volunteers. There are track prep crews, corner flaggers, ticket sellers and those directing traffic. The designers and sellers of programs and tee shirts. Paramedics and all those who spend a day in the July sun placing hundreds of straw bales, then spend another day removing them. Those who phone or visit local businesses begging for financial sponsorship and especially all those businesses, clubs and individuals who answer that solicitation with donations. July 4th is always hot. It's an all-day job and there is no air conditioning at the track. There is precious little shade!

The people who go to this event and especially all those who have gone to it through 100 years of racing heritage, all of them, each and every one, deserves our thanks. There have been so many who have given so much to this event over the years. One who's name is fondly on the tongue of every veteran of Fritchie operations is a man named Charlie Main.

Charlie was totally devoted to his hometown of Frederick, Maryland. The list of community organizations to which he belonged – or founded – is second only to the many awards and accolades he received for volunteer service to the Frederick community. During much of his life Charlie held two or more civically responsible leadership positions at any particular time. For more than fifty-years he was a member of the Lion's Club where he never missed a meeting. He was a former commander of the Frederick state police detachment and from 1952 until 1978, chief of the Frederick Police Dept. A lawman during the 1970's might be expected to have an adversarial view of bikers, but Chief Main had that rare half-full rather than half-empty perspective. We can thank Charlie Main for the Fritchie coming through that period relatively unscathed as other communities took the easy approach of banning races when some incident among participants created distractions.

An incident concerning another Frederick mayor was brought up by Sharon Riley during a visit to Fredericktown Yamaha one afternoon. She related how her husband once learned late in the evening of a long-ago July 3rd that a Kline construction company employee who was supposed to be watering the track after sundown had instead gotten drunk and disappeared to get started on the long holiday weekend!

The July sun had baked the track as hard and dusty as the Sahara Desert and Richard Riley was livid. Sharon was becoming perturbed with him as he stormed through her kitchen while she tried to finish the next day's jumbo batch of potato salad. In desperation Richard called Frederick mayor Jim Grimes. Besides being mayor, Mr. Grimes also ran a commercial truck sales and service company. As it turned out, he had a small water truck on hand that could be used to prep the track. But there was a catch.

The water truck was a recent trade-in and it did not have reliable brakes! A motorcyclist himself, Mayor Grimes recognized the absolute need for watering the track but the smallish tanker would require a lot of trips and he could not allow Richard, or his partner in crime, local racer Donnie Smith, to drive a truck loaded with several tons of sloshing water *and no brakes*! It was getting late and the only answer was obvious to the devoted Mayor Grimes, he drove the truck himself. So it was that the mayor of Frederick watered the track from midnight until 4:00AM rather than jeopardize the race!

Such has been the dedication of generations of Frederick citizens who have gone far above and beyond to make sure this race continues. The vast majority, if not all of them, without expectation of recognition or public thanks. They did it for Frederick.

One group who have been an unsung boost to The Fritchie are the members of a well-known motorcycle club. Publicity is not something they seek, so I hope I am forgiven for mentioning them. Their annual pilgrimage to The Barbara Fritchie Classic though has been an unwavering and much appreciated boost to ticket sales since the 1970's.

Finally, one last overlooked booster in the survival of this race is the outstanding coverage afforded it by the Frederick News-Post. The News-Post has continued to give this race feature story status, thus attracting, and retaining interest by many who are otherwise disinterested in motorcycles. In an age when national AFT races come and go in some cities without non-motorcycle people even being aware it happened, correspondent John Cannon of the Frederick News-Post has annually reported on this event with all the detail given any other major story. The articles through the years have embraced The Fritchie not merely as a race, but as the Frederick heritage it is. That perception of the race is reflected in the race's community acceptance through a period when other races have suffered from a lack of community support. In compiling this book, I am indebted to the archival stories and advertisements found in the Frederick News-Post and the other Frederick papers that preceded it.

The Organizations

R.G Betts
Federation of American Motorcyclis

Through the years the races at Frederick have mostly been sanctioned events. For the unacquainted, there are two types of motorcycle races. Those sanctioned by the American Motorcyclist Association and those which are not. Unsanctioned meets are referred to as "outlaw races."

Sanctioned races afford the opportunity to earn AMA points and status. As well, when the riders show up, they know the universally enforced AMA rules will be in effect without any last-minute surprises or corner cutting, which might impact the safety of the event. The Barbara Fritchie however is older than the AMA!

On September 7th, 1903, three years after the first motorcycle race at Frederick, a group of motorcycle enthusiasts in the northeastern U.S. got together and formed the Federation of American Motorcyclists (FAM). The purpose of the organization was to standardize rules for competition and lobby government on behalf of motorcycle users. It was a grassroots organization conceived and run by motorcyclists. However, it was an all-volunteer organization and within a few years, the burden of their goals proved more than non-paid and unfunded activists could handle.

Another association took shape on November 15, 1916 when the Motorcycle and Allied Trades Association was formed by representatives of the various American motorcycle manufacturers. Realizing that cultivating and recruiting riders would benefit them all, the companies invested in the M&ATA both to address manufacturing as well as rider concerns. The M&ATA took the volunteer FAM under its wing and tried to re-energize the struggling rider association.

By 1918 America had entered WW-I and both industry and citizens were focused on that event. By the end of the war, the motorcycle industry, which had previously counted more than 100 brands just in the U.S., was in trouble. As interest waned even more, the FAM officially folded its tent and ceased to exist. Recognizing that the sport they relied on for bragging rights, innovative design and to draw interest was endangered by the absence of an overseeing authority, M&ATA stepped in to assume regulation of motorcycle racing.

In 1924 the M&ATA officially created a separate body which they named the American Motorcycle Association (a name they had unofficially used previously). While the AMA became the sanctioning body and were supposedly autonomous, they were none the less still owned and operated by the industry operated M&ATA. Both groups were under the direction of a single president.

E.C. Smith executive sec. AMA, 1928-1958

The all-powerful competition committee was made up of twenty-some odd representatives, each one in-turn an employee of one of the major manufacturers. These men with acute knowledge of the sport and its equipment were top authorities. Just the people you want making the technical decisions pertaining to the sport. They had one serious handicap though. As Ed Youngblood wrote in the Dick Mann biography, Mann of His Time, *"each one had a built-in conflict of interest."* This created a situation where, justified or not, some AMA rules would be rumored through the years to have been enacted for the unfair benefit of various brands. It's an accusation that has had a life of its own, especially after WW-II when only two U.S. makers remained (eventually to be one). Although the old committee staffing has been totally revamped years ago, the accusation still comes up in racing related conspiracy theories today.

The new 1924 AMA wasted no time in putting governing rules in place to protect the sport and establish themselves as *the* legitimate authority. Originally, only those employed by a manufacturer as a professional rider and mounted on factory provided bikes could compete for the *"National Championship"* title. These were the *Class-A* riders.

The 1920's were hard for the saturated motorcycle industry. Lesser brands began falling or being absorbed by larger manufacturers by mid-decade. Then, 1929 saw the historic stock market crash and overnight the nation descended into the Great Depression. By the early 1930's, there were only two brands left, Indian and Harley-Davidson. Rather than both companies continuing a mutually destructive head to head competition, something had to change.

Enter "Class-C" racing. It was a brilliant concept that aided both Indian *and* Harley equally, as well as (theoretically) any other manufacturer that may inter the market in the future. Very simply, it was the birth of sanctioned amateur racing. The birth of the privateer.

No longer would a special factory-built race machine be necessary to enter sanctioned competition. What would be required though, in an almost one-hundred eighty-degree turn, was that bikes be bought from regular dealer stock. Suddenly, anyone who could afford a motorcycle could race. And while the bike had to originate as a standard machine, modifying them for enhanced performance began almost simultaneous to the production model rule being adopted. The concept was an immediate and overwhelming success and entries at local and national races reflected the new ease with which one could become a motorcycle racer. It was so successful that special built race-only bikes, until 1930 the only equipment allowed, became *illegal* for competition in 1934!

The famous Joe Petrali retired from track racing in 1937, arguably near the peak of his career when he was 33 years old. Joe cited safety concerns due to the influx of amateurs in explaining his decision to walk away.

From 1934 until 2016, any manufacturer introducing a new bike for AMA (and later AFT) dirt track racing had to produce identical machines and make them, and parts for them, publicly available for purchase. The number made has varied through the years. The idea spurred not only racing but spectating, as non-racing motorcyclists could claim an even closer commonality to their on-track idols. Sometimes it went even farther.

It is class C competition that coined the *"run what you brung"* axiom. Competitors could ride their daily bike to the meet, remove the lights and brakes, and enter the race. Of course, this was more theory than regular practice, though there are plenty of oral histories of men who did just that. One, with his wife as a passenger, is claimed to have rode his Harley from Washington D.C to Daytona, Florida, competed in the 200-mile race and then he and his wife rode the same bike home.

There were other *"exceptions,"* whether official or not before the 2016 entry of the race-only, factory-owned, Indian FTR750's. In fact, the racing committee looked the other way almost from the very beginning. It's still disputed whether Indian was permitted to or simply cheated by entering a race-only engine in class C competition in 1939. That was the year five special "Big Base" Scout engines were produced. (the Big Base did not technically enter production until after the war) This was only five years after both manufacturers agreed to ban race only bikes. There have been similar contrivances of the class C rule throughout the history of flat track racing right up until the entry of the FTR. Most such incidents drawing the same old *"the AMA is biased toward…"* accusations whispered or yelled since 1924.

Only time can tell if the new (in 2019) Production Twins class in AFT competition, which again requires bikes to be built on publicly available engines, will have a similar effect as class C was intended to. With all the other expenses involved in racing today, while the Production Class may be more economical, there is nothing cheap about racing! It is certain though that if you and your wife ride your Production Twins bike to Daytona, chances are you're not going to be very competitive.

There are and have been a myriad of rules applying to who can compete. Who can compete with who. What they can ride and different types of tracks and the restrictions that designate the different types of tracks. All of which are subject to change from one year to the next. From the tires they ride on to the clothes they wear, to the fuel they burn, everything is under the control of the sanctioning body.

As the years went by, the AMA became increasingly independent of the M&ATA. As American motorcycle manufacturers dwindled to two, then one, AMA's ruling board became severely suspect. When non-U.S. brands were allowed to join via their U.S. importers, while not as easy to identify a suspect, speculations and accusations by those who felt slighted by rule changes once again renewed the old pastime of speculating on who was behind it and who stood to benefit. In place of the various old American brands, control of the racing committee was wildly rumored to be under "*The Iron Triangle*" of Harley, BSA & Triumph. While some decisions and rules appear awfully suspect even for a non-suspicious observer, development and advances did proceed despite the accusations or any genuine roadblocks put in place.

By the mid-1960's, the AMA and M&ATA had separate directors for the first time in history. In 1967 the old appointed racing committee was replaced by a "*Racing Congress*" made up of not only industry reps, but also representatives of the riders and especially, from each of the various regional districts across the country. For the first time since the FAM folded in 1919, the various stakeholders of the sport gained an equal voice in decision making and rather than handpicked appointees, the congress was *elected* by their peers.

The new AMA was just in time to reign over the golden age of flat track motorcycle racing. It was the era of the rise of the Honda RS750. The brief but memorable debut of the Yamaha TZ750 and two-stroke Yamaha's near monopoly on short track and TT events. The strengths of the Rotax and the brief domination then sudden demise of the BSA and Triumph triples… and the beginning of the 45-year reign of Harley-Davidson's XR750. In another change of the period, road racing, which had always been one of the five distinct disciplines of the Grand National Championship, was separated from the dirt track aspects of the sport in 1985.

Of course, when racing began in the nineteen-teens, road racing was a dirt surface event to. The 1933 emergence of (American style) TT racing was a sort of short dirt road-course in an easily observed, compact track format. Although some early tracks were exceptionally long. As paved racetracks became more prevalent though, road racing and dirt track slowly began to diverge. While it has been their dirt track background most cited by fans of the legendary American road racers of the last several decades, the dirty, dusty, blue collar atmosphere of dirt track only added to the gulf between it and road racing. A chasm that only grew as American road racing became more attached to European racing than to its dusty roots.

During this golden era, the *Grand National Championship* series truly became a totally different element from the regional, district and privately promoted races held by clubs and civic organizations around the country. While riders were free to run any AMA sanctioned event, the GNC increasingly developed its own cadre of highly skilled, elite riders. The popularity of the GNC, appeared to feed a resurgence of the sport, but it had started to become harder and harder to find local races where new riders develop their skills and above all else, where they develop their desires. In 1970, many cities had a track running weekly or at least monthly races. By 1980, such regular, season-long events were all but gone and if you wanted to race motorcycles, you had to travel.

A perfect storm of unforeseen elements descended on the sport. First, there were the increasing concerns for liability. Such an inherently dangerous activity combined with a previously unheard-of new-found propensity for personal injury claims during the same period caused promoters to begin shying away from racing. Next came the loss of tracks.

Until the second half of the 20th century just about every county fairground had a ½ mile or longer horse racing track. Hundreds of them doubled as motorcycle racing venues at least once a year. Horse racing though was in even more trouble than motorcycle racing and both saddle and harness racing events became more and more scarce. In the absence of horses, the even less politically correct motorcycle races soon fell out of favor with fair boards and city councils. Simultaneously, real estate values began creeping up. 20 – 50-acre fairgrounds situated on prime real estate became too much of a temptation for many fair boards. In some cases not only the races but even the county fair, was left homeless.

Of those that remained, most were within cities, and nearby residents were becoming less and less accepting of the noise and dust of a motorcycle race, even if it was only once a year. Finally, there was a brand-new invader from Europe – motocross.

Motocross tracks (in the early days) were often no more than a very rough scrambles track over natural terrain. The land where they were best suited was often unfit for much else. In fact, the rougher, bumpier, muddier and steeper the land, the better it was for a MX track! These same qualities made the land cheap unlike the wide level expanse of a flat track racing ground. Motocross tracks were typically out of town, so the neighbors didn't complain. There was little to no maintenance, unlike flat tracks which must be continually groomed. A motocross bike could be ridden out the showroom door and be competitive at the local level, while despite class C rules, flat track had become as much a contest of special equipment as it was racing skills. Finally, motocross had become the *"in thing"* for young people. New riders became fewer and fewer on the flat track circuits. Some rode both, but if there was a schedule conflict, moto almost always won. As many have explained it, for those racing purely for fun, they could spend four times as long actually riding at a Motocross event compared to a flat track race. And flat track began feeling the squeeze.

In 1997 the AMA racing congress announced the launch of the AMA *Hot Shoe Series*. This would be an organized national race series, totally separate from the elite Grand National Championship. Some races were held on the same tracks, but not together. The Hot Shoe series was a completely new entity intended to compliment rather than compete with GNC racing. The idea was to attract those amateur and part-time racers who were not ready or able to follow the GNC circuit. It was an attempt to salvage what tracks and promoters were left and give the riders who were still interested a prestigious, titled event to compete in just like the GNC, but on a more affordable level. The interstate highway system was then in place enabling a part-time racer to travel half the country, race on

Saturday and still be back at work Monday morning. Few riders made every race, which often balanced the points chase, allowing a rider to remain in contention without the sacrifice and expense of running the full schedule. It was hoped it would renew interest at the grassroots level to feed a new, continuing crop of up and comers toward the GNC. In part at least, it worked. It did breathe new life into many struggling races and The Barbara Fritchie Classic was one of them.

Other ideas would come and go. Some successful, others not so much but one other factor that nobody saw coming was the maturing of the baby boom generation. Those same young people who craved the excitement of motorcycles in the 1970's, were growing up. They were settling down to careers and families and worrying more about making money than having fun. The largest American born generation in history who had fueled the golden era of the sport from

GOLD CUP SERIES

PROFESSIONAL MOTORCYCLE RACES

(ONE HALF MILE DIRT RACE-TRACK)

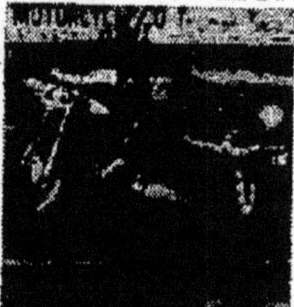

Sunday Aug. 5, 1973

(Rain Date Aug. 11, 1973)

Frederick. Md. Fairgrounds

AMA SANCTIONED

Flat Track & Side Car Racing

GATES OPEN 10:00 AM
Time Trials 1:00 PM
First Race 2:30 PM

ADMISSION $4.00
Grandstand & Grounds
Children under 12 $1.00

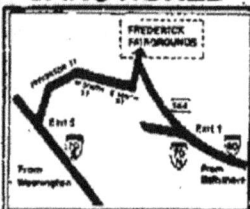

TICKET INFORMATION—CALL 202-223-5996
TICKETS ON SALE AT: Cross Roads Cycle · Blalock Cycle Cycle Inc. · Cycle City · Hersons · Free State · Heyser Cycle Sport Unlimited · Nelber Motors

58

1973   *Souvenir Program*
                          25¢

GOLD
CUP
Professional
MOTORCYCLE
RACES

Sunday 2 pm
May 13, 1973

FREDERICK
MARYLAND
fairgrounds

CYCLE RACING CORPORATION

Cycle Racing Corporation formed in Maryland in the 1970's to promote "regional" races throughout the area including several per year at the Frederick fairgrounds in addition to the July 4th BFC.

1960 to 1990, were losing interest in motorcycle racing. But the sport, and *The Fritchie*, soldiered on.

By 2006 the 883 Series was eliminated and in 2008 the Hot Shoe championship series ended. In 2008 a guy from Paducah Kentucky stepped in to fill the void. Steve Nace's *All-Star National Flat Track* series has been a top-notch operation from the beginning and just keeps getting better. Frederick Maryland has been a key stop on the tour almost from the beginning.

During the Hot Shoe years and the early All-Star events, there was good coordination of the hundreds of races around the country. Part-time, amateur racers who must be back to work on Monday usually don't travel too far. Local races in Maryland and Kansas typically don't impair each other. Pro races and semi-pro races, like the All-Star series, are a little different.

Courtesy Steve Nace Racing

From its 1954 beginning the Grand National Championship series was operated by the AMA. In 2008, AMA sold the Grand National to Daytona Motorsports Group. DMG eventually changed the 52-year-old name of the GNC series to "*American Flat Track*."

DMG and AFT have done tremendous good and have spent incredible amounts of both money and personal reputations to advance this sport. It is an exciting time to be a dirt track motorcycle racing enthusiast on both sides of the track.

It has been tradition and nostalgia that have kept this sport alive through the lean years. That tradition and nostalgia have been used heavily to promote the current resurgence of the sport. The Indian / Harley rivalry in 2020 is the same Indian / Harley rivalry that promulgated the 1920 event that introduced the Delphey's to race promotion. Some recent scheduling conflicts suggest a disregard for this long, established history. An insinuation that lesser races like the Barbara Fritchie, can simply be rescheduled if conflicting with a convenient date for a national. After all, what difference does a day make?

The Barbara Fritchie Classic is the same day every year.

The same day since 1909 on this same track,

Racing originating in this town on this same day in 1900.

This uniquely American sport, celebrated on this uniquely American day, on this unique, historic, American track is not about scheduling convenience. This is an obligation. This is a tribute.

This is honoring the roots of the sport and all the men and women who have kept it alive through the years. On, and off the track.

This is <u>the only motorcycle race in the world</u> with such a connection to a specific day spanning more than a century.

What difference does a day make?

It makes *all* the difference.

The Races

Before the Fritchie

For such a popular sport as motorcycle racing, one of the most frustrating things about researching the earliest period of it is the utter lack of information. Stories and oral histories abound, but hard documented facts are truly scarce. What makes that particularly frustrating is that it has only been in the past generation – my own – that those who were present during the very first years of this history have been lost to us. Yet their stories are largely buried with them, leaving us to speculate and surmise on the "*most likely*" reasons for their decisions and actions as if they took place in ancient times.

The first true motorcycle, as defined by two wheels and a motor, was built well before 1899. The term "***moto cycle***" and its variations though was originally applied to any vehicle combining a motor and any number of wheels. The word "***motorcycle***" (note the "r") was allegedly coined for a machine designed by E.J. Pennington around 1895. Of all places, Pennington came up with this invention in Milwaukee, Wisconsin!

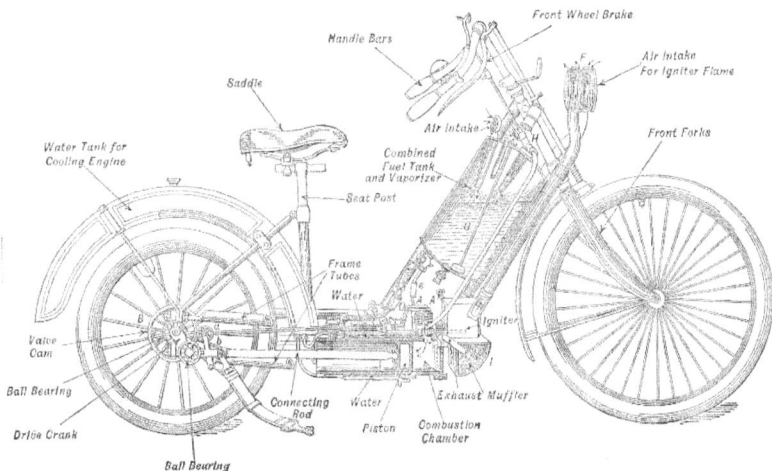

The German Wolfmueller. A circa 1895 two-wheeled, twin cylinder, water cooled design

(No Model.)

No. 574,262.

E. J. PENNINGTON.
MOTOR VEHICLE.

Patented Dec. 29, 1896.

3 Sheets—Sheet 1.

Fig. 1.

Fig. 2.

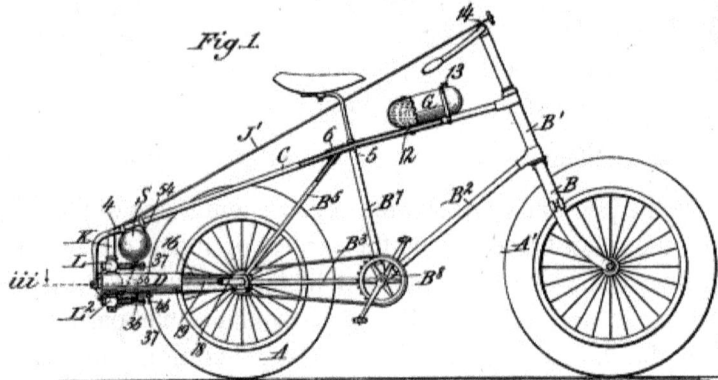

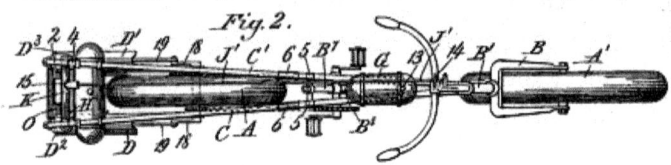

Pennington demonstrated his prototype "motorcycle" in Milwaukee in 1893 but finding few investors, he took his design to England. There he found plenty of interest by investors willing to fund his lavish lifestyle but unfortunately, he never came through with the promised products and rather than the father of the British motorcycle industry he is remembered instead for being a fraud and a swindler. He is reluctantly credited by history though with coining the word "*Motorcycle*" and that at least has stuck.

It is generally accepted that motorcycles developed from bicycles. Motorcycle racing, it seems, developed from bicycle racing as well, but not as we might suppose. Bicycle racing was wildly popular in the 1890's and about the time motorcycles began to emerge, the sport of "paced racing" was hugely popular. The concept of the slipstream, or in racing terms, "*the draft*" has been understood since before motorized vehicles. This is a small vacuum-like pocket of air moving behind a rapidly moving object. Consider how a car speeding past on an autumn day seems to suck fallen leaves behind it. That's the draft!

In paced racing, another bicycle was ridden ahead of the actual racer to create a draft. To assure a faster speed than the racer (and a larger mass/draft) tandem and multi-rider bikes were usually used.

Some employed up to six peddlers! "Motor paced" racing emerged very soon after the origin of motorcycles. These new pacers were more efficient. For those using two riders, the one in front steered and the one in back operated the throttle to maintain minimum distance with the cycler. Thus, the first motorcycles to appear at the earliest races were in fact tools for bicycle races. An article in the Jan. 31, 1900 Tampa Tribune provides a description; *"The motorcycle is a two-seated affair, fitted with storage batteries, looks not unlike a common tandem and has a record of a mile in 1min. 15sec. It is the best pacing machine known."*

An Orient (bicycle Co.) gasoline powered tandem pacer in 1901

A brief announcement in the Frederick News from July 30, 1900 is one early mention of a motorcycle at Frederick.

Grand race meet on Thursday night, August, 2. Three star events and Jack White's "Steam Whirl Wind." The ACME of motorcycle construction.

This was a bicycle race. Whether Jack White's steam whirlwind was used to pace races is not mentioned, but it was not the first motorcycle at Frederick! Fittingly, considering the focus of this book, that first motorcycle rode the Frederick track on Independence Day, *July 4, 1900*. There were bicycle races scheduled 25-miles away at Hagerstown earlier in the day and the bicycles did not make it back to Frederick in time for the scheduled evening races. Spectators came to the track expecting a race. They were appeased with a demonstration of the motorcycle speeding around the track. Like later when "the whirl wind" would be displayed, *"the devil catcher"* was the only motorcycle present on July 4th, 1900, so rather than a multi-bike race, the fans got a timed lap event.

...none of the races advertised took place, owing to the fact that the riders did not get back from Hagerstown. Henry Smith and T.E. Goode rode a one mile and a five-mile exhibition on the "devil catcher." There will be races and exhibitions at the park tonight. − Frederick Evening News, July 5, 1900

The "devil catcher," manned by Henry Smith and T.E. Goode, was the attraction of the evening at Athletic Park last night. A good crowd was present, and the evening was pleasantly spent. ...the two-mile exhibition on the motor cycle was ridden in 4.13, which was very fair time. - Frederick evening News July 6, 1900

Racing, is defined in part as; *"The competitors try to complete a given task in the shortest amount of time."* While in track racing, we revel in the raw competition of riders trying to make a pass for the lead, the race is ultimately determined by a clock. The fastest lap times often being turned in by a hungry rider back in the pack somewhere, trying to race his way to the front. The only way he becomes the winner is if he can make-up enough time to get ahead of the leader on the track - and on the clock.

On July 4, 1900, Henry Smith's devil catcher was demonstrated but we do not have the record of his time that day. The next day, July 5, 1900, by virtue of an existing record of the machine's time for two miles was the first documented motorcycle race at Frederick Maryland despite there only being one motorcycle in the race.

It is said the first *true* motorcycle race took place when the rider of the first motorcycle met the rider of the second and the natural question arose, which one is faster? As that concept applies to Frederick Maryland it is not so spontaneous as the adage suggests. The same thing happened in a thousand cities around the world, but this is Frederick's story. This is how the first two motorcycles met – and raced – in Frederick Maryland.

It was an exhibition. Some may consider such a demonstration as not a real race. Anyone who has ever entered a racetrack with others though I believe will agree that regardless the circumstances, it is *always* a race! The date for that very first multi-bike motorcycle race at Frederick is July 5th, 1901. That is *the day* the first motorcycle rider met the second in Frederick!

MOTOR CYCLE RACES.

An Interesting Exhibition at Athletic Park.

ORDINARY BICYCLE RACES ALSO.

2 mile motor cycle race. French won, with Clark second; time 4.37.
The two-mile open motor race between R. French and F. J. Clark was won by Clark; time 4.15.

This will be the event of the season and an opportunity to witness motor-cycle races.

Clark motor vs. French motor, bowling alleys and shooting galleries. Music and dancing. Frederick Select Band and Orchestra.

Admission, adults, 20c; children, 10c. Free cars to and from park from 7.30 to 11 o'clock. Pavilion and grand stand seats free.

While there were plentiful news stories of pacing motorcycles engaging in "races," this does not appear to be such an event. The first indication is a comparison to the timed event held a year earlier where "Harry Smith *and* T.C. Goode" were clearly riding a tandem pacing motorcycle. In the 1901 stories, French and Clark, while appearing to be the only participants, clearly rode two separate bikes, and each one individually. The local news stories are further confirmed by an item in *"Bicycle World & Motorcycle Review"* magazine for Sept. 1901 which stated, *"...motor bicycle races figured in the events run at Frederick, Maryland"* The article gives the same results and stats as the local paper. Confirming that this is an actual motorcycle race ("motor bicycle") is an article appearing beside it in the same magazine announcing the introduction of Merkel Mfg. Co. of Milwaukee as a brand-new maker of "*motor bicycles.*" The magazine was clearly using this term to differentiate actual motorcycles from the utilitarian machines used for pacing races. This also confirms that Pennington's "motorcycle" name had not yet been universally adopted.

Other articles adjoining the one about Frederick clearly mention "motor paced races" at Hartford, Boston, Detroit, etc.... The clear difference in verbiage between "motor paced race" and "*motor bicycle race*" seems to confirm that the Frederick race is clearly a different type event.

1901 Merkel Mfg. Co. Motor Bicycle

An important explanation is in order at this point. When I originally discovered the early date that racing began in Frederick it was extremely exciting. A quick perusal of other historic racing venues seemed to indicate this as the oldest continually operating motorsports venue – anywhere. I had one unanswered question standing in the way of that assertion though.

These earliest mentions of motorcycles in conjunction with bicycle racing, all seemed to call the venue "*Athletic Park*," rather than the "*Agricultural Park*" as the fairgrounds was then typically referred to. Yet, I could find nothing explaining the discrepancy. Nobody I spoke to or questioned was familiar enough to provide a definitive answer. There was the possibility the two names referred to the same place. Maybe simply a preference by various event people or a reflection of some forgotten disagreement over naming the place?

The mystery was finally solved in late summer 2020. Two articles appearing in the same newspaper mentioning both "Athletic Park" *and* "Agricultural Park" for two different events at the same time. Clearly, they were not the same place!

I discovered that Athletic Park was the property of the Frederick Bicycle Club. The facility was built in 1897 for a meet of the *"Maryland Division, League of American Wheelmen."* It included a ¼ mile oval track located 1 ½ blocks southwest of South Street at what was then the edge of town surrounded by agricultural fields. More land would be added through the years and complimentary facilities built to eventually include the many amenities mentioned in some of the race ads. The baseball field would become home to the "Frederick Hustlers" pro baseball team for many years. Eventually, the ballfield became known as McCurdy Field.

(**NOTE** – While no longer a pro-ball stadium, McCurdy Field still exists. Athletic Park and the former racetrack, however, were developed for residential housing in the nineteen-teen's)

Athletic Park, 1909 courtesy Frederick Magazine, via Heritage Frederick

As well, while the fairground was built, including a racetrack in 1867, the original track was only 1/3 mile. It appears the track was enlarged to the present ½ mile layout by the turn of the 20th century as evidenced by the 1904 Sanborn maps for Frederick that note "*1/2 MILE RACETRACK*" at the fairgrounds. Thus, while motorcycle racing is definitively proven at Frederick as early as 1900, motorcycle racing on the fair ground track has not been proven prior to Oct. 1909. While reducing the margin, that does still leave the Frederick fairground oval as the oldest still operating motorsports track.

(The 1st race at Indianapolis was Aug. 3, 1909, but that was not the same track in use today)

In less than a decade motorcycle racing largely supplanted (track) bicycle racing at Frederick. By the end of the decade, ticket sales were already approaching 2,000 and the news coverage had flip-flopped from that first story about the devil catcher. The cyclers now received a paragraph or two and the rest of the column was devoted to the motorcycles. A Jan. 17, 1900 article in the Indianapolis (Indiana) News speculated on the future of motorcycle racing. The only hope then held for faster racing was on tracks with more than forty-degree banking. Other expectations were special tires treated with ice water to prevent overheating, and tires fastened to the rims with lugs to prevent them coming off at high speed. It was supposed that special masks would be needed so the rider could breathe at such high speed. In all the speculation though, there was not one word about what we would call safety equipment today. Helmets, leathers, even gloves were typically absent in early races. The steep banked motordromes would become reality… and the lack of regard for rider and spectator safety would ultimately be their ruination.

There was a definite interest in motorcycles in Frederick, just as there was everywhere else. These exhibitions with names like whirlwind and devil catcher are sure to have captured imaginations at a time when horses and mules generally defined transportation in Frederick.

An Auto Trade
John Rowland of Hagerstown, traded a one-cylinder Covert automobile for an Indian motorcycle with Murray Brish, Frederick

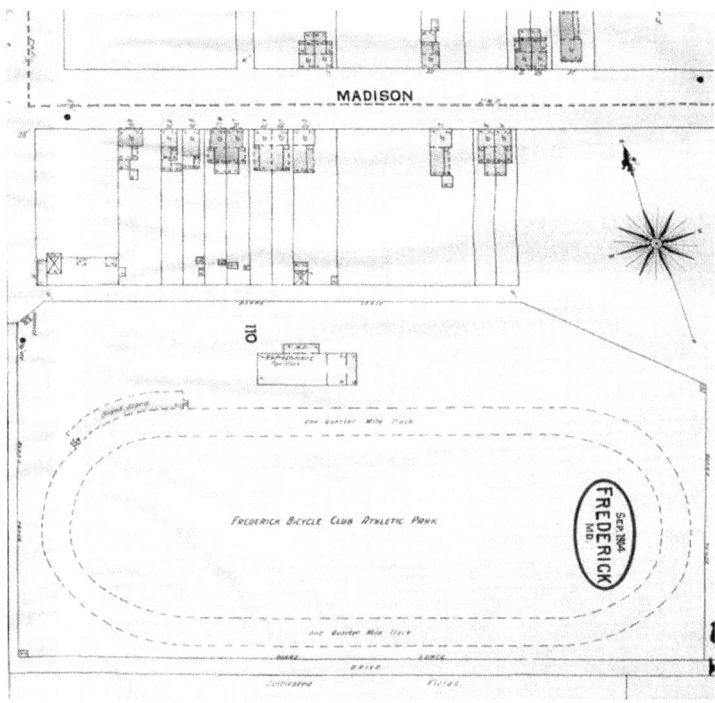

Athletic Park's ¼ mile track in 1904

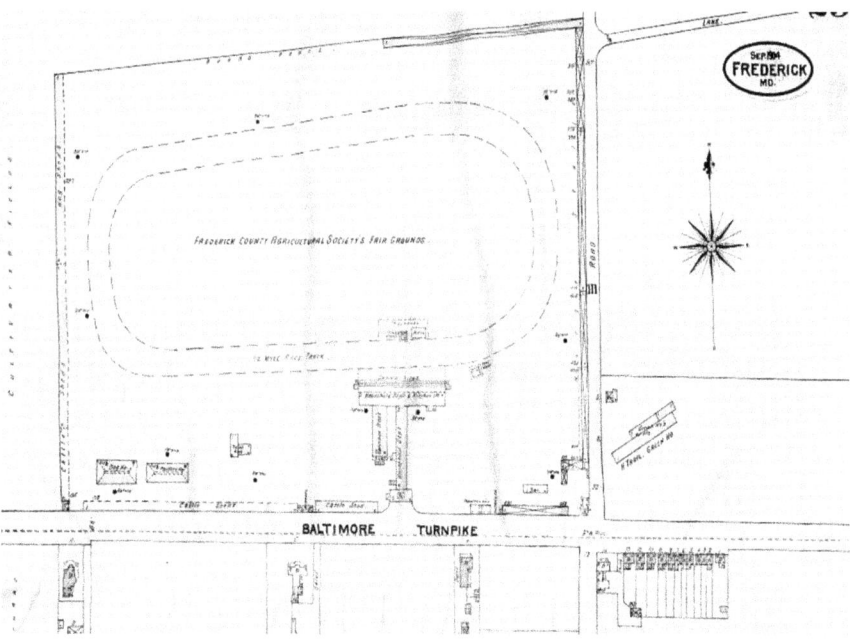

Agricultural Park's ½ mile track in 1904

71

The technological leap associated with the development of the internal combustion engine is comparable to that of the personal computer age a century later. Mr. Roland traded his Covert for an Indian in 1905, only four years after the bicycle races had to be delayed a day for the riders to travel the 25 miles from Hagerstown to Frederick. By 1905 we can safely assume John Rowland rode his motorcycle back to Hagerstown that afternoon and slept in his own bed. Only five years later, the winner would average 22.5 mph during a two-hour race from Washington D.C. to Frederick.

As mentioned earlier, while the 1920 Indian vs. Harley event could arguably qualify as the first race of the annual series that would eventually be named The Barbara Fritchie Classic. The first event solely sponsored by Delphey's, as all future races would be until 1955, was scheduled for Nov. 11, 1921. The provenance of the race from that time until the present is clear.

The current Indian brand bills itself as *"America's First Motorcycle Company."* The original Hendee Mfg. Co., which became Indian (the Indian name was deemed more marketable) can be called the first of any brand name *used* today, but the first Hendee was built in 1901. They did not begin selling to the public until 1902. Motorcycle racing in Frederick, - **on the 4th of July** - began in 1900. True multi-bike motorcycle racing at Frederick began during the same holiday in 1901.

Come to the Park tonight and see the wonderful motor cycles. The French, Clark and Atkinson motors will be here. Your chance to witness their-lightning speed.

By 1909, it was on! Genuine motorcycle races were held during fair week on the ½ mile track in addition to the regular harness races. Frederick Indian dealer, Murray Brish was a member of the fair board and no doubt had a hand in the inclusion of a motorcycle race among the scheduled entertainment. This seems to be emphasized by the fact that all six entries were Indians.

> A motorcycle race was a feature of the afternoon's program. Six Indian motor-cycles were entered in the race, which was a handicap contest, the distance being five miles. The first man off had gone half a mile before "Chick" Thomas, the scratch man, got started, but Thomas overhauled every one of the men ahead of him and won the race in 5 minutes and 50 seconds.
> A consolation race for harness horses which started during the week but got no share of the money was won by Edna Wyoming with Arvie second. In the

Frederick News, October 23, 1909

GREAT FREDERICK FAIR

OCTOBER 18,19,20,21, 1910

SENSATIONAL FREE VAUDEVILLE.
MOTORCYCLE RACES
HARNESS AND RUNNING RACES
FINE STOCK AND POULTRY SHOW

TAKE A DAY OFF AND MEET YOUR FRIENDS
Reduced Rates and Special Trains
on all Railroads

JOHN W. HUMM
President

O.C. WAREHIME
Secretary

(Frederick News, Saturday July 2, 1910)

WILL BE BIG EVENT

Frederick Driving Club plans Large Affair

GOOD RACES ON PROGRAM

These Will Include Harness Events,

Special Races and Motorcycle Race

Which Will Be Held at the Fair Ground July Fourth

"...the motorcycle race will be a five-mile handicap and will feature riders from Frederick and adjoining counties. The winner will receive a handsome gold medal."

74

The Great Frederick Fair, traditionally held for much of the 20th century, during the third week of September, was originally held in October. It was during fair week 1909 that the race between six Indian bikes mentioned previously was held.

The event announced above is a special one. While a function of the horse racing organization, it is an Independence Day event. It is arguably the beginning of what has been *the* Independence Day celebration in Frederick for most of the years which have passed since that 1910 race. Like the 1909 fair race, it is unknown if this was the first July 4th race. It is merely the earliest I have been able to document. Motorcycle racing continued to be part of the fair entertainment. Bicycle World & Motorcycle Review magazine announced in the Sept. 1910 issue under coming events *"Oct. 21, Frederick, Maryland. Baltimore Motorcycle Club's meet at the Frederick Fair."*

The Frederick News tells us on October 22, 1910, not only was there racing but a Maryland State Championship and the breaking of several "track records," thus suggesting previous official racing at the fairgrounds.

BREAK STATE RECORDS

Exciting Motorcycle Races at the Fair

ONE AND FIVE-MILE RACES

Championship of Maryland for one mile in 1.15;

5 Miles, 6.21 – Baltimore Riders Make Fast time –

Gosnell Thrown from Machine

"A feature of yesterday afternoon's track sport at the fair was motorcycle racing... Two track records, one mile and five-mile, were broken by Chic Thomas, with his fast Indian motorcycle. In a one-mile race for the championship of Maryland, Thomas won in one minute sixteen seconds, clipping three seconds from the record made by him on the Cumberland track on October 5."

Following is more of this race report as it may be of interest to those from the local area. *"In a five-mile handicap Thomas was*

75

scratch man, overhauled all the other riders in the first three miles and won in 6.21. This time, it was announced, was the record for five miles on a half-mile track in Maryland. Galt, with a four horsepower Indian, finished second, John Blankney third, John Johnson fourth Augustus Zimmerman fifth, and H.E. Floerkeny of Clear Spring, Md. sixth. Zimmerman, Blankney and Johnson each won an allowance of sixty seconds. Flohrkeny, thirty seconds, and Galt, fifteen seconds.

A three mile novice race was won by Blankney, in 4.15, with Johnson second, C.S. French third, Flohrkeny fourth. The miles were made in 1.32, 1.22, 1.21.

<u>Local Rider Ran into the Fence</u>

Mr. William S. Gosnell, of Frederick, who entered this race, on the second lap after having passed one rider and trying to get ahead of the next, ran into the fence and was thrown from the machine. Mr. Gosnell claims he was fouled by the second rider, being held to the fence. He broke his wrist and was bruised considerably. Mr. Gosnell estimated he was riding at between 50 and 55 miles an hour. The machine was not badly damaged.

FP 10/22/1910

There was also Road Racing!

While only somewhat related, I found this interesting tidbit in the May 30, 1911 Frederick Post. A Road Race from Washington to Frederick. Today, spending two hours getting from Washington to Frederick on I-270, usually means you spent an hour and 30 minutes sitting in a traffic jam.

Motorcyclists Race From Washington

An interesting motorcycle race was run from Washington to Frederick today between W.M. Sweet, Nelvis Bell, Walter Duffey, and George Bell. Sweet, who is well known in Washington as a local rider and who has lately won several road events, added another victory by reaching Frederick first in one hour and fifty-eight minutes. The others arrived in order named – Duffey, George Bell, Nelvis Bell.

The First Outlaw Race!

Maryland had blue laws that kept most businesses and entertainment closed on Sunday well into the 1970's. In the early days, the fair officially opened on Monday and ran through Saturday. Sunday however was a set-up day and open to visitors, although official exhibit's and entertainment was not provided. From an article in the Oct. 11, 1911 Frederick Post however, we learn there were a lot of early fair visitors anxious to examine the then brand-new grandstand. [without having to pay admittance!] While many were seated there enjoying the shade, two motorcycles ridden by a Mr. Hahn and a Mr. Reifsnider entered the track and began racing. After several laps, they were joined, or more correctly challenged, by William Bowers half a lap behind, driving his father's automobile! "*...all the spectators were on their feet cheering their best when the auto passed the two machines and then drew far ahead of them.*"

There would be official motorcycle races at the 1911 fair though, as the Oct. 18, 1911 Frederick Evening Post tells us **"The Hagerstown Motorcycle Club will come down Friday to witness the motorcycle races."**

A large advertisement in the Oct. 14, 1911 Frederick Post newspaper, among other things announced, "**Motorcycle Races on Friday – Two events for Frederick County riders and two open races**." Admission for the grandstand was Thirty-five cents.

Nov. 1, 1911

The Democrat Race

It seems we just can't escape politics today. In reality, politics have always played a large role in America. In 1911, it seems democrats were not particularly partial to motorcycles from an article in the Nov. 2, 1911 Frederick Post that describes the activities at the annual Democrat party picnic at the Fair Grounds.

The event drew a crowd of over 5,000, but many were disappointed when "Monk" Jacobs was unable to provide hot air balloon rides due to high wind that, *"...forced the hot air and smoke from the bag rather than into it"* and then, William Gossnell was the only one who entered the advertised motorcycle race, so the event was canceled. Not to be deterred, Bill Gossnell proceeded to *"give a demonstration of speed"* to those who'd come to see motorcycles.

Note – Gosnell is the same rider who hit the fence and broke his wrist in the Oct. 21, 1910 race

DON'T MISS THE NEWS' AVIATION EXHIBITION!

MARVELOUS FLIGHTS. RAIN OR SHINE

CHARLES F. WALSH, NOTED BIRDMAN

FAIR GROUNDS, MAY 7 and 8

RACES WITH MOTORCYCLE AND AEROPLANE

NOVEL, INTERESTING and SPECTAC-ULAR FEATURES

Lowest Charge Ever made for a Curtiss Exhibition

Usual Price of Admission, $1

Only 35 Cents to Grounds; 25 Cents to Grandstand.

JOIN THE THRONGS at the GREAT AIRSHIP DEMONSTRATION

May 4, 1912 ad

"The Frederick News" newspaper hosted what would have undoubtedly been the strangest race in Frederick history. In terms of modern equipment this seems quite the joke. At that time, it was not.

As the two fastest things imaginable at that time, the motorcycle vs. aero plane race was a popular exhibition in the nineteen-teens. This one scheduled for Frederick would have to be canceled though due to heavy rain the previous day and night which left the surface of the fairground track *"flowing like mortar"* when patrons walked across to the infield for a closer look at the plane according to the report by "the News" on May 9th.

Interestingly though, from an unrelated article originating in England in November 1910, a similar event was held but on a two-mile track. The motorcycle in that race was the hands-down winner!

"...the motorcycle traveled at a rate of between sixty and seventy miles per hour. The biplane could not go faster than forty-five."

1912 July 4th race Ad

1912, which is the earliest documented attempt at a July 4th race, promised to be the biggest and best yet. Unfortunately, in a turn of events all too familiar to flat track fans and racers alike, mother nature had other ideas.

"Motorcycle races are being filled and several very lively races of these speedy machines are promised." (Frederick News, July 3, 1913) While the schedule for this event still included horses, bicycles *and* motorcycles, the degree to which public interest had leaned toward technology in the decade that had passed since the first motorcycles appeared in Frederick is evidenced by the report in the next morning's paper. While it was only as an aid to bicycle racers that originally brought motorcycles to the track, the July 5, 1913 Frederick News describes the motorcycle races as *"the feature event"* [outside of horse racing] in 1913. The best bicyclers in the state barely get as much press in this article as Harry Smith and his devil catcher did in 1900. The report for the July 4th event mentions what would become familiar names of Frederick area riders. Fred Smith, Leslie Brandenburg, Robert Reifsnider, William Gosnell, Charles

Stull… Motorcycle racing had taken a definitive place in local racing circles. Then something strange happens.

From 1914 until 1919 there is scarce information concerning local racing. At least part of this interruption can be explained by WW-I. Racing was suspended for at least two of those years due to the war. By 1919, racing had resumed and the various ads in the Frederick newspapers suggest interest in racing motorcycles was as keen as ever. It also suggests some degree of competition between the Indian dealership of Murray Brish and the Harley dealership of Paul Delphey that would bode well for Frederick racing history.

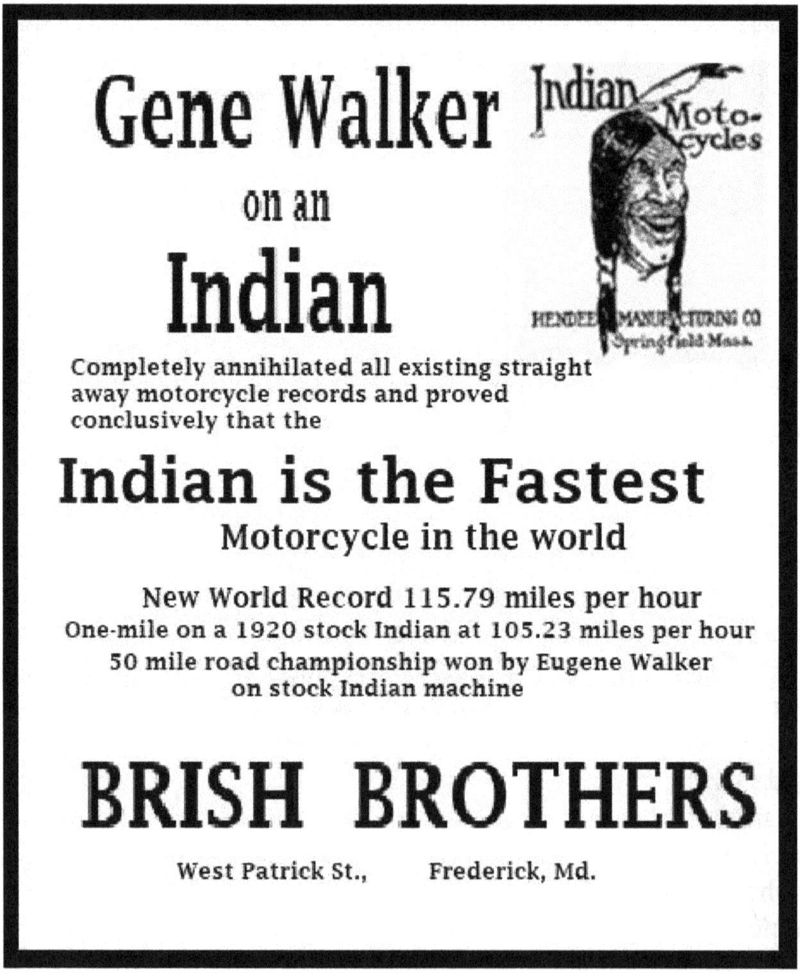

May 1, 1920

80

Returning doughboys fueled the market for adventure. Business was driven by creating excitement in the *new* models and would be a proven tactic for years. The Delphey's though, were not content to simply *tell* customers about their motorcycles. Whether for business or sheer competitive spirit, J. Paul and Chester continued to get out on the track and *show* people what their bikes could do.

MOTORCYCLE RACES
ARMISTICE DAY, NOVEMBER 11, 1920
AT THE FAIR GROUNDS
2:30 o'clock, Admission 50 Cents

The INDIAN and HARLEY-DAVIDSON MOTORCYCLE Dealers of Frederick are going to put on the best motorcycle races ever held on the local track. There are going to be four big events.

2 SIDE CAR EVENTS and 2 SOLO EVENTS

All entries must be made to BRISH BROS. or J. PAUL DELPHEY, both of Frederick.

FALL IN LINE   EVERYBODY'S GOING

Unidentified riders, 1921

MOTORCYCLE RACES!

TODAY
ARMISTICE DAY

Frederick Fair Grounds

2:45 P. M.

All Professionals
DON'T MISS IT!

J.PAUL DELPHEY, Promotor

The July 4, 1922 Driving Club race resulted in Charles Eyler clocking 2.58 in the two-mile sidecar race with Chester Delphey second in 3.12. The track however had an overabundance of sand that particular year which the judges determined made it too dangerous to hold the scheduled solo races. Chester though, had reserved the track the following week for another race.

Big Motorcycle Races

FREDERICK FAIRGROUNDS SAT., JULY 22

RIDERS YOU READ ABOUT

HOT COMPETITION - REAL SPEED

DON'T MISS IT

ADMISSION 75c   CHESTER DELPHEY

Promoter

The 1922 race was held on an at first unusual date, July 22. However, since this was a *"National Championship"* race, that may have played a role in scheduling. The Delphey's were still new promoters and had yet to establish an annual race date. Some of the entries mentioned offer some insight through. There were already races scheduled in Baltimore and Winchester Virginia on July 4th. Several of those listed are on the Baltimore entry list for the 4th and Grove of Chambersburg Pennsylvania won the Winchester race held the same day. Then of course there was the established harness racing meet at Frederick on the 4th.

Motorcycle racing by local riders had been part of the annual July 4th harness race meet at Frederick since at least 1912 and the annual fair even longer. Professionally promoted races had been held with Delphey involvement the last two Novembers. This 1922 event though was no local race. A sanctioned, national championship event with serious prize money and riders straight out of the newspaper from all over the country. This was undoubtedly the first **BIG** race at Frederick and may account for why 1922 is sometimes pointed to as *"the first"* Fritchie. In 1923 Chester Delphey brought a second National Championship race to Frederick. Records were falling at almost every meet around the country as equipment development was progressing at a fever pace. Several new records were set at Frederick that July, but more impressive is the entry list from our perspective. Included are names viewed as icons of the sport typically associated with motordrome racing. Famous names appear throughout the Fritchie's history up to the present. It's humbling to step onto the Frederick fairground track today after realizing those men raced this same track almost 100-years-ago. Gene Walker, Bill Minnick, Gilmore Oaks, Dynamite Scott, Tom Connor… By 1924, Chester Delphey's event would attain established race status together with an identifiable date – Decoration Day (May 30).

BIG MOTORCYCLE RACES BEING PLANNED

Promoter Delphey announces that $390 in prizes will be offered

Chester Delphey, this city, middle Atlantic states motorcycle champion, announces that on Saturday afternoon, July 22, at 2:30 o'clock, he will promote a number of events at the Agricultural Park track which promises to be interesting. There will be four races, two solo and two sidecar. Cash prizes totaling $390 will be awarded to the winners. The meet will be sponsored by the M. & A. T. A.

Professional Motorcycle Races!

FREDERICK FAIR GROUNDS
FRIDAY, MAY 2
2.30 P. M.

World's Best Riders
In Hot Competition
Don't Miss It!
FOLLOW THE CROWD
RAIN, DATE SATURDAY, MAY 21

CHESTER F. DELPHEY
Promoter

STAR RIDERS WHO WILL BE SEEN IN THE LINE UP:
PAUL ANDERSON, Harley-Davidson
JOHN SEYMOUR, Indian
BILL MINNICK, Harley-Davidson
DYNAMITE SCOTT, Indian
TOM CONNER, Harley-Davidson
JOHN FISHER, Indian
AND OTHER STAR RIDERS

Johnny Seymore famous Indian motorcycle racer and holder of
many half mile dirt track records is shown above. Seymore is
one of the most talented and nerviest riders today. He will ride
in the motorcycle races at the Frederick Fair Grounds
Decoration Day, May 30.

Title Holder To Race Here

Anderson, who will be seen on the local in the Motorcycle races Friday, was the first rider to make a mile a minute on a 1/2 mile track and is now holder of the ten-mile record

Paul Anderson, May 27, 1924

MOTORCYCLE RACES
FAIR GROUNDS
Saturday, May 30, 2:30 P. M.

Four Big Events, Including

10-MILE SIDE CAR NATIONAL CHAMPIONSHIP

WORLD'S BEST RIDERS

IN HOT COMPETITION

Auspices Chester Delphey

G DAY FOR FREDERICK

Ball Game Morning;

Motorcycle Races Afternoon

Frederick Daily News, Saturday, May 31, 1924

LARGE CROWD SEES MOTORCYCLE RACES

3,000 people line track

The unusually large crowd, the masterful riding of Paul Anderson, Milwaukee, Wisconsin, and Dynamite Scott, Springfield, Mass. and an accident during the tuning up process preliminary to the events, featured the motorcycle races held Friday afternoon on the half-mile dirt track at the fairgrounds under the promotion of Chester F. Delphey, this city.

...The ten-mile national championship was then run off. This was won in easy fashion by (Paul) Anderson, riding a Harley, in 11 minutes 59 and 2/5 seconds. An Indian driven by Herbert Webb, Roanoke, Virginia came in second; while Johnny Vance made third on his Harley.

Prizes awarded; Ten-mile solo championship, first, $85, second $40, third $20.The races were efficiently handled by Amour Anderson, Reading Pennsylvania, official referee of the M. & A. T. A. under whose sanction the event was conducted.

1925

The 1925 races were set for Decoration Day, May 30th and over 3,000 spectators cheered as Dynamite Scott brought his Indian across the line in the Ten-Mile National Championship sidecar race just ahead of Delphey's Harley-Davidson piloted by Bill Minnick. It was no easy win with Scott making the last seven laps holding his carburetor in his hand after it had fallen off.

87

He kept the carb pressed to the manifold and worked the throttle butterfly with his thumb while he continued with only one hand on the bars. Minnick won every other race that day but notably, in the class B event, Charley Halley from nearby Brunswick placed second. Halley also won the amateur class. Races would be held at Reading on July 4th, 1925 and Bill Minnick would set a new ½ mile world record on Delphey's rig in that race.

1926 Ad

Bill Minnick setting the world record sidecar time in 1927. Note the passenger totally tucked in the flexi sidecar and Bill's right foot braced against the sidecar body.

88

During the 1927 Decoration Day race Bill Minnick of Wilmington DE riding a Harley-Davidson set a new world record for a 21 cubic inch (350cc) motorcycle on the half mile with a 31.5 second lap time. The main event was a ten-mile solo class A race won by Art Pechar on an Indian. Pechar's average lap time was 34.05 seconds. Pechar and Minnick fought fiercely for the lead with Minnick eventually falling off which allowed Pechar the win. Two years later Pechar would move to Great Britain where he would enjoy a successful career as a speedway racer.

Others who rode the 1927 Frederick race include:

Walter Stoddard, Hagerstown – Harley, Rudy Adams, Washington – Harley, John Bodnar, Pittsburg – Harley, Arthur Lotts, Baltimore – Harley, J.H. Fisher, Hagerstown – Indian, Art Pechar, New Haven – Indian, William Minnick, Wilmington – Harley.

Missing Years 1929-1931

There is one single mention in the July 7, 1928 Frederick paper announcing that *"Motorcycle races will be held at the Fairgrounds, July 14."* That is the extent of the announcement and I have found no follow-up articles, but area baseball games are reported as rain outs the 13th & 14th. As there was rain late in the day July 4th, it is unknown if this was a rain date from the Harness racing club's normal race, or one of Chester Delphey's races scheduled later in the month of July as he had previously done. Assumedly in conjunction with the National Rally, in Washington, D.C.

1929 through 1931 are a bit different. The absence of any mention of racing in conjunction to the Delphey's or any of the other events typically including racing, has been a mystery. The easy explanation is the stock market crash of 1929 and the ensuing Great Depression, but the market didn't crash until September! Motorcycle sales continued, or at least advertisements did. As mentioned elsewhere, there were races nearby sponsored by a Pennsylvania promoter. There were local riders racing elsewhere.

The only suggestion of an explanation is in August 1930 when this snippet in the *"do you remember"* column of the Frederick Post confirms it is not simply a dearth of publicized reports.

Do you remember -
When the Delphey brothers staged motorcycle races annually at the Fairgrounds? ...the races were discontinued about three years ago.

Despite extensive searching, I have not been able to answer why racing disappears from Frederick for these three years. It could very easily be due to the financial strain of these opening years of the great depression. Unrecorded construction or rule changes at the fairground are all possibilities. New rules or ordinances by the city could have played a role. Since race dates were still fluid and we do not have any data on potential schedules, even weather could explain the mystery. All are *possibilities*, but none can be documented. Even suggestive evidence is lacking. One major occurrence in the Delphey race program that is documented precisely during this period may be a *contributing* factor, but again, cannot fully explain it.

This racing draught follows immediately on the heels of Bill Minnick's world record run in Frederick on May 30, 1927. How was such a crowning glory followed by... nothing?

On August 26, 1928, just over 15 months after his record setting Frederick run, Bill Minnick riding his Delphey sponsored Harley-Davidson at a track formerly located in Carrollville, Wisconsin, approached a turn three abreast with two other riders. It was a classic 3-way shutoff contest.

Bill Minnick won the contest but lost everything else. At about 100mph, he crashed through a trackside wooden barrier and was killed instantly. Three spectators were also hospitalized with serious injuries. It is unknown if any of the Delphey family were in Wisconsin with Minnick, but it is unlikely. The news, however, would have surely been crushing. This coming six-years after Chester and Oscar Lidie's crash ended both of their racing careers, may well have made the brothers think twice about involvement with racing in any form or at any level of engagement. It seems to make sense, but then there is the fact that Minnick did not have his crash until *August* and J. Paul and Chester's races were held in *May and July* respectively… *except for this year.*

There is also evidence that by 1929 J. Paul was sponsoring another rider. Walter Stoddard of Hagerstown moved to Frederick from his hometown of Hagerstown, Maryland so that when he was not racing a Delphey bike, he could work in the Delphey shop.

There is a three-year gap. Racing, on the same dates by the same promoters (the Delphey's) does resume though. There have been other similar gaps that are "forgiven" regarding the longevity of this event. I believe the evidence supports the absence of racing was not because it was unwanted. It was not resumed by someone else, or as different events. Despite not being able to ascertain why this gap exists, I maintain that it should not be considered a genuine abandonment and resurrection of the race, but rather an unwanted interruption like the war or the several spats of bad weather that caused similar gaps.

1930's

It would be during the unexplained interruption of 1929-31 that racing on the fourth of July by the harness racing club would cease. When J. Paul Delphey resumed Frederick racing in 1932, it was on this iconic date. Thus, racing on July 4th at the fairgrounds track continued essentially unbroken from 1919 (at least) under "the Frederick Driving Club," into the era of the Delphey Brother's Classic. Chester & J. Paul Delphey's national championship race moved along with the date. One likely reason for the date change is the National Motorcycle Rally then being held at Washington D.C. over the July 4th holiday.

1932 Ad

July 9, 1932, July 4, 1933 & 34

The Delphey brothers, J. Paul and Chester, congratulating Joe Petrali.

Courtesy of Betsie Handley

The 1932 race was set for Monday July 4th, but a heavy rain shower resulted in postponement of the event. With the agreement of the riders, the race was re-scheduled for Saturday the 9th. Joe Petrali would be the star of the day, winning three of the four classes he entered. The one race Petrali did not win was the coveted six-mile national championship won by "*The Texas Comet*" Rural Murray of San Antonio. It was a classic Harley (Petrali) vs. Indian (Murray) race. Petrali got the hole shot but Murray passed him in turn two on the third lap and Petrali ceased being a threat. By the fifth lap Petrali dropped to fourth where he would finish the race. Emerson Rawlings, Bloomfied N.J. second, Tony Catanzio, Long Island NY third. Pertali would recapture the championship in 1933 only to lose it again in 34 to Louis Balinski of Kalamazoo Michigan. (both on Harley's) Third was Fred Toscani of Garfield NJ. On an Indian. Bringing up the tail of the field in sixth place was local Hagerstown MD rider Clarence Fegley. Nothing to be ashamed of considering he was riding against the absolute best in the country and finished only 2.28 sec. behind the winner!

LOUIS BALINSKI

From 1934 race advertisement

1934 was a big change to the Fritchie and motorcycle racing in general as the first year of the new class C racing rules. In three class C events, only four of the nine podium positions were taken by riders from farther than 30 miles from Frederick. The rule was intended to promote racing by common men on standard bikes rather than full-time pros on special built machines and it certainly had the desired effect from the very first year.

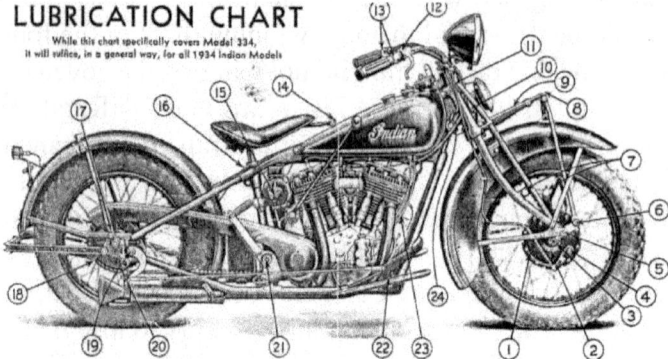

LUBRICATION CHART

While this chart specifically covers Model 334, it will suffice, in a general way, for all 1934 Indian Models

1. Front Hub—Few turns of Alemite Gun every 1000 miles.
2. Important—Keep drain hole clear to allow escape for excess lubricant in hub.
3. Friction Washer—Keep free with a few drops of oil every 200 miles.
4. Brake Cam Bearing—Few drops of oil every 200 miles.
5. Bell Crank Pivot Bearings—Grease with Alemite Gun every 200 miles.
6. Bell Crank End Pins—Grease with Alemite Gun every 200 miles.
7. Brake Anchor Link Bearings—Grease with Alemite Gun every 200 miles.
8. Spring End Bearing—Grease with Alemite Gun every 200 miles.
9. Spring—Grease leaves when they squeak—see Care of Spring Fork.
10. Lower Head Bearings—Grease with Alemite Gun every 500 miles.
11. Upper Head Bearings—Disassemble and pack with grease every season.
12. Hand Brake Lever and Cable—Oil hand brake lever pivot every 500 miles.
13. Grips—Unscrew protector sleeve and inject a few drops of oil monthly.

14. Saddle Front Connection Bearing—Grease with Alemite Gun every 200 miles.
15. Generator—Few drops of light oil in oiler at each end of generator every 400 miles—see Care of Generator.
16. Seat Post—Grease with Alemite Gun every 200 miles.
17. Rear Hub—Pack with grease twice each season—see Care of Wheel Bearings.
18. Chain—See Care and Adjustment of Chain.
19. Brake Cam Bearing—Grease with Alemite Gun every 500 miles.
20. Brake and Clutch Rod Clevis—(Clutch rod on left side)—Few drops of oil on front and rear clevis plus every 200 miles.
21. Kick Starter Segment Bearing—Grease with Alemite Gun every 500 miles.
22. Brake and Clutch Pedal—(Clutch pedal on left side)—Grease with Alemite Gun every 500 miles.
23. Magneto—See Care of Magneto.
24. Controls—Few drops of oil inside upper end of leather casing once a week.

Preventative maintenance was a daily job.

1923 H-D advertising photo

94

Joe Petralli winning the ½ mile National Championship

Courtesy of Betsie Handley

PETRALI WINS!

"Outriding the field in two of three features at Frederick Joe Petrali left no doubt..." So began the report in the Hagerstown Morning Herald for July 6th, 1936 on the previous day's races at Frederick.

1937 promised even more excitement

7 MOTORCYCLE RACES MONDAY...

In the last year for class-A competition, Fred Toscani won at Frederick for the second and last time.

Federico Toscani in the last Class "A" race at Frederick. 1938

1938 ad

The fair races on Friday October 14 were particularly well challenged in 1938 with 34 entries. The fierce competition however took an equally unusual toll. The anticipated favorite in the class C race was the previous year's class A national champ, Bob Beaty of Wilkinsburg, Pennsylvania. Beaty was on his way to fulfill that expectation when he collided with Cumberland Maryland rider Richard Fox. Neither were injured seriously, but both were out of the race.

As the track was being re-prepped, a truck pulling a drag was struck by Bill Huber who had obviously entered the track a bit prematurely for a practice lap. Huber was not seriously hurt but his bike was out for the meet. In the worst crash of the day, Vernon *"Red"* House, who sold Indian motorcycles in Washington, D.C., came off the back straight a little too hot and hit the fence outside turn three sending he and his bike summersaulting west of the track. Red was taken to Frederick Memorial hospital by ambulance, then transferred to Garfield Hospital in Washington, D.C. to be treated for various injuries including a broken collarbone and broken jaw.

1938 Great Frederick Fair Ad

The new class"C" racing was decidedly different from the "professional" class "A" When is the last time you saw a racer wear a necktie – in a race?

Two interesting *firsts* employed in this October race were a handicapped starting order, whereby the bikes were lined up single file for the start of the race, from the <u>slowest</u> qualifier to the quickest, who was at the rear of the line. The other development was use of an *"electric eye timer."*

Apparently, there was some difficulty with the new electronic technology, but all felt the handicap start was a fair idea. Interesting that time would ultimately prove the opposite for each idea. While this race was still a function of the fair, Indian Dealer Murray Brish was then on the fair board and perhaps feeling the squeeze of Delphey's success in race promotion, the 1938 fair race was a quality production. However, it appears to have been the last of the fair's motorcycle races. The crashes and injuries may have played a role. This was not long after public sentiment had essentially shutdown the huge motordrome racing industry and the fair board may not have wanted the negative publicity anticipated from these incidents.

Author's note – The portion of the track where House crashed is elevated, which resulted in his going airborne for a considerable distance after hitting the rail. It is unknown if he was transferred to the Washington hospital due to the severity of his injuries, or merely to be nearer his home and business in D.C. He did fully recover.

Vernon "Red" House at Frederick

as another racer's sponsor, more than ten years after Red's crash.

RACES FRIDAY
IN FREDERICK

Delphey Brothers staging annual
cycle meet on fourth...

Thus, began yet another announcement on July 1, 1941 for what had become an expected annual event at Frederick. Nobody would suspect it yet, but this would be the last race for several years.

June 5, 1942

On June 5th, 1942, J. Paul Delphey walked down the street from his Harley-Davidson shop to the Frederick News offices to issue a press release and interview. A month before the already scheduled race and six months after the attack on Pearl Harbor, while the Delphey family endured the weight of anticipation as son Julian's deployment orders were expected any day, J. Paul had made an important decision.

The previous day, Paul explained, he had mailed a letter to AMA headquarters in Ohio requesting that the sanction for the July 4th race, and for any motorcycle race at Frederick, be indefinitely suspended for the duration of the national emergency. Delphey stoically expressed "*It would be un-American*" to use valuable resources for racing while the country struggled to supply its own and its allies' soldiers needs for the war. Paul was quoted saying that; "*After seeing the crowds attending all types of races, it is my opinion we would undoubtedly make a financial success of the races here this year, however, I don't need money badly enough to act contrary to ...the requests of the president and the governor of Maryland*" Another point which Delphey expressed his concern for was the possibility of young men being injured racing, which would prevent their ability to serve in the army if called to.

At the end of the interview Paul expressed his hope that racing could resume for the 1943 season. We can understand his various reasons for wishing it, but it would prove half a decade before motorcycles would return to the fairground.

Shortly after Delphy's request had been made, the AMA suspended all sanctioned racing in the nation. How much that decision may have been influenced by J. Paul Delphey can only be speculated. As J. Paul mentioned, President Roosevelt had asked for such activities to cease. Interestingly though, the official press release from E.C. Smith and AMA used the same "*un-American*" comment J. Paul Delphey had used in his previous letter to Smith.

July 4, 1947

July 4, 1947 was a huge event in the history of The Fritchie. It was the first race of the historic series since J. Paul Delphey patriotically suspended racing in 1942 due to WW-II. Racing was clearly missed by the Frederick fans as more than 7,500 crowded the fairgrounds on that hot July afternoon.

Many of the icons of motorcycling are traced to the adventure hungry vets returning from the war in the 1940's. The bike clubs, customizers and of course, racers. The seventy-five hundred spectators buying tickets that day would not be disappointed. There were 45 entrants for the class C racing event.

Of the 33 who had entered as novices, ten were moved up to amateur status before the qualifier. Among them was a young man from nearby Hanover, Pennsylvania. There with his brothers, 32-year-old Armin Hostetter was lined up on a hot new machine for the Frederick track. A big 500cc single, overhead valve Matchless G80 with newfangled "*teledraulic*" forks instead of the girders and springers used by the competition. Armin didn't win the race that day, but he never forgot it! He would be better remembered throughout the region for operating Trail-Way Speedway near Hanover, Pennsylvania. In 1972, Armin, a farmer, built the slick clay 3/8-mile track beside his house in the middle of his 250-acre farm. It remains a popular track today with a full, season-long schedule of both motorcycle and auto racing in the real-life "*build it and they will come*" strategy.

PROFESSIONAL
MOTORCYCLE RACES

FREDERICK FAIRGROUNDS

MONDAY, JULY 4

Time Trials Begin 12:15   Races 2:00 P. M.

DELPHEY BROS. PROMOTERS   A.M.A. SANCTION

101

Courtesy, Richard Lyons collection

103

Armin traveled the race circuit as he was able and his mastery of the Matchless from the beach course at Daytona to the mid-west soon caught the attention of AMC (Associated Motor Cycle) who made both Matchless and Norton brands. As a result, Armin rode for several years as a Norton factory sponsored racer. In January 1978 Hostetter would essentially invent the sport of arena cross when he hosted the first "Motorama" at the Harrisburg, PA farm show arena. Joining Hostetter in traveling from Hanover that day in 1947 was a Harley rider, Lloyd "Bud" Laugerman, who while finishing last in his heat would none the less eventually be known by generations of Harley riders as the owner of Laugerman's Harley-Davidson at York, Pennsylvania.

Motorcycle racing was officially back in Frederick and back with a vengeance! The fans were eager to watch, and the riders seemed to have multiplied and become even more eager and daring during the wartime lull. Exemplifying the changes that had taken place during this short but technologically catapulting hiatus from racing is the experience of the day's race announcer, Pat Brooke of Harrisburg, Pennsylvania who had first come to the race in 1922 as a competitor on a borrowed motorcycle.

Brooke had not been to Frederick since before the war and decided to fly in his private plane rather than take the narrow roads still suffering from wartime neglect. However, when arriving at Frederick, he discovered the anticipated airfield on the national guard grounds was now the barracks and associated buildings of Camp Dietrich!

Brooke and his wife circled Frederick looking for a suitable landing spot. They found the brand-new municipal airfield, which had been carved from a farm field next to the fairground only a year earlier, but the field was unattended and lacking radio communication, they chose to look farther. Brooke eventually found "Steven's airstrip" near Lewistown, seven miles from the city where he finally landed the plane. Pat Brooke contacted an old friend who, just like 25 years earlier, loaned him a motorcycle and Mr. & Mrs. Brooke finally made it to the races just in time.

Armin Hostetter on a Matchless, 1947

The above photo, while not at Frederick is used none the less as one indicative not only to racing, but specifically to the local mid-Atlantic motorcycle community. Ray Texter and Bud Laugerman would go on to operate neighboring H-D Dealerships in Lancaster and York, Pennsylvania. Ray's son Randy and his grandchildren Cory and Shayna would all have promising GNC & AFT pro racing careers. This was a transition time in motorcycling. While Indian as a brand, would hold on for three more years, they were feeling the squeeze. Delphey's Harley shop was the only motorcycle dealership in the 1950 Frederick phone book. The Indian franchise had gone through several homes after being dropped by the Brish brothers several years earlier and finally disappeared even before the brand did. The British marques had not yet gained the foothold they would briefly embrace several years later. There were occasional Continental brands seen at meets, especially CZ and Bultaco, but the Japanese names were still largely unheard of.

105

1950

July 10, 1950, (rain date) novice main at Frederick, Maryland. L to R; #37c Bill Balderson of Baltimore, MD., #76u Don Gouker of Hanover, PA, U/K, U/K, #176c Charlie Miller, Hagerstown, MD., U/K

The above Richard Lyons photo comes with the explanation that Balderson is riding one of three "big base" Scouts, which Bob Lyons had built and tuned over the winter of 48/49 for use at Daytona that year. He, along with Al Moran and Joe Burroughs raced them throughout 1949. Lyons, Moran and Balderson raced the same three bikes in 1950. Each of these special bikes had a unique black and white paint scheme. The fenders were gloss black with a wide white stripe down the center and the tanks were the same black with the white stripe 2/3 way down on each side, running the length of the tank with the Indian logo on it. The Indian script logo was only used on Lyon's bike. The other two used Scout and Scout TT decals. Bladerson campaigned the bike all season but only for that one year (1950). The distinctive black on white paint job can clearly be seen on Al Moran's bike in Don Emde's excellent book on the Daytona 200.

Richard goes on to explain that Charlie Miller was also an Indian rider but switched to BSA mid-way through the 1950 season. He is on a BSA in this photo in the pole position. Miller rode for Twigg's Cycles in Hagerstown. H. William Twigg's shop had originated as an

106

Indian dealership in the 1930's, but by this time was selling BSA. In less than five years, nobody at Frederick would be running Indians …until Brandon Price in 2019.

1950 was well before the advent of the ubiquitous race van. Even pick-up trucks were rare. This was the era of the race trailer. Several can be seen in the preceding photo in the infield, some attached to some rather stylish automobiles. Particularly though, note the white convertible just behind the starting line. In absence of a trailer the motorcycle's front wheel has been removed and the forks attached to the car's bumper for towing the bike on its own rear wheel.

Indian particularly was feeling the push of the British bikes and many Indian loyalists were switching to them. July 4th was a Tuesday in 1950. However, rainstorms caused a postponement and in a rare turn of events, a rain date was set for the following Saturday, July 8th. Richard Lyons pointed out the paucity of cars in the infield indicating fewer race entries resulting from this rescheduling.

BLICK'S INDIAN
CYCLE SHOP
Cushman motor scooters - Mercury outboard motors
Repairs of all kinds a specialty
Rear of 413 N. Market St. Frederick, Md.

EXPERT MOTORCYCLE RACES

SATURDAY, JULY 8
Frederick Fairgrounds
RACES 2:30 P.M.
RAIN CHECKS HONORED
General Adm. $1.00 tax incld. Grandstand $1.00 tax incld.
Promoted by
Delphey's

July 5, 1950

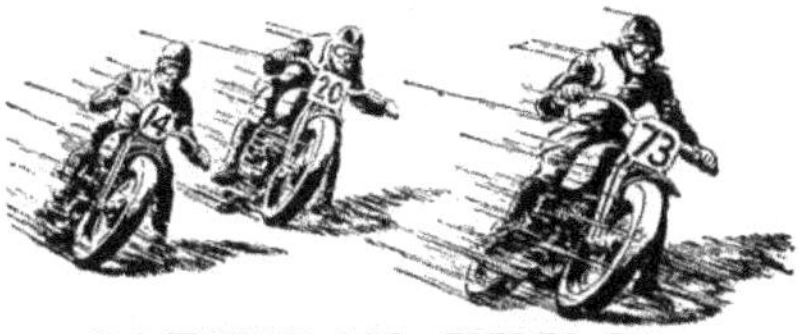

With the various British brands among the greatest pressures compressing Indian's market share, the ultimate irony would be when one of those companies, Brockhouse Engineering of Southport, UK, acquired the remaining assets of the "Indian Motorcycle Manufacturing Company" and the last "Indians" sold in the U.S.A. under the original marque would actually be rebranded Royal Enfield's made in England.

1951 & 52

3 ★ RACE MEET   1/2 Mile
Dirt Track

9 EVENTS

WEDNESDAY

JULY 4

FREDERICK FAIRGROUND, FREDERICK, MD.

Time Trials 12 Noon - Races 2 P.M. D.S.T

45 MILES NORTH OF OUR NATION'S CAPITAL

Promoted
by

DELPHEY'S

Frederick
Maryland

1951 Advertisement reproduction

"Frederick will have the only AMA sanctioned motorcycle races to be held on the entire Atlantic seaboard."   So began a Frederick News article on June 29, 1951. A pre-entry had been received recently from a rider returned from early retirement, John Butterfield, and J. Paul Delphey stated that he was sending an express telegram to Billy Huber in Reading Pennsylvania alerting him to the competition so Huber would be sure to get his entry in and attend the Frederick races. Ma Nature would not be outdone though and 1951, despite a scheduled rain date, is a scratch in the records due to rain.

Julian Delphey did as good a job hyping the 1952 race as his dad had done the previous 32 years. There was lots of talk that year about three riders from Frederick, one in each of the novice, junior and expert classes that year. A true rarity at Frederick even today. John Droneburg would race expert. Johnny Esworthy would race in the amateur class and Doggie Hiltner would run the novice class. It would be a Baltimore rider though, who would take top honors. Bob Boutwell and John Droneburg had a sort-of rivalry going that summer in the regional races and it would be a special coup for Boutwell to take Droneburg's hometown race.

Bob Boutwell and his fast Triumph

Boutwell's Cycle Center in Baltimore and later Cockysville, would be one of those familiar incubators of famous racers. First it was Bob himself. His general manager, also a racer in the 50's Norm Farris, is a man unfamiliar to many today, but Norm's son Rodney was a force to be reckoned with in the 80's & 90's! Rod's development under Bob, Norm and the others hanging around Boutwell's Triumph & Yamaha shop got a huge boost from a transplanted Marylander named Gary Nixon who had coached and advised Rodney.

1953

Bob Boutwell would win the Fritchie again but not in 1953! That was to be the first Fritchie win for another multiple Frederick winner, Thomas L. McDermott. Tommy was a factory BSA rider who would go on to road race in Europe for the company, but in 1953 the Glen Falls New York rider would be showing em how it's done in Frederick Maryland.

Tommy McDermott Sr

Bob Boutwell was back in 1954 with a goal in mind. That goal was to add his name to the short list of those who had won this race more than once. He would not go home disapointed! Boutwell was the first of another list relevant to the BFC. John Droneburg would continue to compete throughout the region but like other Frederick racers, he never did achieve his goal of keeping the winner's trophy in Frederick at the end of the day.

Author's note - There was other motorcycle racing near Frederick. From approximately 1948 into the 1960's there was a TT track owned by Heart of Maryland Motorcycle Club named *Mountain Top*, at Braddock Heights 3 ½ miles west of town that held district races. For 53 years there was drag racing 8 miles east of Frederick at the "*75 & 80 Dragway*," which opened in September 1960 and closed in Sept. 2013.

OFFICIAL PROGRAM
MOTORCYCLE RACES
FREDERICK, MD.
FRIDAY, JULY 4, 1952
A. M. A. SANCTION 17965
PROMOTED BY DELPHEY'S

Welcome to Frederick   Thank you for your Patronage

DELPHEY'S
EVERYTHING WE SELL · · · WE SERVICE

Authorized Dealer for the Famous

HARLEY-DAVIDSON MOTORCYCLES

COLUMBIA   TROJAN &
    &   ARKANSAS
SCHWINN   TRAVELER
BICYCLES   BOATS

EVINRUDE OUTBOARD MOTORS

140 W. PATRICK ST.   FREDERICK, MD.

TIME TRIALS

111

3 miles   *Time 5-44-1*

NOVICE - FINAL

2-52c *Moara - H.D.*   7c *Durban Ind* 4
Spilled 110 *Simmons Tri*   88c *Berthold Ind*
1-65c *Miller BSA*   56B *Papp* 3

5 miles **AMATEUR - FINAL**   *Time 5-41-2*

2-16B *Willet HD*   4-76u *Younker HD*
1-53A *Hammer Tri*   3-79u *Angelo Tri*
5-12B *Cravener HD*   6-88A *Cravens HD*

5 miles **EXPERT - FINAL** *Time 5-27-8*

1-57 *Bantwell Tri*   24c *Droneburg HD*
4-58 *Smitty Ind*   3-27 *Burkhart HD*
2-87a *Bordo HD*   190 *Taylor Tri*

Courtesy, Richard Lyons collection

112

1955

There is some intrigue concerning 1955, but the questions are as much about the AMA as the BFC. In a casual perusal of the records it immediately becomes apparent that the July 4th event, while scheduled, advertised and planned for by J. Paul Delphey, was ultimately canceled 12 days before the race.

The AMA was experiencing a transition period from 1953 – 1958. The organization, the races and the industry were essentially unchanged since 1934. While AMA maintained the status quo, the market changed exponentially! The range of motorcycle styles had grown, and these various styles had their own market shares. Racing, even under class C, had also grown both in size and the development of the bikes being raced. With only one American manufacturer left, and a current assault by imported motorcycles, AMA needed to make some changes. There would be growing pains along the way.

After 30 years of service with the organization, E.C. Smith, the director of the AMA from its 1924 beginning, announced his retirement at the season opener in Daytona in 1958. It was not a surprise. Smith's successor, Linton Kuchler, had been hired in 1955!

One of the first big changes was instituting the Grand National Championship Series. With that series also began the current-style system of accumulating points at each race on the GNC schedule throughout the season. This meant that riders looking to win the championship, or a factory paycheck, tried to make as many GNC races and earn as many points as possible.

Prior to this season-long point accumulation system, "class C" riders were essentially free to choose their races across the country. The "Grand National Champion" was chosen annually from 1937 until 1953 by the winner of the single race held at the Springfield Illinois State Fairground each summer.

During the first two years of the GNC (54 & 55) there were 18 and 17 races on the schedule. This mirrored pre-GNC schedules for "nationals" since WW-II and did not suggest much change. In 1956 however, the total for GNC dates dropped to only 7 races. According to flat track historian Bert Sumner, the reason given was "safety *concerns"* a justification Bert attributes to the research of Greg Pearson.

In fact. There had been discussion within the AMA about abandoning racing altogether among fears that racing injuries and deaths were negatively impacting the general public's acceptance of motorcycles and hence, sales of motorcycles – remembering that AMA was still a function of the manufacturer financed M&ATA trade group.

There were seven races again in 1957. The schedule did not rebound to surpass ten races in one season until 1960. Racers of course did not become any fewer just because GNC races did. Top tier riders would show up to compete in any race that was relatively nearby during this period and some that were not.

Everyone in Frederick including the promoters had every expectation of a race on Independence Day, 1955. A sanction from the AMA guaranteed a promoter the only sanctioned race within 100 miles. Of course, that distance is of little consequence to most motorcycle racers, even in 1955. New Jersey, Pennsylvania, Maryland, Delaware, and Virginia are somewhat of an unofficial racing region. There has traditionally been a lot of racing *and racers* in these contiguous states that despite being different "districts" in the AMA designation, share more commonality than they do differences. Thus, scheduling often became more about *where* than *how far*.

Most of the regional races, such as The Fritchie, soon had iconic dates. One of the notable benefits of a recognized annual date was avoiding schedule conflicts. The reasons why are lost to us today, but those traditions and expectations seem to have been disregarded in 1955.

In this racing region, the Reading Pennsylvania ½ mile had become established as *"The First Race in the East!"* Its annual date in the locally rainy month of April was always risky though. Not surprisingly, *"The Billy Huber Memorial"* race at Reading was rained out on April 17th, 1955. It was rescheduled for June 17th… and rained out again.

114

AMA approved a (second) rain date for July 3. Ordinarily this would have been an advantage for Frederick's race the next day just 112 miles south. However, in 1955 a ½-mile national race was scheduled for the fourth of July at Heidelberg in western Pennsylvania.

---

15 MILE NATIONAL CHAMPIONSHIP
HEIDELBERG RACEWAY
Heidelberg, Pa., located eight miles South of
Pittsburgh, Pa., on Routes 519 and 28

July 4th 2:30 p. m.

CAMPSITES AVAILABLE

PITTSBURGH RACING ASSOCIATION
718 Hope Hollow Road   Carnegie, Pennsylvania

Due to the fourth falling on Sunday in 1954, the Frederick race had been scheduled for Saturday the third. According to Delphey, the Pittsburg promoter had seized on this opportunity as leverage with the AMA to grab the coveted July 4th date for 1955.

This explanation does not seem to be totally valid as an AMA sanction only offered a 100-mile radius of protection and Heidelberg was far outside that limit. This is emphasized by the fact that Delphey did obtain his usual July 4th date when he got his sanction that spring. The Reading race being rescheduled for the day before the Fritchie certainly had some unknown bearing (the Reading race had over 100 entries!), but the result was the same. A lack of pre-entries and the expressions of many riders that they would be going to Heidelberg instead of Frederick on the 4th left Paul Delphey unwilling to risk the new promoter's money. Yes, "*new promoter.*"

While 1956 has long been the accepted date for the Frederick Lion's Club adopting the BFC, an obscure notation in the race announcements of the June 1955 "*American Motorcycling*" magazine instead of listing "J. Paul Delphey" as promoter, it lists "*Frederick*

Lions." It used the address of the Delphey shop, but clearly, the race had been handed to the Lions Club. J. Paul and later his son Julian and grandson Jay would assist in running the race for the Lions club for years to come employing their long-standing industry connections. This year for the first time though, J. Paul Delphey appears to have been risking someone else's money rather than his own. It may explain his being more hesitant about taking a chance on a race date when the racers said they were going somewhere else! Whether this was an intentional snub of the Delphey's, or merely an oversight by whoever was responsible for scheduling at AMA, the result was the same. On June 23, 1955, J. Paul Delphey once again called the Frederick News to make an unwanted announcement. There would be no race.

There have been no city sponsored fireworks in Frederick for 15 years. "The Big Shoot" got too expensive and city officials began to feel the money could well be spent elsewhere. However, the Delphey brothers have sponsored motorcycle races at the fairgrounds for years on the fourth of July. This year, major riders had signed to appear elsewhere...

Lead-in to Frederick News article announcing the cancelation of the races.

CLASS "C"
RACE MEETS   PHONE NO.   WHERE
JULY
2—3* Allegan Racing Assn., R. #2,
      Allegan, Mich.   OR-3-4840   Calhoun Fair Gnds.
3—2* Quaboag Riders MC, P.O. Box #54,
      Monson, Mass.   CO 7-5586 Stafford Springs, Conn.
4—3* Rib Mountain Riders MC, 819 S. 10th Avenue,
      Wausau, Wis.   VI 8-1255
4—2* Winfield Lions MC, c/o R. E. Gardner,
      1042 S. 56th Terrace, Kansas City, Kans.
4—3* Owensboro MC, 2570 W. 2nd. Owensboro, Ky.   Owensboro
4—4* Mansfield MC, RD #3, Mansfield, Ohio
4—4* Frederick Lions MC, 140 W. Patrick Street,
      Frederick. Md.   MO 3-9271

Upcoming race schedule in AMA's "American Motorcycling" magazine for June 1955, indicating the sanction had been granted. This listing also demonstrates the new promoter of the race, "_Frederick Lions MC_ (motorcycle club).

There have been other years when the race was called due to rain and unable to be re-scheduled. The events which led to canceling the 1955 race, less than two weeks in advance appear to have been as much out of the promoter's control as the weather was. As such, it is my own opinion that this missing race should be forgiven in the same way as a rainout or the war, when calculating the series' age and continuousness. The planning and efforts to hold the race are well documented. The sanction was obtained. The race advertised and the track rented. The measures taken the following year reinforce the devotion to the event and the desire to see it continue. If not for factors beyond the control of the Delphey's, there *would* have been a race held in 1955.

1950's Pit scene

Bob Myers collection, via David Sites

A New Chapter

1956 would usher in a brand-new vision for The Fritchie, in more ways than one. J. Paul Delphey and his son Julian were members of the Frederick Lion's club, a civic organization of local businessmen that engages in various community benefitting undertakings. The hallmark project of the organization for many years has been one that provides free vision care to those who cannot otherwise afford it.

Today the reasons why are unclear. Even the date has become less obvious than previously accepted. 1956 would mark the first year

117

of a new chapter of race sponsorship by the Frederick Lions club. Julian Delphey would manage it as before, but the Delphey's would publicly give the race, and the proceeds, to the Lions club.

For the first time since the race began, the Delphey business would be separate from the event they had stewarded for 34 years. A race that had progressed from a ploy to promote motorcycle sales into a genuine community event. Even serving as the city's Independence Day celebration when the city couldn't afford one. Father and son would continue to do much of what they had been doing to organize the event and passed that knowledge on to others within the club as a reliable and continuing funding source.

It was an event that had made Frederick Maryland known to many who would have otherwise never heard of the city. An event that brought the city itself together. And yes, it was an event that fueled interest in motorcycles. The classic had fulfilled the goals

EXPERT MOTORCYCLE RACES

WEDNESDAY, JULY 4

FREDERICK FAIRGROUNDS

TIME TRIALS 1 P. M.   RACES 2 P. M.

sponsored by the

LIONS CLUB OF FREDERICK
BEBEFIT OF CHARITY FUND

Eight Big Events   Free Parking

Children Under 12 Admitted FREE!

Frederick News June 22, 1956

envisioned for it by Paul Delphey on that long ride home from Marion Indiana in September 1920. No longer a business venture, The Classic had become a community venture and through the generosity of the Delphey's, the community would now own it and benefit from it. Thus, on July fourth, 1956 The Frederick Lion's Club became the official promoter of motorcycle races at the fairgrounds. It was a relationship that would continue for another 50 years. It may have been a new chapter for Frederick but for the racers, there was nothing different. It was the same race. Emphasizing that, Tommy McDermott came back south from New York to win his second Fritchie in 1956.

1953 & 1956 winner Tommy McDermott

(<u>not</u> @ Frederick) **Bill Davis of Washington D.C. is one of, if not the 1ˢᵗ African American to hold an AMA license. Davis rode for Herb Rieber's Indian shop in D.C. The bike Bill Davis had so much success with however, as evidenced by the distinctive black & white paint scheme, was one of three built by Bob Lyons of Falls Church Virginia. This particular "big base" Scout was Bob Lyons' personal race bike (identified by the red Indian script-style tank decal). Photo & Davis background courtesy Eddie Boomhower. Bike history provided by R.L. Lyons, the son of the bike's builder, Robert Lyons.**

1958 ad

George Roeder Sr.

121

1959 was "*Bad Bart*" Markel's only win at Frederick despite always being fast there, to include retiring George Roeder's track record in 1966 until Markel's own record was broken three years later by Royal Sherbet in 1969.

Bart coming out of turn-two in 1967. That track would be considered unrideable today. Bart set a record that day.

122

The 1960's

"Ask not, what your country can do for you. Ask what you can do for your country." President John F. Kennedy, Jan. 20, 1961

President Kennedy's inspiring suggestion epitomizes an atmosphere that was prevalent in the 1950' and 60's in America. Kennedy was a member of a generation who were born on the heels of the greatest pandemic since the medieval black plague and immediately preceding the Great Depression – or into the depths of it. A generation who had narrowly saved the free world during World War II. A generation that resumed their lives during a period of the greatest individual prosperity in the history of the world. A generation who were now comfortably enjoying the fruits of those circumstances. As Kennedy suggested, many had already begun an era of intense community engagement.

Religious, political and fraternal organizations had been important to society for centuries, but the mid-twentieth century witnessed an explosion of interest in completely volunteer clubs whose aim was to make a group effort for the betterment of all. The clubs provided the same sort of camaraderie and joint effort these men had experienced during the war. The goal was similar as well, progress of the whole of society, and they were not just men! The many, many organizations spread across the landscape included women either as auxiliary organizations or outright members. They were truly what journalist Tom Brokaw rightly named, *"the greatest generation."* The Lions club is one such organization.

The race proved to be a huge success for the Lions club. It became *the* primary fundraising endeavor of the organization and resulted in considerable income to finance the charity programs of the club. They shared the revenue with organizations such as the YMCA, Salvation Army and other community aid organizations. The Lions club's sponsorship coincided with a new injection of interest in motorcycle sport.

Unknown race team in a 1960's pit scene

1960

The first expert race of the new decade was won by South Carolina resident Richard Croach. The amateur and novice classes were won by Carlo Monosteri and Marshall Lamm, respectively.

Marshall Lamm novice class winner. 1960

1961

The expert main was won by national #50, Tony Murguia all the way from Key West Florida. As is typical, the story is much more interesting than mere results. When the green flag flew George Roeder (Sr.) grabbed the hole shot and a comfortable lead that he easily held for nine laps of the ten-lap main. On that last lap Roeder's engine blew and all he could do was watch Murguia and Bates Molyniaux who had seconds earlier been battling for 2nd and 3rd, fight over 1st and 2nd. This same situation had just played out in the Amateur main when Thad Coleman capitalized on the leader's blown engine in the last lap. David Estep was the novice class winner.

Tony Murguia at Frederick, 1961

Bob Myers collection, via David Sites

1962 - 1964

Mother nature must have had the Lions wondering about their commitment to the Fritchie in the early 1960's. For three consecutive years the race was cancelled due to violent thunderstorms passing through the area. In 1964, even a rare tornado touched down in Frederick county. Finally, clear skies and good racing returned.

1965

1965 BFC winner Larry Palmgren.

Bob Myers photo via David Sites

Larry Palmgren would take his first of two Fritchie wins in 1965 when the expert main was ended in the ninth lap due to... what else? A thunderstorm rolling down from South Mountain. Local favorite Don Twigg would secure a runner up position, the best ever by this local rider. Twigg's sponsor – his dad – was a former Indian dealer who ran the BSA & Yamaha dealership in nearby Hagerstown. Twigg was not only well known in racing circles but many fans at the Fritchie were Twigg customers, making the local boy doubly popular. The Twigg shop has sponsored and supported many racers from the early days of the business in the 1930's, up until the present.

National #31, Don Twigg

Bob Myers photo via David Sites

Larry Palmgren's brother Chuck would win the 1965 amateur class main event. George Longabaugh and Charles Hildebrand would fill out the top three in that class. There is no mention of the novice class in the record. It is noted as running *after* the expert main in other 60's race reports and if that were the case in 65, the class would have been a total rainout.

During the 1960's, Willie Moye from the Philadelphia area and riding a Triumph, was among the earliest African Americans to be allowed to participate in AMA sanctioned competition. It would be another 30+ years before a man of color *won* The Fritchie but that is an accomplishment that would have undoubtedly happened much sooner if the talented Moye had not lost his life in a crash at the Heidelberg Pennsylvania ½ mi. in June, 1965.

1966

Dirt track legend Bart Markel from Flint Michigan had set a new Frederick record of 29.4 seconds during qualifying. It beat the previous record of 29.7 set by George Roeder, from Monroeville, Ohio, but during the race Markel's Harley-Davidson KR's engine blew taking him out of contention. The main was then handily won by national #9, Gary Nixon of Wheaton, Maryland on a Triumph.

Another mention in that 1966 article is of amateur class winner, Eddie Adkins. Who after a decent racing career of his own, went on to make a long and respected name for himself as an expert race tuner for various Grand National Championship riders well into the 21st century. The races had not only proved successful for the Lions club, but for the fans and the many riders as well.

128

Another "Free State Cycles" rider, Malcolm Doying, novice class July 4th, 1967

Eddie Adkins sharing a pit with fellow BSA rider, Don Twigg #31

Bob Myers photos via David Sites

Frederick, 1966, Earl Myers (brother of Bob Myers) in his first year as a national number. Earl was a big guy who traveled with and supposedly, served as quasi bodyguard to, Gary Nixon. Bob Myers collection via David Sites

1968

1967 was another rainout in a replay of the story that had become so familiar during the early 1960's. That missing year made the Lions club and the charities that depended on this event even more eager for the 1968 race meet. So much so, that when an organization approached the mayor and council about a lucrative contract to lease the entire Frederick airport to stage an air show the week of July 4th, 1968, the contract was tentatively approved but with a caveat.

Mayor John Derr noted the annual motorcycle races held the same week and the council stipulated in the contract that the corporation staging the air show, in addition to the airport rental, if the tickets sold for the motorcycle races fell below the highest attendance recorded for that event, the air show promoters would be responsible for paying the Lions Club the difference! I have wondered if the mayor and council realized the highest attendance year was *1947*. In that year admission was $1 but in 1968 it was four dollars! I have not found any documentation of conflict between the race and airshow, or if the air show had to pay up, but Even the mayor and council of Frederick were protective of the Barbara Fritchie Classic.

I do not know if the air show made any money but the devoted fans at the Fritchie did not seem to notice there was anything else going on. Chuck Palmgren took the trophy back to New Jersey that night like his big brother had done three years earlier.

Leading the 1968 Expert main with Grand National Champ #1 Gary Nixon breathing down his neck, Chuck Palmgren's expression says it all. A friend of Palmgren and Nixon, Triumph marketing manager Ron Adkins crashed near this very spot earlier that day and received injuries that would prove fatal. Bob Myers photo via David Sites.

1969

Larry Palmgren

Chuck Palmgren's brother, would be back in 69 to win his second BFC title and the lion's share of the $15,000+ purse. Despite besting the record set by his brother the year before, it was anything but an easy win for Larry Palmgren. His main competition would be the legendary – even at that time – Bart Markel. Making it even more interesting, Palmgren jumped the start for the main and was moved to the penalty row for the restart.

Bad Bart was having his own issues though. Not the least of which was the fact he had already shipped his primary bike to California for the upcoming (July 6) Sacramento mile. The back-up Harley that Markel was riding just wasn't running the way Bart wanted that day. Despite that and a bad start, Markel did pull ahead of the pack by the second lap and maintained his lead as Palmgren fought hard to work his way to the front from as much as 150 feet behind the leader during the 1st lap. By the eighth lap of the ten-lap race, Palmgren was all the way up to second place.

Then, entering turn one during lap nine, right in front of the grandstand where everyone came to their feet cheering for the underdog, Larry Palmgren went low, taking away the inside line Markel planned on through the apex and out through turn two. By the time they hit the back straight Larry was 32 feet ahead and never left off till he got the checkered flag. Norm Robinson was third, more than half a straightaway behind the 1st & 2nd riders.

The Amateur winner was Royal Sherbet from Largo, Florida. Sherbet had taken a chance during qualifying and discovered a fast line around the track, breaking the track record in the process. During the main he pulled far ahead of 2nd place Mike Sponseller to win by half a straightaway. Mike Sponseller was obviously paying attention because it was another half a straight behind him to third place, Al Grande.

Sponseller and Sherbet became good friends on the race circuit and even now, more than fifty years later, they stay in regular contact. Sponseller good-naturedly refers to his old friend as *"Ice Cream."*

The 1969 novice event was won by a man who remains a force to be reckoned with in dirt track motorcycle racing yet today, 51 years later. That novice's name was John Goad.

Mike Sponseller (sr.) Frederick, Maryland ½-mile, 1969

Earl Myers on the same day. Earl was the brother of Bob Myers, the man
responsible for so many of these photographs.

Mike Sponseller and Don Castro. Rumor has It there were some top-secret British race bits hidden in that crate that they were not supposed to know about. After all, what's a race paddock without a conspiracy theory?

Present day riders are directed to the portable hippie-era, "green energy" air compressor lying to the right of the crate.

Bob Myers Photo, courtesy David Sites

<u>1970</u>

Motorcycle Races To Be Held In Frederick

July 2, 1970, Frederick News

Multi-race Fritchie alumni Jess Roeder mentioned during an interview that the generous purses at Frederick always made the riders feel appreciated. The $15,000 purse in 1970 when adjusted for inflation, is the equivalent of more than $100,000 in 2020! Consider that the median family income was $9,870 in 1970 and it is no wonder there were 75 entries for this race! The boomer generation was under 30 and all those young people were looking for excitement.

The bikes were seeing what a few years before would have been unimaginable performance changes. Despite Indian's departure in 1953, we now had BSA, Triumph, Norton, Ossa, Bultaco and others from Europe. There were also beginning to be a few promising entries from Japan. And of course, there was Harley-Davidson, to include some who were then starting to race lightweight 250 and 350cc bikes manufactured for H-D in the Aermacchi factory in Italy. As well, in response to changes in 1969 by the (AMA) race committee, 1970 marked the year Harley-Davidson introduced a new race bike that would change how many people viewed the sport. It was a bike that would come to dominate the sport for the next 45 years. Enter the XR 750!

Like 1969, Bart Markel was again leading the race when he got into turn one a little hot and went down, allowing Jack Warren to take the win. Bill Finn won the amateur class.

National #82* (that year!) Jack Warren for the win. BFC 1970.

Bob Myers collection via David Sites

135

1971

In 1971 Grand National Champ Bart Markel, was expected to challenge 1970 winner Jack Warren of Cornwall, NY, but Warren didn't appear, and Markel was injured a week earlier at the Charity Newsies race in Columbus, Ohio. That left the door wide open for a fast 2nd year expert from Largo, Florida. Royal Sherbet Jr. riding a nearly stock BSA model A65, handily won the 50th BFC. More on that race is found in the chapter devoted to Royal Sherbet.

* Jack Warren normally ran #82, but in 1971 he was #62.

Royal Sherbet (before getting his national number)

Larry Darr national #94 (taken at Reading PA 1969)

Bob Myers photos via David Sites

1972

As mentioned previously, there is and has been considerable confusion over exactly what year the Fritchie began. Since the series existed for years before having a lasting name attached to it, that confusion essentially continues to exist. The 50th anniversary of the Fritchie was *celebrated* on July 4, 1972.

The expert main was won by National #94 from Mansfield, Ohio. No, not George Roeder Sr. who had recently retired and given up the number, but another Ohio farmer (like Roeder), 25-year-old Larry Darr. It would unfortunately be Darr's only win at Frederick. It was the following spring when he was involved in the horrendous, fiery crash with Mark Brelsford at Daytona that has taken on a life of its own thanks to the internet. Darr raced with H-D factory support and so, was one of those who was running the new alloy XR 750 in 1972. In fact, he rode a brand-new alloy XR in the bike's maiden

137

race at Frederick in 1972. The alloy XR had only been approved by AMA less than three months earlier. Larry's details of that event appear in a later chapter devoted specifically to it.

Denny Varnes from Cochranville, PA won the 1972 Junior class taking the checkered flag just as he lapped the last rider in the field.

Buddy Barnes and Bobby Widner, Hagerstown & Monkton, Maryland racers.

Bob Myers collection, via David Sites

50th ANNIVERSARY

BARBARA FRITCHIE CLASSIC

FREDERICK, MARYLAND
☆☆☆☆☆☆☆☆

☆☆☆☆☆☆☆☆
FREDERICK FAIRGROUNDS
JULY 4, 1972

Souvenir
Program
$1.00

1973

1973 expert winner, #41 Bill Eves

Richard Lyons photo

To the amazement of everyone, Larry Darr was back to defend his Fritchie win. As mentioned, Larry had been involved in a serious crash earlier in the season and while still far from fully recovered, he was good enough to set a new lap record. Denny Palmgren got the holeshot and led the first five laps before suffering a mechanical that took him out of the race. Darr also suffered mechanical problems. The win wasn't a gimme for Eves though with Jimmy Manes coming on hot with victory his goal as well. Manes would give it all he had coming dangerously close, seeming to brush the fence several times. It was a slip during one of these highline moves that cost Manes some ground he never made up. In the meantime, Tony Sterling of Quantico Virginia was gaining on Maness! The race turned into a contest for second and third between Manes and Sterling who eventually finished in that order while Eves checked out ahead as Manes and Sterling battled each other.

The junior winners were T.L. Yarborough, David Singleton 2nd, Richard McConachie 3rd . The novice winners were Mike Eades, with Steve Freeman 2nd and Bill Ehinger 3rd.

140

Larry Darr (post-national number) on his way to a track record in 1974

novice winner Mike Eades and junior winner T.L. Yarborough

1973 was near the peak of the so-called golden era of Dirt Track motorcycle racing. When you consider that the Fritchie was merely a *"regional championship"* before the Hot Shoe or later All Star series' began, with no national status, points, or recognition and it is interesting to consider some data for the 1973 BFC left us by Frederick News-Post's 70's era motorsports correspondent Betty Lester.

There were 130 total entries. Twenty-six nationally ranked experts. More than half of them did not qualify for the main event! There were thirty-two juniors and 72 novices entered in the event. The Frederick police department estimated there were well over

6,000 spectators in attendance and an unknown number of team and family members along with track and event workers in the infield in addition to the 130+ racers. *That* is the level of activity in this sport during its peak period.

1974.

Barbara Fritchie Classic
Motorcycle   Race
THURSDAY, JULY 4, 1974
Frederick Fair Grounds
Sponsored By The Frederick
Lions Club
Advance Tickets $3.00
Tickets Purchased At The Gate
$4.00 Get your tickets at Blue
Ridge News Agcy., Fogle's, Del-
phey's, Dutrow's Honda, Shockley VW,
Schroeder's, Carmack-Jay's two
locations, or any Frederick Lion.
All proceeds for benefit
of the
Frederick Lions Charity Fund

Expert main 1974 staging (partial lineup) #62s Johnny Goad, #26s Rich Schroeder, #58s Eddie Adkins, #99s Steve Dalgarno, #14u Johnny Leale

Richard Lyons photo

Starting line, 1974 Expert main. 4s Denny Palmgren, #96 Billy Schaeffer (winner), #10n Rocky Simmons, #41 Billy Eves, #62s Johnnie Goad, #58s Eddie Askins, #14u Johnny Leale, #33 Paul Smart Richard Lyons photo

Novices 88s Jimmy White & 29s Chuck McCurry in turn one, 1974

Bob Myers photo via David Sites

Over 5,000 fans watched Larry Darr set a new lap record during time trials and another record during the six-lap heat. Billy Schaeffer got the hole shot in the main though, and Darr battled 1973 winner Billy Eves for second place. Larry was not able to make a pass on Schaeffer and Schaeffer, Darr and Eves finished in that order.

The Junior class was won by Mike Edes and the novice class by 16-year-old Phil Roper of Petersburg, Virginia.

As seen in this 1974 photo by R.L. Lyons from the grandstand, the fans on the back straight have been part of The Fritchie for a long time. - Richard Lyons photos

1975

Flagman Al Wilcox sends them off in the expert main 1975. Front row seen here, #68c Steve Freeman, #36s Brent Lowe, #41 Bill Eves, #42 Steve Morehead (winner) and #37s Al Grande
Richard Lyons photo

1975 Junior class winner Bill Roper #14s returning from his victory lap to flagman Al Wilcox (r) and announcer, Dave Warren (white trousers).
Richard Lyons photo

While the focus of this 1975 Richard Lyons photo is obviously the BMW airhead in the foreground. The photo is indicative of the tradition of riding motorcycles to this race. This is in fact overflow bike parking. The main area reserved for them being behind the photographer on the blacktop nearer to the grandstand. Further, this is all in addition to the bikers on the back straightaway. There are still a lot of cars, but it is the motorcycle riders who supported The Fritchie that truly kept this race alive. Many of those guys are

146

still maintaining this tradition of riding to the race every July. Some of them on the same bikes! For many, just walking around admiring those machines is as popular today as it was in 1975.

1976

1976, the two-hundredth birthday of the United States of America was a celebratory year. Every city and town held festivities and of course, July fourth was *the* premiere day for it. The Barbara Fritchie Classic had a lot of competition, but as both a Frederick *and* a racing tradition, the celebrations elsewhere didn't diminish the crowd loosely estimated at "over 5,000."

That day Margo King was the first woman to race at Frederick, but she wouldn't be the last. Her entry into what *had* been men's territory and doing it on that special Day at the race named for such a heroic woman, bears an allegorical significance that few in the stands or lining the fences, or even Margo herself gave much thought to. Like every woman who has rolled onto the track since then, Margo was just there to race. The racetrack is no place to make social statements or even a place to be if you're not deadly serious about the real reason for being there – racing. Margo was not a woman racer. She was a racer, who just happens to be a woman. More on this amazing racer can be found in a separate chapter devoted to her.

Margo King

Brent Lowe of Wakefield, VA would win the expert main of the 1976 Fritchie. Bill Eves was dominating the track that day, but after a re-start, Lowe got the hole shot and never gave up the lead. Due to the configuration of the track turns 3 & 4 at the west end of the track are typically drier and slicker than turns 1 & 2. It can create issues for many riders. It was cited as *the* factor by almost everyone interviewed after the 1976 race but for some reason, Lowe described that very same situation as beneficial to him. Eves took second and #52, Scott Rader, third.

Brent Lowe, #36c lined up beside #68s Steve Freeman - Richard Lyons photo

1977

The results for 1977 show six different brands of motorcycles in the three main events (Expert, Junior, Novice) - Harley-Davidson, Ossa, BSA, Yamaha, Triumph, and Bultaco. The XR750's were definitely foretelling the dominance to come, but Triumphs were still in contention and the Yamaha's were making their presence known to all. Harley's lightweights were in evidence as well in the novice class.

#41 Bill Eves coming to the line for the 1977 Expert Main.

Richard Lyons photo

For those who've followed this sport and its stars, some of the names mentioned in the 1977 BFC results may be recognized.

Expert: 1st Bill Eves (H-D) 2nd William Schaeffer (HD) 3rd William Crabbe (H-D) 4th Stephen Freeman (H-D) 5th Jay Livingston (Yamaha) 6th Brent Lowe (H-D) 7th Dave Singleton (BSA)

Junior: 1st Lance Jones (Triumph) 2nd William Donaghy (Triumph) 3rd Joseph Purdue (Yamaha) 4th Mark Cox (H-D) 5th Stephen Powell (H-D) 6th Delbert Busche (Triumph) 7th Robert Griffin (Triumph) 8th James Williams (Triumph)

Novice: 1st Peter Berthauer (Ossa) 2nd Leroy Meyer (Yamaha) 3rd Thomas Duma (Yamaha) 4th Robert Crabbe (Bultaco) 5th Larry Sweeten (H-D)

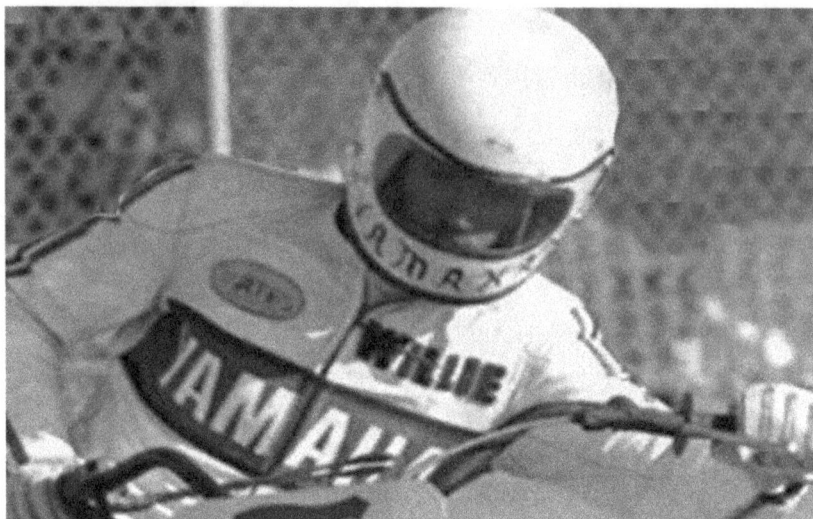

Local favorite Willie Crabbe finished 3rd in the 1977 and second in 1978.

1978

Despite days of threatening weather, 1978 saw more than fifty riders and 3,500 fans for the races. The Harley XR750 was firmly in control of the sport and all the top experts were riding them. 1st was Joseph Purdue of Richmond VA. 2nd was local favorite Willie Crabbe, 3rd was Dave Singleton.

Junior class – 1st Richard Mendenhall. Novice - Darren Erichsen.

#37, Joey Perdue was the 1978 winner

1979

The 70's were arguably the all-time high point for dirt track motorcycle racing in America. The traditional motorcycle genre was riding the crest of a wave powered by the bulk of the baby boom generation. But the monopoly of dirt track racing was also beginning to be attacked from all corners. This last year of the golden 70's would be a washout in Frederick. Literally. A heavy thunderstorm during the night of July 3 left the fairground track unsalvageable in time for the Wednesday races and the Frederick News-Post reported the next day that the races would not be rescheduled.

1980

(Photo not from 1980)

1979 was a rainout but 1980's expert main was won by national #72, Steve Hall. The majority of the talk around the Fritchie in 1980 though was about an attractive young blonde-haired girl who everyone kept staring at. For the second time in history, a woman had entered the BFC.

Novice Tammy Kirk had a tough reputation for being a top-notch competitor. She won her heat against nine other riders. All men. She would finish in second place in the novice main.

LIONS CLUB OF FREDERICK

READY FOR THE RACES — Final preparations are being made for the 59th consecutive running of the Barbara Fritchie Classic, the oldest continuous half-mile dirt track motorcycle race in America. The race is to be held at the Frederick Fairgrounds on Saturday, July 4th, the rain date is July 5th. Shown above from left are, Jay Delphey, race chairman; Kyle Enloe, program chairman; Mike Kehne, track committee; Mike Vantucci, sponsor; Julian Delphey, race chairman; and Richard Riley, sponsor. (Photo by Tony Casadonte)

1981 Lions club publicity photo

Despite all the preparations and expectations 1981 would be a total rainout. The Maryland State Police recorded just short of 1 ¼ inch of rain at the Frederick Barrack on Saturday afternoon when the race was supposed to be running. The races were tentatively rescheduled for the next day but the rain did not move out of the area completely until Monday morning and a decision was made Sunday to cancel the whole event.

The Lions Club had again increased the purse by 30% for 1981 and the pre-entries attracted by that move seemed to indicate it was the right way to go.

FREDERICK

FAIRGROUNDS

1/2 MILE TRACK

MOTORCYCLE

★ ★
★ 4 ★
★ ★

Star
Event

RACES

THUR. JULY 4 th

RACES START AT 2:30 P. M.   TIME TRIALS 1:00 P. M.

ADVANCE TICKETS $3.00   AT THE GATE $4.00

—————— FREE PARKING ——————

PROMOTED FOR CHARITY BY

FREDERICK LIONS CLUB

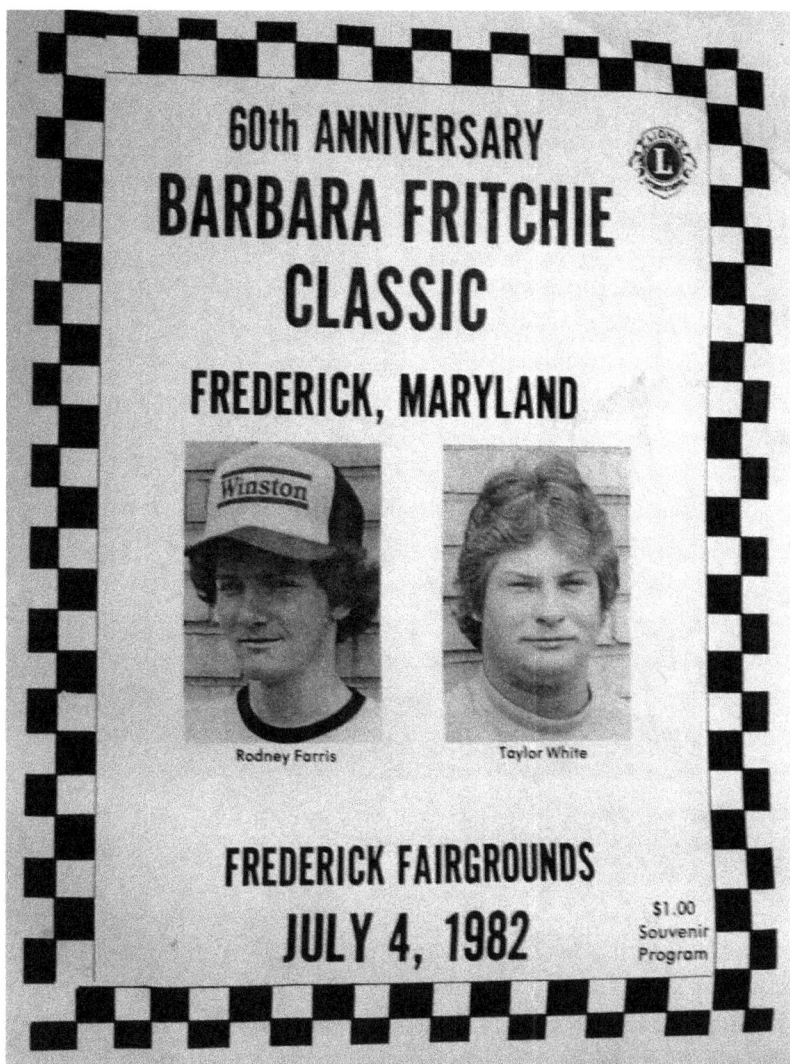

Cover of the 1982 program

1982

July 4, 1982 was a Sunday and five-hundred couple miles west of Frederick, all the pros had run The Indy Mile the day before. It was uncertain how many of them would make the rocket ride east through the night, but a few hundred miles between races is not unusual in the dirt track world. The purse included a guaranteed $3,000. Another $1,500 contributed by the three major bike dealers in Frederick (Fredericktown Yamaha, Harley-Davidson of Frederick and Dutrow's Honda). A $250 fast lap prize and other enticements to make the stop at Frederick quite inviting in 1982. Two up and coming local friends were the guys many had their eye on in 1982. Taylor White and Rodney Farris grew up racing each other and both had learned the lessons well.

There were hometown heros on the cover of the 82 program, but the winner would not unexpectedly be an Ohio guy, Darren Erichsen

The local guys would be there come hell or high water and the promoter's strategy to attract the pros worked as anticipated. In addition to all the expected riders there were some unexpected names at the top of the lists compiled by longtime race fan Julien Delphey as he watched from his coveted perch in the announcer's booth at the top of the tower adjacent to the finish line. The expert main was won by Darrin Erichson from Ohio. Sammy Sweet came all the way from Texas to win the Junior class, but second was Chris Evans who

156

made the equally impressive trip south from Canada! Ron Andrews from Virginia took the win in the ever popular Novice class.

Darren Erichsen #24f takes a victory lap for the 1982 BFC

1982 Junior winner Sammy Sweet telling Dave Warren how he did it.

1983

The expert main started like a tornado touching down as #38 Rob Crabbe grabbed the hole shot but #50, Fran Brown passed him before they made a full lap. Brown then held the lead till the end. Crabbe held on to second place and #92 Rod Farris filled out the podium in P3. The rest of the 1983 expert field was Matt Rozawicz 4th, Darren Erichsen, the previous year's winner P5, followed by Randy Texter, Gary Conkling, Billy Norfleet, Taylor White, Scott Davignon in that order. Half of those riders held national numbers! Junior and novice winners were, Mark Hartley and James Oliver.

The Lions Club of Frederick, MD. Presents

61st Annual

Barbara Fritchie Classic

AMA's Oldest Running
1/2 Mile Race $3,000
July 4th AMA Purse

Frederick Fairgrounds located off
East Patrick Street,
Frederick, MD

Practice 12 noon
Time trials 1 P.M.
$250 Lap Money Race 2 P.M.
for Final Event

Call Mike Kehne
Dutrow'sSales & Service
301/478-8117

Tickets $6 at the Gate
Rain Date July 5

158

1984-1990

Except for Doug Davis (#41) who grabbed the win in his rookie expert year of 1985, the Fritchie went back and forth between Steve Morehead #42 (2nd from left) and Rodney Farris #92 from 1984 until 1990. Morehead and Farris are seen here with tuners Mike Wheeler and Dick Sears. The majority of the decade stacks up as Farris, Davis, Farris, Morehead, Morehead, Farris.

Doug Davis & Steve Morehead

As a local boy, national number 92, Rod Farris, was all too familiar with the hole shot being key to this track and he made a pretty good stab at it as the flag dropped on the 1987 BFC. Obscured from view behind Farris in the above photo is Rod's friend, #42 Steve Morehead. The remainder of the grid is #68 Darrin Erichsen, #71 Dave Miller, #66 Geo Roeder, #57 Rusty Rogers. Second Row, #63 Gary Conklin, #79 Tony Pitcock, 75a Brad Haas, #75 Nickie Fontana, #83 Mike Reid. Another photo of the grid prior to the start shows #13 Mickey Fay at the inside second row position. It is unknown if this photo is a restart or Fay is missing for some other reason.

#42, Five-time Fritchie winner, Steve Morehead

Courtesy Will Hyser

John Goad on the red on white XR 750 Rod Farris rode for him

Announcer Dave Warren and Dick Sears (pushing bike) share a laugh with Steve Morehead. Dick Sears was Steve's tuner for the day on the XR750 loaned to the visiting Morehead by Tom Hyser (on corner of the stage) of "Hyser's Cycles" in Laurel, MD. Courtesy of Will Hyser

Farris went on to get the win in 87, but it was well earned. Rusty Rogers, national number 57, was a second-year expert who was immensely popular with the Frederick fans and from fast qualifier he was not giving up to the veteran Farris without a fight. Considering that he did it on an XL500 Honda against everyone else on Harley XR750's, and Rusty's drive and determination is only more apparent. Rogers was one of those guys who seemed to always be riding right on the edge. There was no "*good enough*." It was all or nothing with Rusty Rogers.

Rogers was back to win the BFC in 1990!

1990

It is almost a legend today, like King Author or even Barbara Fritchie, but once upon a time in America there was a Japanese motorcycle brand that put a serious kink into the outstanding record of the Harley-Davidson XR 750. From 1983 into the early 90's, the NS then RS750 Honda was the only consistent challenger to the Harley-Davidson XR750... and many times it was the XR that was the challenger!

Even before the XR 750, ever since Murry Brish's Indian dealership stopped participating after the 1920 Armistice Day race, the Fritchie had always been sort of a Harley event. Whether it was the origins with the Delphey dealership and heavy advertising using Harley-Davidson literature or something else, there was always just an unspoken aura of Harleiskness surrounding the event. In the 1980's & 90's there was a special "Dash for Cash" for XR-750's only. To spice things up, and encourage those campaigning Hondas to come to Frederick, Mike Keene, then working at Dutrow's Honda, organized a group of Maryland Honda dealers to underwrite a special contingency prize fund for anyone who could win the Fritchie on a Honda.

164

Rusty Rogers, 1ˢᵗ Honda RS750 winner of the BFC, July 4, 1990.

(1989 photo riding CR500 Honda)

Bob Myers collection via David Sites

Cash is a great incentive but the chance to put your name in the record books as *The First...* is always inviting. It is a record that can never be broken. *The First* is forever! Add to this the satisfaction of one side of this brand rivalry being able to de-throne the other and it should be no surprise there were almost as many Hondas on the grid in 1990 as there were Harleys. It would be a Virginian who normally rode Harleys who would claim the title of "*first*" to win the BFC on a Honda.

Not just any Honda either. Rusty Rogers came to Frederick to ride Johnny Goad's Honda! George Roeder was in Frederick that day but there was a problem that kept Geo out of the main. George was there to ride Tom Hyser's loaner XR 750 despite "Hyser's Cycles"

165

1990 Junior winner Jason Fletcher, being interviewed by the familiar BFC announcer Dave Warren

being one of the participating Honda dealers!   In retrospect, one is left wondering if that *"problem* "may have had something to do with this being Honda's best shot at winning the Fritchie and Roeder's ride for that day being furnished by one of the contingency sponsoring Honda dealers? His fellow dealers were probably not terribly happy about Tom Hyser being the biggest threat to their first win.

Robert Majeski was second in the 750 main and Larry Pegram was third on another Goad Honda.   Rod Ferris' Harley had a mechanical issue that took him out of contention as well.

1991

In 1991 Larry Pegram would take a turn on the Frederick podium.

30 years later, Pegram is *still* competing in National Championship racing!

The very first motorcycle races ever held in Frederick 90-years earlier in 1900 and 1901, were brought here by people from Baltimore. The Fritchie may even have originated because of moving a race date from Baltimore to Frederick in 1921. Various racers calling Baltimore home have competed and won at Frederick. In 1991 the 750-expert winner of the BFC would be an up and coming 18-year-old from Baltimore – Baltimore *Ohio!*

Larry Pegram did have connections to Maryland though. The owner of his Skip Eaken tuned Honda RS 750 was BFC veteran and

167

ex racer, national number #99, Mike Sponseller, who lives at Frederick, making the win particularly sweet. Even sweeter was that the up and coming young Pegram was riding the RS750 Honda, which Mike Sponseller had bought from Wayne Rainey's team. The Pegram/Eaken/Sponseller effort would be known as *"Team Jesus"* by some with either admiration or scorn depending on whether you were watching or following Larry "the Worm" Pegram.

July 4, 1991 was not a typical BFC race day. Cloudy threatening skies kept the normally scorching temperatures comfortable and the moisture in the track. That made it a racers day at Frederick!

Pegram was not many people's favorite to win that day as the flag dropped on the start. Larry was in the middle of the front row with George Roeder on the outside and Rodney Farris on the pole. This was Farris' home track where he had won multiple times and Roeder, who had won the Dash for Cash that day, would soon become the winningest rider in the history of the Fritchie. Pegram was not there to watch though.

When they crossed the stripe on the first lap, it was Roeder, Pegram and Farris, 1-2-3. So close, as the saying goes, *"you could throw a blanket over them."* Exiting turn four on lap three, Farris drafted by both Pegram and Roeder for the lead with Larry following him past George. A quick learner, on the next lap, Pegram used the same move to pass Farris and held the lead till the end. Roeder however was already suffering from mechanical issues and continued to fall back, ultimately finishing the race in 7th place. National #51, Craig Estelle took 3rd. Pegram and 10th place finisher Michael Scott, were riding the only two Hondas in the field. All the other experts were mounted on XR 750 Harley-Davidsons.

In the junior division Georgie Price IV checked out to take an easy win with Kenneth Mohler and Eric Johncox fighting it out for second and third. Junior ranked Jess Roeder, little brother of George Roeder had a nasty get-off during his heat race and while bruised and sore, he was not seriously injured.

In a field of teenagers and twenty-somethings, in the novice class it was a thirty-year-old former racer who had just come back to it in

1990 who checked out, half a track ahead of most of the competition. Even lapping the last-place rider at the finish line.

So, what made #78ᴍ Rodney Mashue special? Other than being an obviously talented rider, Rodney did it with one foot. He had a bad racing accident several years earlier that ultimately resulted in his leg being amputated just below the knee. Dismissing his handicap, Rodney instead blamed it only for his being several years behind in the ranks when compared to other riders his age.

When asked if it made any difference in his racing, Rodney jokingly replied that it makes him lighter so he can go faster. Announcer Joe Kelly not giving up so easily, asked if Rodney ever encounters situations where his prosthetic causes problems. Mashue, finally admitted that "*if it comes off the foot peg things can get a little scary*." Eleven months after this win, on June 20, 1992, Rodney Mashue would unfortunately lose his life in a racing incident at the Darke County fairground in Ohio.

Mashue's Honda has a brake lever just above the clutch lever on the left handlebar.

Bert Sheppard photo

70TH ANNUAL

Classic

Frederick Lions Club

July 4, 1992

Now

Then

Dame Barbara snatched the silken scarf
She leaned far out on the window-sill
And shook it forth with a royal will
"Shoot if you must, this old gray head
But spare your country's flag," she said
A shade of sadness, a blush of shame
Over the face of the leader came
The nobler nature within him stirred

Barbara Fritchie

EASTERN REGIONAL • PURSE $5,000 • FREDERICK FAIRGROUNDS

170

Lap one, turn one. 1992 BFC

Mike Hacker's Victory Lap

1992 Pro-Am winner, Mike Hacker talks to announcer Joe Kelly

1992

During this period before the 1997 launch of the AMA Hot Shoe series, the Fritchie ran as a "Regional Championship," which was essentially a meaningless title... unless *you* won! If not for the tradition this race had become in the mid-Atlantic motorcycle community and the degree which it had been embraced by many mid-west riders, together with the existence of an inviting purse, it is unlikely it would have survived this troubled period.

The top spot at Frederick would go to Geo Roeder in 92 & 94 with Rusty Rogers picking up a second win in 93. Ninety-five was a rain out and Steve Morehead won the next two years but 1992 was George Roeder's first win at Frederick. That story is told by him in detail in another chapter. There were two restarts in that expert main. George led the first lap before a red flag. Randy Texter #65A got the hole shot in the second restart but did not hold it long. He was passed by Steve Morehead and Ricky Graham as they battled and eventually took each other out. The last attempt at a race was all Geo Roeder! The podium would for the first-time feature three brands from three different continents with Geo's Harley XR 750, Kris Kiser on a Rotax and Dan Ingram on a Honda.

In the junior class James Hart #16P grabbed the hole shot and held the lead through the turns. #55P caught up to him and the pair rode

side-by-side through the straights through most of the race, with James continuing to hold the lead in the turns. Both riders mounted on Woods Rotax bikes were evenly matched mechanically, which is understandable when it is realized that they are brothers, James and Roy Hart! The brothers would finish just as they had ran, 1 & 2 with Jess Roeder 3rd.

Mike Hacker won the ProAm class with Shawn Clark second. The record oddly does not mention third place.

1993

July 4th, 1993 was a rare Sunday race. It was also typical Maryland 4th of July weather. The mercury in the thermometer would push past 100F that day and the water truck could not keep the track wet enough. The water truck also provided a welcomed respite for some trackside fans who lined the front straight rail for a welcomed shower as the truck passed on its frequent missions to quell the dust..

The previous day was a GNC race in Michigan and not many top riders made the long ride east for the "regional" Fritchie. One who did was a Frederick favorite, Rusty Rogers who set fast lap time for the day and went on to lead, and then win the expert main. George Roeder coming off a bad day in Michigan stopped off at home in Ohio on the way back Saturday night and stayed there as his dad and brother Jess drove on toward the rising sun. Trying to put the Roeder name in the book for consecutive years, Jess came into the corner a little hot on the first lap and laid it down. He made the restart though and still managed to finish second behind Rogers. David Rayburn would be third. The 93 Pro-am class was fraught with red flags, blamed on the "dry slick" track under the blistering sun. That situation eventually (after four red flags) brought a decision to end the race early by AMA referee Harold White. Shawn Clark would be declared the winner due to his position when the race was called, but the crowd favorite was a young racer from Connecticut, #32u Kenny Coolbeth Jr. who would go in the book as P2.

1994

George Roeder II was back for another notch in his Fritchie belt. After getting the all-important hole shot George pretty well checked out after the first lap but there was plenty of talent in the field! Scott Stump took second and Dave Rayburn won a battle with Georgie Price for third.

What was then the "600 class" was won by Robert Majeski. Eric Kinsey #38F was second and 90B Les Washburn was third. In the Pro-am class, Todd Winsett jumped ahead to an early lead. Todd checked out as the laps ticked off, five, six, seven, eight, then, as he was about to lap the last place rider on the ninth lap of the ten lap main, at the farthest point from the grandstand, Todd Winsett disappeared from view with a puff of dust on the dry slick turn three. Matt Auxier, would capitalize on Winsett's bad luck by winning the 94 Pro-am event with Gary Stogsdill second and Dave Lesniak third. 1995 was a rainout.

1996

Another name familiar to Fritchie fans came east for some Lions club money in 96. Steve Morehead's 41st birthday was only a month away but as though demonstrating the adage about age and experience vs. youth and exuberance, Morehead, who was the oldest rider on the circuit, had his toughest competition from 17-year-old Paul Lynch. The youngest rider in the expert class. *"Experience and a lot of laps. That's what made the difference right there."* Steve said when asked how he had held off Lynch. Advice from Morehead is as relevant today as it was twenty-four years ago. *"We use a lot of races like this to test things on the bike. Every adjustment you make, you learn from it."* Steve Morehead's notebook, like those of many, many other racers, is a coveted artifact of the sport.

Lynch was positive about his 2P finish. *"Anytime you can keep a guy like Steve Morehead in sight, you're doing good."* He said after the race. *"We came here with high expectations but did a little better than expected!"*

James Hart and Ken Mohler battled for third throughout the expert main but Mohler managed to hang on to it for six laps of the ten-lap race. Then, on the seventh lap, Hart squeezed around Mohler and was able to maintain the position to the checkered flag.

In the 600 main, Georgie Price jumped out front and held the lead the whole race until a risky, last lap, last chance, highline pass by Kevin Varnes to win. It really wasn't unexpected or even new. As Varnes stated during the victory interview, *"It's kind of a rivalry between Georgie and me. We been racing each other since we were seven years old. So whenever one of us get's the lead..."*

174

Yet another of the familiar Winsett brothers won the Pro-am class. John Winsett, third past the line on the first lap would work his way into the lead and hold it to the end. Marco Novello was second and Scott Slimm third.

The 1996 dash for cash, a year after his death, was named in honor of the late #92, Rodney Farris. It could not have been more appropriate for anyone else but Rod's friend, Steve Morehead to win the first ever, *"Rodney Farris Dash for Cash."*

Of special note to current fans, Betty Lester & John Cannon of the Frederick News Post leave us this report on the 50cc class;

In the Pee Wee race, John Lewis overcame a slow start off the line to win the three-lap race. Lewis who lives in Brandamore, PA, turned 7 on July 1. In the fall of 2020 AFT Pro, operator of the "Moto-Anatomy" dirt track racing school along with the Royal Enfield "Slide Academy," and factory racer / bike developer for Royal Enfield (in 2020) remembered the race as his first ½ mile race.

1997

Steve Morehead was back in 97 to do some more testing on a new chassis. Morehead low-sided in turn one during his qualifier but used that same highline to pass the entire field on the first lap of the main. This would be Morehead's last Frederick win. He retired from racing at the end of the season to take a job with GNC/AFT. *"He's an old, smart dog"* Georgie Price, who finished a distant second said of Morehead. Mike Varnes claimed third place.

Robert Lewis won the 600 class with Chris Hart second and Garth Bastian third. This was the first year an 883-class race was staged at Frederick. First and second place winners were Chance Darling, & Tom McGrane (no P3 was noted in the record).

Pre-national number, John Nickens, Richmond, Virginia, the 1998 takes a victory lap in 1998 as the rain comes down at Frederick.

1998

Richmond Virginia has long been a hotbed of rider development and National number 17, John Nickens was one of those to come out of that incubator. Nickens was in his first year as a 750 Expert rider, still carrying his 11s district number. He had some bad luck here in 1997 when he crashed during qualifying. Then his throttle cable broke taking him out of the 600cc main but July 4, 1998 was one of those days when things simply clicked. He got the hole shot and never looked back. Mike Varnes from Reading Pennsylvania echoed a sentiment heard often in Frederick; *"The start is everything here."*

John Nickens attributed his quick starts to a history of drag racing. Roy Miller took third in the rain shortened main, but the star of the day was John Nickens and his XR750 Harley-Davidson. It was Nickens' first expert win and the first time a man of color had won the main event at the Barbara Fritchie Classic. It is thought by flat track historian Bert Sumner that this was the first main event of a significant AMA sanctioned race anywhere won by a man of color.

The well contested, 1998 minibike race won by 7-year-old

Tommy Mudgett Jr. of Sykesville.

1999

July 4th, 1999 was a rare BFC held on a Sunday. There was a national the previous day at Indianapolis, Indiana. Many riders made the all-night drive from Indy to Frederick to do both races. One of them was Expert winner, "*Revin*" Kevin Varnes.

Varnes of New Holland, Pennsylvania joked that he decided to stop by the race; "*since it was on the way home.*" After a bad day out west (Varnes finished the Indy mile in last place) he almost missed Frederick, not arriving until 11:00AM. It was soon enough though. It was Varnes' first win at Frederick on a 750. Second was Steve Beattie from Ontario Canada. 3rd was Dave Rayburn and Shawn Clark finished fourth. A name which hadn't become too familiar yet won in the 600cc main. Kenny Coolbeth Jr. had stopped on his way home from Indiana to. Hot Shoe points leader, Coolbeth was in contention for his 3rd straight title in the series and hungry for the points to be had at Frederick.

Chris Hart won the 883 class, but it was the second-place finisher who would get all the crowd's attention. Michele DiSalvo of Modesto California was the third woman to race The Fritchie and the Frederick fans made sure she knew they liked her. Michele would later remark that she could hear their cheers even while her Sportster screamed down the front straight past the grandstand. DiSalvo would go on to become an international race sensation and later, a respected tuner who teamed with Briar Bauman to help the fellow Californian win the AFT national championship in 2019. Rookie Cory Roth won the 600 pro sport main, beating Tom McGrane. Just prior to that 16-year-old Roth won the 250 main.

The Frederick News-Post correspondent tried to interview the winner of the minibike race, but the champ was a little shy. His dad Rick explained that 10-year-old R.J. Hart had seen Bruce Brown's film, "*On Any Sunday*" and decided that was what he wanted to do. Rick said it was R.J.'s favorite movie, "*he must have watched it 80 times.*" Second in the mini was Justin Walker, a six-year-old from Wintersville, Ohio and stepson of Dave Rayburn who finished 3rd in the expert main. Third and fourth were a pair of five-year-old rookies in their first race, Jake Keeney and Marshall McMillion.

Michelle DiSalvo at Springfield in 2000 courtesy Paul Haney

178

2000

After a four-year absence from Frederick, Geo Roeder was back in the first year of the new millennium and his presence was well noted. Defending Fritchie champ Kevin Varnes, nursing a shoulder injury from early in the season, slipped high in turn two and Roeder took full advantage to grab the lead and not look back. It was Roeder's third win at Frederick. 1998 winner John Nickens was third behind Varnes.

2001

Wednesday July fourth, 2001 didn't look like a good day for racing, but the show went on with racings optimism. Practice, heats, class after class... Then, barely into the first lap of the 750-expert main, large raindrops began to sporadically splat onto rider's visors. Whether the bikes were faster or the rain slower, it took seven laps before Ma Nature forced a premature checkered flag. It was more than enough time for Geo Roeder to defend his Fritchie crown though. Steve Beatie was second, Paul Lynch, third, Robert Lewis 4th, Rick Winsett 5th, Jess Roeder 6th. In the 600-expert main it was Johnny Murphree, Dominic Beaulac and Mike Hacker, 1-2-3.

2002

The 02 expert win was another notch in his Frederick belt for George Roeder II of Monroeville, Ohio. One of the hottest Fritchie's on record, the temperature hovered around 100 degrees Fahrenheit during most of the day, but the competition was no cooler. Kevin Varnes gave Geo a real run for the win but came up just a bit short. Roeder joked that he was just going fast to stay cool. *"When you stop, its hot!"* Out there Roeder said, *"...you're getting an 80 to 100 mph breeze."* George said one of his favorite parts is driving back to Ohio from Frederick on the evening of July 4th every year, *"we get to see every town's fireworks show from Maryland to Ohio."* Those fireworks must have truly been memorable. During another interview, eighteen-years later, Jess Roeder said the same thing to me as one of his favorite Fritchie memories! Win, lose, break, or crash,

179

I suppose witnessing that with his dad and brother would have been a memorable way to cap a long day at the track.

Geo Roeder owned The Fritchie from 1992 to 2004.

Besides the ambient temperature, Kevin Varnes was a hot rider in 2002. He was scoring well in almost every race, both hot shoe and GNC. That day he won the 505 class and took second in the 750 before noticing oil dripping from his XR750. It proved to be a mechanical issue that prevented him from running the dash for cash. Varnes later admitted he was kind of happy to see the leak and getting out of another race after running two mains, back-to-back in 100+ degree heat.

2003

The third Fritchie of the new millennium saw some changes, and some memories. The second year of the experiment to make the track faster by removing the cushion almost killed the race as AMA placed restrictions on the track barring 750's for competition.

The 2003 main was a 505cc race won by Dominic Beaulac of Quebec Canada in a rain shortened five lap race. Second was a name that would be heard many more times for years to come, Jared Mees. Rick Winsett took third and Frederick resident Joey Tyerar while deep in the field at 11th place, was notable just the same as he'd been a regular at the hometown race as he moved through the ranks from minibikes, all the way to expert. A Tyerer heritage that goes back to when his great grandfather announced to the Frederick community that he was adding bicycles and bicycle repairing to his gunsmith business in 1899.

#30, Dominic Beaulac taking the highline around turn one.

In the 505 pro sport class, Scott Lowery narrowly made the win as his bike was barely holding together. *"When you're out front like that, you go until you blow up. You don't get a second chance."* Lowery said.

The vintage class report shows two familiar names from 1999 and perhaps a record for The Fritchie. A father and son in the same race. Showing no mercy for dad, 14-year-old R.J. Hart not only beat Rick but as the elder Hart said, *"He almost lapped me!"*

2004

04 marked the year the cushion came back to Frederick. Along with it, the 750's were back as well. Thomas Kline and his road construction men had worked a miracle to hear the comments from the riders who had rode the Fritchie in previous years. After the stone dust was installed and conditioned, Richard Riley and Eddie Adkins

assessed the track with Paul Lynch as the test rider and determined the project to be a success. It was an assessment echoed by the racers in July. *"They made quite an effort to improve it. And they did!* (improve it) George Roeder II said.

For George II, it was a bittersweet win at Frederick that day. It was the first time he had been back since the passing of his dad, the legendary George Sr. in May 2003. Roeder the Ohio cushion master, made it look easy, lapping several riders in the main *"I knew I had to beat him off the line"* said Jared Mees. But Roeder got the hole shot and was gone as expected. Despite having the seeming advantage of being the test rider to tweak the track for the Independence Day race, Paul Lynch finished third with Dan Gideon 4th and Rick Winsett 5th. Winsett had suffered a serious crash a couple years earlier and was undoubtedly one of those happy to see the track improvements.

Geo Roeder #66

Yet another familiar name pops up as the winner in the minibike race. A second generation, racer nicknamed *"Fly'n Ryan"* by his dad Kevin Varnes. Hauntingly reminiscent of a scene in a film just recently released (*"Fast and Left, A Flat Track Film,"* Evan Senn, 2019) six-year-old Ryan Varnes was quoted by Frederick News-Post correspondent John Cannon as saying; *"I like racing because you win trophies."*

2005

Geo Roeder was back in 05 looking to add number seven to his career wins at Frederick. He worked extra hard at it but thanks to luck, it was not to be. That luck was bad for Roeder who threw a chain in qualifying and had to start the main from the back row. The luck was good for young Jared Mees. As he'd predicted a year earlier, Mees *"had to beat him off the line,"* and due to George's starting position, Jared did exactly that this time, and never looked back even as the Roeder brothers were coming on hard. Jared Mees ended George Roeder's streak at Frederick with Geo and brother Jess filling out the podium as numbers 2 & 3.

Craig Shipp photo

As has become common, one of the names in the minibike race would become well known in Frederick. Unfortunately, not with the ultimate results we all hope for. The winner that year was 6-year-old Kyle McGrane of nearby Gap, Pennsylvania. Kyle would keep racing and become an outstanding rider as he progressed through the ranks. Sadly, during his second year as a GNC2 pro, Kyle would lose his life in a racing incident in California in 2016. The #2 & 3 minibike riders in 2005 were names familiar to motorcycle folks from Frederick, Cole Dutrow and Jensen Riley.

2006

The 2006 BFC was close to the GNC's swing through the east leaving Odessa Michigan after the ½ mile there on July first and heading to Parkersburg, West Virginia only 200 miles from Frederick. Not next door, but near enough that several pros sent pre-entries with intentions of picking up some easy Fritchie bucks.

Among those entering the BFC that year are Jared Mees, George Roeder, Joe Kopp, Kenny Coolbeth and Paul Lynch. In part due to lots of riders experiencing difficulties in Michigan on the first, most of those pre-entries would DNS in Frederick. That dark cloud seemed to come east with them. Paul Lynch fell during the main, taking him out of contention. Ricky Marshall would win the main that year with Jess Roeder second and Chris Hart third.

2006 winner, Ricky Marshall Craig Shipp photo

While he did not finish, the fastest man that day ended up being Sammy Halbert. Thanks to a Maryland State Police helicopter, he made it from Frederick to Baltimore in about five minutes. The first-time Fritchie racer discovered rather rudely how close that outside fence is. The impact left him unconscious and suffering a badly sprained neck, a torn ACL and numerous contusions. Rather than a warning, Sammy took it as a challenge.

2007

07 was another of those years when the afternoon showers swept down from South Mountain to threaten the race. Ma Nature did a great job of watering the track, giving consistent wetting. The rain was deemed not enough to cancel the race, but the abundant moisture made the otherwise frequently dusty track *very* messy. Expert main winner Dan Gedeon later stated that he was out of tear-offs for the last three laps, able to see little more than the white rails around the inside of the track. Gedeon was running second the first four laps then, between turns three and four race leader Jared Mees slipped wide and Gedeon squirted under him for the lead. Mees would later say; *"He wanted it more than me today."* Third was Paul Lynch and fourth was John Raun Wood.

2007 winner, Dan Gedeon Craig Shipp photo

Mees did win the 450 expert race with Don Taylor second and Dan Gedeon third. Shawn Ford of Ontario Canada won the 450 Pro Sport class with Brandon Robinson second and Dennis Flynn third.

2007 was also the last time then 88-year-old AMA Hall of Famer *"Airborne Al"* Wilcox would wave a flag at Frederick. Wilcox, a former racer from Trenton New Jersey, raced The Fritchie 19 times in his career and won it in 1957. In 1966 Al gave up racing and became a promoter and popular starter at races all over the country. His leaping, acrobatic antics earning him the name "airborne Al."

#43 Sammy Halbert hot after Dan Gedeon #13 between turns three and four. 2007

<u>2008</u>

One of the rare scheduling conflicts took place in 2008 when a national was scheduled on July 4th in Topeka Kansas. This was the first year of AFT management of the Grand National Circuit and assumed at the time to be a simple oversight. The Fritchie was moved to July 6th the Monday of the three-day Independence Day weekend. No harm / no foul.

AMA NATIONAL HOT SHOE SERIES

★ 86TH ★

BARBARA FRITCHIE
CLASSIC

JULY SIXTH 2008 ★ 10AM

PRO 750/1000
PRO EXPERT
PRO SPORT

AT THE FAIRGROUNDS

GATES OPEN @ 10AM
HEATS START AT 12
PRO 750/1000 PRO EXPERT PRO SPORT

FREDERICK
★ MD ★

Website BarbaraFritchieClassic.com
Designed by AccessMediaLab.com
For more info Call 301-663-8333

Shayna Texter, 2008 450 Pro winner <small>Craig Shipp photo</small>

July 6th, 2008, Shayna Texter became the second woman to win at Frederick and the 1st to win a main event when the 17-year-old from Willow Street Pennsylvania took the 450 Pro Sport checkers. Another 17-year-old rider, this one from the mid-west named Jeffry Carver Jr. got the hole shot but Texter stayed with him the whole way. At the half-way point, Shayna slid by and never looked back. The 750 and 450 Expert classes were won by Jared Mees and Matt Weidman respectively. (Tammy Kirk became the 1st female winner at Frederick in 1979 when she won her heat race)

<u>2009</u>

Dan Gedeon made 2009 his second checkered flag in the 750 main at Frederick. Sammy Halbert and Matt Weidman took second and third with Cory Texter and Ricky Marshall rounding out the first five in the field. Halbert won the expert singles (450s) narrowly beating Jared Mees in the first of many classic Halbert/Mees battles at Frederick. The lead changed between them several times in the exciting race where Matt Weidman even slid out front at least once as Halbert and Mees fought each other, but it was Halbert who held the lead on the all-important last lap.

188

AMA NATIONAL HOT SHOE SERIES

OLDEST RUNNING HALF MILE IN THE COUNTRY

THE BARBARA FRITCHIE CLASSIC

87TH ANNUAL

4TH OF JULY

FREDERICK FAIRGROUNDS
FREDERICK, MD

GATES OPEN @ 10AM
HEATS START @ NOON

PRO 750/1000
PRO EXPERT
PRO SPORT

AMA

2009 Pro Singles,

#21 Jared Mees, #20 Matt Weidman, #41 Ricky Marshall (hidden), #65 Cory Texter, #43 Sammy Halbert, #72 Tim Eades

In the Pro classes, Jeremy Higgins won the pro singles with Cory Crawford and Brody Miller two and three. Evan Baer won the pro-twins with Cory Strickler second and Garrett Wilson third.

2009 750 expert main starting grid

#41 Ricky Marshall, #57a Ken Yoder, #65 Cory Texter, #43 Sammy Halbert, #13 Dan Gedeon, #14 Bryan Hazel, #44f Nick Evans, #32 Shawn Baer, #72 Tim Edes

2010

The second decade of the new century witnessed some major changes for the Fritchie. 2010 was the first year of the new **American All-Star National Flat Track Series**. The new co-promoter introduced some new classes that offered more racing. Prior to this change, it was rare for a local name to appear in the program. Afterward, several locals compete in classes for vintage bikes, 450 and 250 amateur categories and "senior" riders. The All-Star series would prove to be a resounding success for developing a new wave of grass roots interest.

Defending GNC champion Kenny Coolbeth Jr.& 3rd place Jethro Halbert Craig Shipp photos

The pro racing is still the main show of course. That year, Sammy Halbert won his first Fritchie main in the Twins class narrowly beating Kenny Coolbeth the defending AFT champion. Third was Luke Gough from Hilltop Australia. Sammy also won the expert singles with Jared Mees second and Sammy's big brother Jethro Halbert third. Other winners were Jason Isennock, Pro-Twins, Brad Baker, Pro-Singles, Tom McGrane Jr., 450 Open Amateur & 450 Amateur, Cole Yauchzee, 250 Amateur and Nick Taylor Open vintage.

2011

Sammy Halbert was back in Frederick for the fourth of July 2001 and he had a claim to defend. Halbert would defend his title, defeating Luke Gough and Jared Mees 2 & 3 in the main event. The

191

results for the expert singles was the same with Gough and Mees trading for 2 & 3.

Sammy Halbert, July 4th, 2011, on his way to another Fritchie win.

Other class winners included Cory Crawford Pro-singles & Pro-twins, Brody Miller 450 Open Amateur, Nick Taylor Open vintage, Brett Friedel Veteran 30+, Colton Smith 450 Amateur and a new name from Ohio, Jarod Vanderkooi 250 Amateur 2nd & 3rd in that class were Tristan Avery and Colby Carlile.

Tristan Avery (L) Jarod Vanderkooi (Ctr.) and Kolby Carlile (R) being interviewed by Richard Riley.

192

Brad Baker, the 2012 BFC expert winner

Courtesy Craig Shipp & Frederick.com

Halbert was back trying to make it three in a row but he came up just a bit short after maybe trying just a bit too hard. Sammy went down in lap one when the backend tried to pass the front in turn four as he was looking for a way around Mees. From the last row on the restart, Halbert still managed an enviable 4th place in the main. The winner was a complete surprise though, another Northwesterner like Halbert, Brad Baker, riding a borrowed bike edged out Mees and #3 Luke Gough.

With a thrilling drag race to the finish, Cody Miller and Colby Carlile gave the crowd a little more than expected when Carlile went into turn one way to hot, rode across the top of the bales and slammed into the fence. Walking away with some minor scratches, it looked a whole lot worse than it was. Winners in other classes included; Ryan Wells Pro-Singles, & Pro-twins, Jarod Vanderkooi 450 Amateur, Jerry Steele open vintage, Tristan Avery 250 Amateur and Thomas Englehart Veteran 30+

Sammy Halbert, Pro-singles, Frederick Maryland, 2012

2013

Lucky #13! It's a popular sticker or patch around bikers and hot rod guys. For Sammy Halbert, it sure was lucky. He became the holder of the second-place record for wins at Frederick when he took his third in four years. But he also made a clean sweep of the Frederick meet with wins in Expert Twins, Expert Single and Dash for cash. Coming off major knee surgery just four months earlier, it was a miracle he was here at all. Second-place winner Kyle Kolkman gave him a run until the third lap when Halbert pulled away and Kolkman never regained the ground. Brandon Robinson took third place in the main. In expert singles, Halbert won, Mikey Martin took second and Robinson who professed his preference for clay tracks, was third. Kolkman was right on Halbert to the end in the dash but couldn't quite get by.

The 2013 pro-singles winner was Dan Bromley, 450 Open singles, Colton Smith, 250 & 450 Amateur, Tristan Avery, Open vintage, Billy Worthington, Pro Twins, Cody Johncox and veteran 30+ Brody Miller

Courtesy Craig Shipp & Frederick.com

Expert Main, 2013, #14 Briar Bauman in his 1ˢᵗ year as a national number, #89 Evan Baer, #49 Chad Cose, #7 Sammy Halbert, #19k Adam Bushman, #32 Shawn Baer

2014

The grand marshal for the 2014 Barbara Fritchie Classic was Mary Nixon, the widow of former grand national champion Gary Nixon from nearby Cockeysville, Maryland. Gary's number of course was #9, the same number Mees used. During opening ceremonies while addressing the crowd Mary Nixon mentioned that *"I sure do like that #9"* referring to Mees' bike. It was an emotional moment and while I'll keep my favorites to myself, Mees needed to win that race for no other reason than to make Mrs. Nixon proud. Following the race, Mary insisted on making the considerable walk through the infield pits so she could personally congratulate Mees.

Halbert put on an incredibly hard charge after a re-start and made his way up to second. In his words, *"The pass for third and second was a little bit sketchy just because this track is so narrow. I was going around the outside of guys and just kind of hoped they left me enough room to get by. And then, luckily there was enough room and I survived."* That's a pretty ballsy statement from a guy who was medevac'd out of here by helicopter eight years earlier. It wasn't quite enough though. Mees won by less than a bike length, but he won. He and Halbert were then 3 - 3 at Frederick. Rob Pearson and Ben Evans was 3rd in the expert twin main.

Another new name came up on the winner's list this year. Jeffrey Carver Jr. of Alton Illinois won the expert singles. Jeremy Higgins and Sammy Halbert finished 2 & 3. In other racing Brandon Price won open singles amateur, Austin Woodruff 85cc, Jarod Vanderkooi pro singles, Colton Smith 250 Amateur, Jeremy Higgins super singles, Dallas Baer senior 40+, Joseph Maher open vintage and Jamison Minor pro twins.

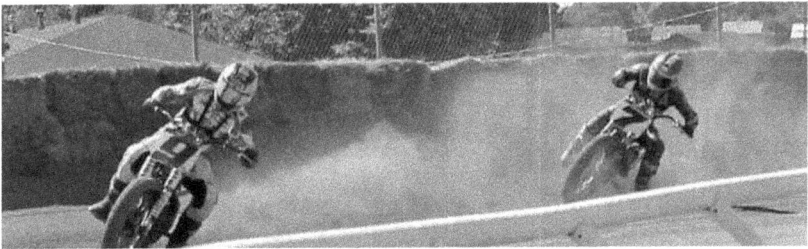

2014 Expert main, Mees #9, Halbert #7, between turns 3 & 4

FOR MORE INFO CALL 240-285-9012

2015

THE YEAR OF THE GROUNDHOG

It was 2015 that AFT scheduled the Du Quoin mile on the fourth of July. Not just a competing race but a mere (in flat track terms) 12 hours away. Even if the message wasn't intentional, it *was* clear. July 4th was just another day to AFT. Barbara Fritchie beware. While the top tier racers with points to gain all headed to Illinois, do not get the impression those who did come to Frederick were any slouches! The winner in fact was the winner of the previous year's dash and the super singles class when there *was* plenty of other pro competition. Jeremy Higgins won the day in 2015, but he won it by being fast, not because the competition wasn't. Danny Koelsch took second in the main, his XR750 Harley screaming to catch and pass Ben Evans and then pursuing Higgins to the very end but running out of laps before he could catch him. In the final results, Mike Poe was third after also squeezing by Ben Evans like Koelsch had done. Evans was 4th and Jason Isennock 5th. Higgins also won the dash for cash and narrowly missed a clean sweep when Chad Cose won the expert singles.

Courtesy Craig Shipp & Frederick.com

Mike Poe (3rd), Jeremy Higgins (1st), Danny Koelsch (2nd)

2015 Expert main

2015 Pro singles & Pro twins Jesse Long. Open singles amateur, 450 amateur and open vintage Joey Alexander. Senior 40+ Dallas Baer. 250 Amateur Brandon Newman. Super singles John Long. There was also a special pre-1930 class in 2015. Bikes that would have been right at home here in the earliest years of The Fritchie. The rolling start for these clutchless bikes was unaccustomed to the modern race fans and while the speeds were slower, they were as serious as anyone on the track that day. John Rhodes #26, of Richmond, VA. was the winner on a 1925 Excelsior.

Make no mistake! This was not some mere exhibition.
This *was* a genuine *race*.

So… what's this about a groundhog you ask? Recent as it is in the long history of the BFC, "*THE groundhog*" always seems to come up whenever Fritchie regulars get together and start reminiscing.

Baby groundhogs are born in early spring. By June they can care for themselves and by July, most are searching for new homes of their own. So it was that a wandering young groundhog had apparently taken temporary shelter under the stage adjacent to the start/finish line at the Frederick fairgrounds. By late-afternoon, he had, had enough of this noisy bunch of humans and their machines. Just as the main event was lining up, Woody decided to see where that white line led to. Maybe he thought it was a crosswalk? It *was* a hot day. Maybe he just wanted a snow cone? It was the guy who would eventually win the race, Jeremy Higgins who first noticed the little guy sneaking out from under the podium.

Even a juvenile groundhog is a compact animal of more than five pounds. Suddenly finding one in your path at 90mph is not a scenario to be entertained if avoidable. So began the great groundhog chase of 2015. Several of the track workers and a few infield spectators joined in trying to avert tragedy. Woody didn't want to go back where he came from and as each rescuer got near, he would suddenly be confronted with the problem of, "*how do you pick up a frightened, wild groundhog?*"

A brave fellow finally made a fast grab of Woody's tail and lifted him off the ground. The fearless rescuer, Ted Trey, had the groundhog at his mercy. Woody was carried to a fence that separates the stage area from the rest of the infield. Trey expected the fence to be enough to keep Woody off the track until the 8-lap main could be run, but Woody had other ideas. He knew where the gate was! As Mr. Chuck slowly made his way toward the gate, another infield spectator calmly walked over and dropped an inverted trash barrel over him. That did the trick. By the end of the race however, the barrel was lifted and found to be empty! Woody had already burrowed out from under the barrel and disappeared while everyone else watched Jeremy Higgins win the race.

Woodrow trying to sneak back in after being ejected for being in the pits without a wristband.

<u>2016</u>

This year gave us another installment in the continuing Mees / Halbert battle for Frederick. Halbert had won the expert singles heat against Mees but Jared got by him and won the main, before Sammy had an opportunity to repay the act in the expert twins main Mother Nature said, "not today!" The rain which had been threatening all afternoon finally began in earnest. Not a passing shower this time, the rain poured, and the track surface began raising from water running between the stone dust cushion and clay subsurface and the race was called. As fast qualifier, Mees was awarded the race. Halbert by no surprise was second and Chad Cose third.

Also completed were the pro-singles main – Dalton Gauthier, Brandon Price and Cameron Smith, and the 450 amateur – Zach Mullen, Jake Fell, Tyler Mullen

Expert singles class 2016, Halbert #69, Mees #1, Cose #49

Curtis Fisk leading Billy Worthington into the front straight under the increasing threat of a mid-summer thunderstorm.

95 YEARS OF RACING

BARBARA FRITCHIE CLASSIC

THE FREDERICK FAIRGROUNDS

FREDERICK MD

JULY 4TH

Adults - $20
Kids 7 -12 - $10
Kids under 6 - Free

Gates Open at 10am
Heats Start at Noon
Race Ends by 5pm
Free Fireworks Downtown

WWW.BARBARAFRITCHIECLASSIC.COM

FOR MORE INFO CALL 240-285-9012

2017

Sammy Halbert evened up the score against Jared Mees for Frederick wins on July 4, 2017. Sammy putting notch #4 in his Fritchie belt. Despite Jared not showing up to contest the race, Halbert didn't have any easy time of it. #23 Jeffry Carver Jr. followed closely by Chad Cose made this one of the most exciting Fritchie mains in recent memory. Carver and Halbert swapped the lead several times in incredible passes until Sammy finally pulled it out in the last corner of the last lap and beat Jeffery across the line by less than a bike length. Adding to the show was Halbert's borrowed Baer Racing Products KTM 1000, nicknamed "The Beast." It's a powerful bike but it's a bit unwieldly. At five foot-four inches and 140 pounds, Halbert certainly had his hands full but you'd have never known it watching the race.

Super singles – Chad Cose, 450 Amateur – Brian Wass, Pro singles – Brandon Price, 250 amateur – Mike Poe, Open vintage – Shane Livingston, Senior 40+ - Richard Mellinger, Open Amateur singles Brandon Newman.

Halbert #69 and Carver #23, turn one, Expert main 2017

Sammy Halbert and Daryl Baer taking a hard-earned victory lap on the Baer Racing Products KTM 1000.

2018

Cory Texter had been coming to Frederick for half his life. Both as a racer and with his dad Randy, who was also a racer. His little sister had won the 450 pro sport class in 2008, but Cory had never won in Frederick. 2018 was one of those years when things just turned bad wherever he looked. There was one of those little dark clouds following Cory Texter and he just couldn't shake it... until the fourth of July! Experiencing a mechanical in the first lap, he got lucky and there was a restart. He was on the last row, but his bike was running again!

Always good on the start, from the third row Cory Texter managed to get into third place by turn one. He passed 2nd place Dalton Winkler then finally the leader, Ryan Varnes. It was one of those days when things just clicked into place for no obvious reason.

All-Star All-Star

BARBARA
AMA
OLDEST RUNNING HALF MILE RACE
FRITCHIE
Classic
JULY 4TH

MOTORCYCLE
RACE

barbarafritchieclassic.com

20 FREDERICK 17
MARYLAND
USA

$1 $1

Souvenir Program

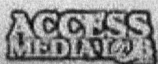

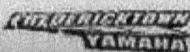

Expert pro singles – Cameron Smith, Super singles, open singles amateur, 450 amateur – Trent Lowe, Senior 40+ - Richard Mellinger, Open vintage – Michael O'Neal, 250 amateur Billy Ross

2018 winner Cory Texter between turn 3 & 4

Cory Texter on the podium being interviewed by announcer, Scottie Deubler
Criag Shipp photo

2019

During years when there has been a GNC race anywhere from the heartland east in the month of July, there have typically been more top ranked riders in Frederick. Whenever they are not already in the neighborhood, a chance for a Frederick payday becomes less attractive. And yet bucking that trend, 2019 gave a good field of top-notch professionals. Cory Texter from nearby Willow Street Pennsylvania was back and someone came through with an XR750 for Sammy Halbert to ride. Chad Cose and Ryan Varnes were back as well. Marylander Dalton Winkler was unfortunately sidelined after a serious crash several weeks earlier in New Hampshire. Another Maryland pro who'd come up through the ranks at Frederick was Brandon Price.

When Price opened the doors on his van that day a new chapter began at the Frederick fairgrounds. July 4th, 2019, Brandon Price of Whitehall Maryland was racing an Indian FTR750 on the same track where this 98-year-old series had emerged from a Harley-Davidson / Indian duel in 1920. Price would be racing against a Harley factory rider. Price's historic win that day is only slightly dampened by him having raced against the 50-year-old XR750 model instead of the up to date Harley. Additional Fritchie facts for 2019 are.

- The first Indian to compete in at least sixty-five years.

(last time estimated to be approximately 1955 via Richard Lyons)

- The first Marylander to win in 30 years.

(last was Rod Farris 1989)

- 1st, 2nd & 3rd place expert class winners were riding different brand bikes. Indian, Harley-Davidson and Yamaha, respectively.

Other winners included All-Stars singles & super singles – Dallas Daniels, Open singles amateur – Aidan Roosevans, Senior 40+ - Rick Winsett, 250 amateur – Logan McGrane, Open vintage – Darryl Jakubowski.

Brandon Price on an Indian, "FTR 750 Scout." July 4th, 2019, the first Indian brand motorcycle at Frederick in more than 65 years.

Indians at Frederick

Archeologists have identified two ancient native American village sites dating back thousands of years less than a mile from the fairground track. Indians, both the native variety and the motorized ones have each had storied histories at Frederick. The latter though, has made a noteworthy return. Murray Brish, motorcycle enthusiast, Indian dealer, and fair board member was instrumental in the first races at the fairgrounds.

#37c Bill Balderson, July 10th,1950 on a Bob Lyons built "big base Scout" The last photographically documented Indian at Frederick until July 4th, 2019.
Photo courtesy of RL Lyons

2020

Fans, Racers, and longtime friends of the Fritchie.
It is with a heavy heart that we must announce that the 99th annual
Barbara Fritchie Classic has been cancelled.

So began the message posted by the promoters of The Fritchie on the Race's website, Tuesday, June 9th, 2020. The message continued... *Over the past 3 months of dealing with the Covid 19 pandemic and its subsequent government intervention, we have waited patiently and optimistically hoping that we would be able to give the fans and racers a safe place to be on the 4th of July this year. Maryland has been on the forefront of safe measures to protect its residents and in doing so has implemented a tiered system of reopening businesses and activities. The current phase that is in place does not allow for events to be held that are the size of the Barbara Fritchie Classic. After going through various channels to seek approval and offering various scenarios to potentially try to hold the event, we have not been able to receive 100% verification that Maryland and Frederick County's Executive would allow the race to take place under the current reopening phase.*
We appreciate the patience and support from all those who have attended the race year after year, both fans and racers. We will now turn our efforts to preparing for the 2021 event, which will be the 100th Anniversary of the oldest and greatest Motorcycle races in the country.
Thank you for your understanding
The Friends of the Fritchie

It was an unwanted announcement but not a totally unexpected one. Nobody was prepared for the restrictions unexpectedly put in place in March of 2020. Those restrictions began to be relaxed in stages, but by the second week of June, Maryland Governor Larry Hogan and Frederick county executive Jan Gardner decided virus transmission was of greater concern. And so, it was like June 1942 and June 1955, when just days before race day, the 99th annual BFC was canceled. **If not for factors beyond the control of the** ~~Delphey's~~, **RILEY's there would have been a race held in** ~~1955~~ **2020.** This should not be held against the longevity of the series any more than a rain out would be.

212

A Few Good Men

I've touched lightly on those who are responsible for this race through the years and as we know it today. What follows is just a slightly closer look at a few of them.

The Delphey's

While previously touching on who they were and the role they played in the Barbara Fritchie Classic, it would be a disservice to this story not to give just a bit more background on the Delphey brothers and their family. After all, for the first 35 years, this race *was* the Delphey Brother's Classic!

Cornelius "Grant" Delphey came to Frederick as a blacksmith. His trade was in a state of transformation in the late 19th century as new methods and mechanization of the industrial revolution were taking over what had up until then been cottage industries. Grant had the foresight to learn, grow and adapt with his trade of metal working. He was the first in Frederick to use the then new, acetylene gas equipment, particularly for welding. For the first time in history metal work became somewhat portable instead of tied to a blacksmith's forge and anvil. Grant Delphey's home and shop were at the corner of N. Market and 7th street. His sons would grow up around the business. They would learn and understand the intricacies of metal work, as well as becoming acquainted with the then new metal working machinery.

As young men, Paul and then Clarence went to work down the street in the machine department at the Ox Fibre Brush company. Company owner McClintock Young was an innovator himself who wanted to automate his new factory. Mr Young's problem was that automatic broom and brush machines didn't exist, so he had to invent the machinery then build it, in order to automate. J. Paul and Chester Delphey, along with their brother in-law Joshua "Fred" Shipley would be responsible for improving, maintaining, repairing and modifying the equipment and occasionally we might assume, building a whole new machine.

(No Model.)

6 Sheets—Sheet 1.

McCLINTOCK YOUNG.
BRUSH MACHINE.

No. 456,610.

Patented July 28, 1891.

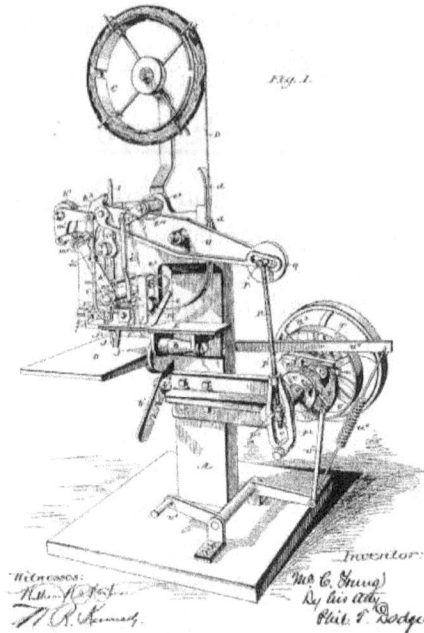

Fig. 1

Witnesses:

Inventor:
Mc C. Young
By his atty
Phil. T. Dodge

U.S. Patent office drawing of McClintock Young brush machine

As noted elsewhere, Chester Delphey's daughter recalled that the brothers had first begun buying, repairing and re-selling used motorcycles in 1914. Their first business location being on Chapel alley between 2nd and 3rd streets.

Fred Shipley, who had married the Delphey's sister Naomi, was the brother of Harry Shipley, the first Harley-Davidson dealer in Frederick. At the time of Fred's death in 1955, he and Naomi were living at 138 W. Patrick street, next door to the Delphey store. While I have been unable to discover exactly how the dealership transitioned from Harry Shipley to Paul Delphey, this connection certainly sheds some light. The 40-year period from 1880 to 1920 saw an incredible leap in technology. The Delphey brothers caught that wave and rode its crest. In 1918 they opened a motorcycle shop in the old Ebert's carriage works warehouse on W. Patrick Street and grew the shop into one of the most popular and recognized businesses in Frederick for most of the 20th century.

Avid sportsmen, the Delphey's soon branched out into all types of sporting goods. The store was decorated with numerous taxidermy animals hunted by the Delphey's. Behind the store was a menagerie of live game including white tailed deer, black bears and of course racoons. On Julian's "farm" just outside town, he kept bison, elk and more deer. They were among the first to sell factory produced aluminum and fiberglass boats and canoes and they sold Evinrude outboard motors from early on. J. Paul turned the business over to his son Julian in the early 1960's while the business was near its peak of popularity. J. Paul would die not long afterward in 1965 from a sudden, unanticipated heart attack.

Courtesy of Heritage Frederick

The above photo, like the one in chapter two, appears to be from the fairgrounds from the picket fence, the linier (stable) building and the ticket booth at the gate. This photo, also like the previous one, is marked 1919. As the group and the motorcycles do not appear alike, it is my opinion these are not the same event and probably, not the same year. The notation on the photo, along with the year, identifies

215

J. Paul and Julien Delphey as appearing in the photo. The notes are clearly incorrect since if this is 1919, Julien would only be two years old! While I suspect J. Paul and probably at least one of his brothers are pictured, and while I have my own opinion on which is Mr. Delphey, the names and date remains uncertain.

J. Paul Delphey about 1925

Courtesy of Betsie Handley

When he took over, Julian continued with the proven business model except for adding even more sporting goods. In 1970 Julian successfully ran for election to the Maryland house of delegates where he served until 1982. Julien Delphey volunteered with various civic organizations as well as his years of service as a legislative representative. One of his proudest accomplishments was securing scenic river protection for Frederick's Monacacy River. Julian was also instrumental in Frederick's flood mitigation plan. During this period while Julien was busy with civic matters, the business was gradually turned over to his own son Jay.

In the late 1990's, in accordance with revitalization plans, the city of Frederick decided the Delphey store was the ideal location for a six-story parking garage. An offer was made to buy the property and promptly refused. The city then instigated condemnation proceedings which in addition to the threat of losing their property, added the expense of defending against a protracted court battle just because the city wanted what they had.

As always, eventually, the city prevailed. The Delphey's were paid a fraction of the land's value. The Delphey's store closed in 1998 and the building was razed soon afterward. Four generations of Delphey's who had demonstrated such devotion to their hometown and played an integral part in the city's journey over 100 years' time, would understandably have felt betrayed. The urban revitalization that took their home and business was only possible due to the flood control measures Julian Delphey himself championed in the Maryland legislature on behalf of all of Frederick.

Downtown Frederick and the former Delphey's property, 1998 & now.

Images courtesy MD. DNR / MERLIN GIS

The Lions club race committee - Jay Forney, Kyle Enloe, Doug Warfield, Jay Delphey, and Julien Delphey in the Delphey store at 140 W. Patrick Street. (approx. 1980)

Chester Delphey race starter approximately 1925

Courtesy of Betsie Handley

140 W. Patrick St. approximately 1920

(courtesy Frederick Magazine via Heritage Frederick)

The ghosts of W. Patrick St. today

The Delphey's were a family who turned an old carriage warehouse into one of the anchor stores defining Frederick's business district. They gave the city so much, only to see their business closed and their property taken and turned into a parking garage by the same city which they had faithfully served for four generations.

The Delphey's were much more to this town than mere businessmen. They were part of the heart and soul of Frederick. From patriarch Grant's modernization of metal work and manufacturing to the elaborate holiday displays at Delphey's Sports Store. Their participation in organizing and holding parades, celebrations, bicycle rallies and other community events. Through their service to charitable organizations. Julian Delphey's years of service as a member of the state legislature and especially the family's role in giving us The Barbara Fritchie Classic. This family's contribution to Frederick is deserving of a much more suitable legacy, but I believe J. Paul, Clarence and Chester would be quite proud that at least the race - *their race* - lives on a century later.

For the record, the fourth Delphey brother was named Ray. An exceptionally talented musician, he moved to Washington D.C. after his celebrated return from the war in October 1919. In Washington, Ray had a long and successful career as an extremely popular musician in various bands and orchestras. Ray is typically not thought to have been involved in the motorcycle business. However, when Chester opened the Hagerstown store, the license was in both he and Raymond Delphey's' names!

The Riley's

I have known who Richard Riley is for quite some time, but it has only been in recent years that I have finally made his acquaintance. What a shame it took so long! It is pure speculation on my part but I have this mental picture of an adolescent Richard Riley appearing for all the world to be the inspiration for "Happy Days" Richie Cunningham, complete with a Fonzie-like buddy.

As he has often told the story, a teenaged Richard Riley once caught a ride with a friend on an old Indian motorcycle, and Richard was hooked. His mother however said; "*You'll never have a motorcycle as long as you live in my house!*" (Marion, is that you?)

220

Being the respectful son he was, Richard moved out. Problem solved!

Richard served in the U.S. Navy and true to form, during a port call in Barcelona Spain, he checked out a bike show where he met Sr. Francesc Bulto… *and bought a motorcycle*. Richard rolled the bike onto ARS-40, "**the U.S.S. Hoist**," before sailing back to Norfolk Virginia. During the peak of the cold war, "The Hoist" had been in Spain that spring of 1966 to locate and recover something the Air Force had lost in the Mediterranean Sea before someone else found it – *an H-bomb!*

As dangerous as his mother had previously found motorcycles, by comparison to the duties her son had with Uncle Sam, my guess is that mom was happy to find out Richard had left the navy and taken a job in a local Virginia motorcycle shop.

It was during this time that Richard saw his first Barbara Fritchie Classic after riding up from Norfolk for the races in 1968. Less than ten years later, he would open a motorcycle shop of his own - *in* Frederick.

On September 7, 1975, Richard and Sharon Riley opened Fredericktown Yamaha & Triumph on the corner of Grove Road and Urbana Pike, which was then on the outskirts of town. The largest of the few neighboring businesses was a stone quarry! Richard and Sharon's children would grow up in the shop with their mom often working the parts counter. Much to many (male) customer's embarrassment in the 1970's, Sharon sometimes had to explain to them what parts they really needed to fix whatever problem they were experiencing. Their initial shock soon turned to respect when they realized this little lady knew what she was talking about.

From the very beginning, the Riley's embraced the racing side of motorcycling. On an unusually slow winter day at Fredericktown Yamaha Richard and Sharon's son Ian told me about riding all over the map with his Dad to motorcycle races as a small boy. Sometimes in an XS 650 Yamaha *with a sidecar*. Months later someone sent me a photo from a 1972 race program. I do not know who the photographer was and apologize for that. The location, was Reading Pennsylvania. The Fredericktown Yamaha logo is on the chest of

Donnie Smith's leathers. Right behind Donnie is Richard Riley and sitting on dad's shoulders as if to confirm what he had told me that day at the shop several months earlier, is a pre-school-age Ian Riley. The Riley family connection with racing runs deep!

Harrington Delaware class winners, 1978.

Junior Tommy Duma 26f, Expert Corky Keener #62, Novice Donnie Smith #98s

In those days, most racers, both amateur *and* professional, drew most of their sponsorship from local motorcycle shops all over the country and from early on the Riley's supported riders they could believe in. It is a tradition they continue today even as much larger businesses have backed away from racing and national racing itself has gravitated to larger – and fewer – specialty sponsors.

Emphasizing the Riley family connection to the Fritchie is of all things, potato salad. Yes, potato salad. That iconic 4th of July picnic staple. In the late-1970's Richard asked Sharon to make some food for the track workers and among other things, she made a big batch of her special potato salad for the employees and volunteers. Today, forty-odd years later, it's claimed that expectations of her much-anticipated potato salad is the only reason some of them still come to help out at the race.

When you pull into the parking lot at Fredericktown Yamaha and Triumph you know instantly that this is the kind of shop where tradition runs deep. Where tradition, rather than a word, is a way of life. The Fredericktown Yamaha logo can be seen today on the bikes and leathers of top tier American Flat Track riders and those of weekend amateurs riding everything from MT 07's, to YZ 450's and 250's, on down to PW50's with training wheels.

Riley's chose the historic spelling of *"Fredericktown"* for the name of their business. Frederick's history is long and storied, but there are few things remaining that have stood the test of the years. The Barbara Fritchie Classic is one of them and The Riley's are immensely proud to have played a role in that often overlooked and enormously underappreciated bit of historic preservation.

Before leaving this family, who carry the current Fritchie baton, I am compelled to remind everyone that as much as Richard and Sharron Riley deserve our admiration, their son Ian who works in the shop with his dad, has been an under-recognized pillar of this event. While every member of the Riley family is part of this effort, during the many hours I spent with Richard and Sharon in their Frederick shop, Ian unassumingly sat nearby at his desk and floating around the shop answering phones, assisting customers, and generally attending to the day-to-day business of Fredericktown Yamaha & Triumph while politely appearing to ignore that I was monopolizing his #1 employee's time while he (Ian) was so busy.

Then, as some long-ago event was recalled, or more often, when Richard or I frustratingly *tried* to recall something, Ian would politely speak up, filling the blank or miraculously and enthusiastically producing some souvenir or piece of one-of-a-kind memorabilia emphasizing the incident or scenario we were talking about. Dirt track racing is popular again. It is about as close to *"fashionable"* as flat track has been since 1980. The eagerness and excitement which exudes from Ian Riley though, is genuine. He is the real deal, but then he didn't have much choice while growing up!

Richard and Sharon Riley may today carry the weight of this race, but should Ian decide to shoulder the Fritchie's burden into the next chapter of history, the race will be in good hands!

Richard Riley, at the BFC Podium, July 4, 2017

THE TRACK

In dirt track racing every racetrack is unique. The surface changing even from lap to lap. Over the lifetime of this race, the track has remained static in shape and location. The original 1867, 3/8-mile oval updated about 1900 to a ½ mile is the same track still raced today. Since 2004, the track has had a limestone "pea gravel cushion" surface. The cushion though is sort of thin and the base – under the cushion – is well known as a hard-packed, fine, amalgamated clay that begins taking a groove if the cushion gets pushed off by too many fast bikes. There is mention from the nineteen-twenties of the track then having a cushion of sand. For several years at the turn of the 21st century, the cushion was graded off and it was raced on the bare clay. When traffic does brush off the cushion and the track grooves up, the cush remains on the outside. This has resulted in some great racing and some spectacular passes as racers ride essentially, two different tracks, side-by-side. Regardless the surface though, this has been the same track in every other way since 1904.

The front straight is wider and just a bit longer than the back. There is a very slight elevation difference from west to east so that the back straight is ever so slightly downhill, and the front slightly uphill. (*It should be remembered this track was designed for harness racing, which races clockwise, thus, downhill on the front straight.*)

Turns one and two are less exposed than 3&4. Thus, 1&2 hold moisture better, creating different traction situations on opposite ends of the track. Turns 3 & 4 are on an elevated berm with an infield tunnel beneath. This isolated high point causes more drying if there is any wind at all and there are no shading buildings as there are around turns 1&2. This west end of the track is well known for being "dry slick" on all but cloudy, rain threatening days.

The tightest spot on the track is over the tunnel where the track is only 30 feet wide. Through turn four the track widens so you come out onto the widest part of the track, the 50-foot-wide front straight like being sprayed from a spigot. When that straight-a-way tightens back down in turn one it can be discerning to those approaching at full speed! There is an ever so slight double apex in 1&2 rather than the consistent radius of 3&4. This "flat spot" in the middle of the turn allows riders to keep the power on… if they have the room between other riders and the nerve to trust in the already questionable traction.

The entire track has a highly visible white plastic barrier around the inside and a chain link fence around the outside. There is **no** runout. The fence is lined with hay bales, but while adding some measure of safety, they also take two feet off the already conservative width.

The Fritchie requires finesse, but it gives the grandstand crowd an incredible show. Screaming engines bounce off rev limiters right in front of the stands as the bikes pitch into turn one at around 90mph during the expert main, Dust and gravel are slung through and over the fence all the way around to the back straight. Riders either love or hate this track, but all of them, universally, compliment the Frederick fans. Frederick, Maryland, *is* a motorcycle racing town.

Frederick Maryland
1/2 mile

Grandstand

Courtesy of Heritage Frederick

This photo, courtesy of Heritage Frederick, is during the construction of the Frederick fairgrounds track. It depicts the construction of the berm on top of which the west end (turn 3&4) sits. For that and other reasons, it is thought this was during original construction of the track in 1867. All the construction is being performed with either horse or human powered equipment. Particularly, a lot of shovels and rakes!

The circular confines of the camera lens surround the perimeter of the photo to confirm the presumed age. Photo exposure was controlled in cameras of that period by manually uncovering and recovering the lens on the front of the camera rather than using an internal "shutter" as later cameras do. This crude exposure method also "burned out" (over exposed) the mountains and city rooftops in the background of the center of the photo.

25th race 1947

John Butterfield

(unidentified photo of John Butterfield, not at Frederick)

Those attending the 25th annual BFC (then "the Delphey Brothers Classic") would no doubt be quite surprised to learn how long the series has continued. John Butterfield was a well-liked racer and Harley-Davidson dealer from Roanoke Virginia. Racing historian Eddie Boomhower stated that John was particularly well known for his sliding. Butterfield would travel the country following the racing circuit on two-lane roads in the pre-Interstate highway era while hauling his race bike and equipment in a modified sidecar attached to another Harley-Davidson! Judging by the (stripped) brake drum on the front wheel and pie pan number plate, this photo may actually be the hauler pressed into service rather than the race bike.

Johnny Butterfield was also noted for racing the same Harley-Davidson throughout his career. When he finally retired to his Virginia Harley shop, he shipped the race bike back to the shop in his home state of Maine where he originally bought it.

Note – information & photo for this article courtesy of Eddie Boomhower and his "The Racers' Reunion Book" 2009

50th race, 1971

Royal Sherbet

Royal Sherbet in 1971 riding a BSA, A65

In the winter of 2020 while researching this book, I tried to find the 50th anniversary winner for an interview. I chased quite a few questionable leads until taking one last shot in the dark. The next morning when routinely checking my email, there, ten-minutes ago, was a message – from Royal Sherbet! We would meet later that year but to establish my purpose in reaching out, I briefly asked if he remembered winning the BFC in 1971.

What follows is the reply I received to that question. Fifty years later. Royal's memory of the day is as fresh as if it was yesterday. It's a phenomenon among racers that's amazed me for years. In another racer-esque phenomenon, Royal Sherbet had the world by the tail in 1971. He was in dreamland. He'd earned the fabled *national number*. Royal was on. He was burning up tracks across the country. Then, after a win in New York, he curiously took off his leathers, loaded up his van and just went

231

home to Florida in the middle of the season. He'd had some injuries. He'd seen some others. His dad had passed in April and he had a wife and two small children at home. It was just time.

A racer's decision to walk away is one of the most personal decisions a person can make. But when the racer knows it's time, it's time. Where and when it comes are irrelevant. They owe us no explanation beyond... it's time. Royal has remained active in motorcycle racing though. He's a talented engineer and fabricator. Among other talents, his hand built Bultaco Astro is a work of art.

[author's note – most of this recollection concerns Royal's record setting lap at Frederick in 1969.]

[TE] July 4, 1971, Frederick, Maryland. Do you remember?

[RS] *Yes, I remember that day in 1971.*

I was a second year Expert and first year National Number and if I remember correctly I won the Expert main event that day but did not break my all-time one lap track record that I had set there as a Junior during time trials in 1969.

The man that used to announce those races came up to me during Daytona Bike Week many years later & told me that, that track record that I had set as a Junior in 1969 had stood for many, many years before anyone was ever able to better it.

I would be interested in knowing how many years that record stood before someone on a much more modern & higher HP motorcycle broke it.

The bike I did that on in 1969 was a standard bore 650 BSA A65 with only 32mm Amal carbs and only 1.5" TT straight pipes. Knowing what I know now I doubt if it had much over about 50 HP compared to the HD XR750's that were into the low 70 HP range by 1972 and are now up to at least 100 HP and in some cases slightly over that.

The day I set that Track Record in 1969 turns 1 & 2 was a rough damp cushion but turns 3 & 4 was dry slick because of how the sun shines on that track during that time of year.

During Time Trials when I came down the front straight & got the green flag for my one lap. I thought I might be able to hold it wide open going into the corner because of the damp cushion there. However, as I went into that first corner without ever even letting off I got the feeling that I

232

might be able to just keep it pegged if I could come off of turn two on the inside because of that pole on the outside of turn two.

As it turned out I was able to go in high without ever shutting it off at all, then squared it off and came off two so as to barely miss that pole on the outside.

Then, even though it was dry slick, I was able to run turns 3 and 4 wide open as well. "Boop boop" (as he twisted his right hand forward then back, as through blipping a throttle) That was all I did.

When I came back to the van and everyone told me I had just set an All Time Track Record that was even faster than ALL the Experts......I just couldn't hardly believe it.   The only thing that topped that was when one of my AMA National Number Expert Heroes [Bart Markel] stopped by my pit and said he sure was glad I wasn't an Expert that he had to race against.

[author's note – That was quite a compliment from Bart Markel. The Hall of Famer and Grand National Champion.]

The detail in this fifty-year-old memory is amazingly not unique. In fact, it is common to many, perhaps most racers. And yet, few are those who get to experience those stories.

It is an unexplainable trait seldom mentioned by those whom it applies to. Yet among themselves or their own, the stories flow. They shrug off and joke about bad experiences. The racer's camaraderie is guarded and protected, but intense. When those stories are shared, they are a glimpse into the racer's soul.

The evolution of the sport at the top level has become so dependent on team backing, external sponsorship and public perception, especially the ever present and prying "social media," that top riders have been even further forced to develop two distinct personas. One public and one private. While some, so accustomed to the necessity of "selling themselves" may seem brash publicly, all whom I have ever met are in fact very personal people. "Quiet" may not define many but applies to more than can be called braggarts. Typically, if you manage to get through the racer's cultivated public persona, you'll meet a very different person.

Royal Sherbet #30D in turn two followed closely by his pal, #99c, Mike Sponseller during the 1969 Amateur class race.

50th race, ver. 2.0, 1972

Larry Darr

As has resonated throughout this history, prior to now the actual beginning of this race has been uncertain. That situation reached its peak in 1972 when the Lions Club celebrated the 50th anniversary of the Fritchie. It is speculated that this is a result of the *25th anniversary* being celebrated a year late in 1947.

On July 3rd, 1972 Larry Darr and Bob Frank stopped by the Harley-Davidson factory on Juneau street in Milwaukee to pick up a new bike. Then Bob drove straight-through, 1,500 miles to Frederick. It was not until they rolled the 1972 XR750 out of the van in the Frederick Fairground infield that Larry Darr first sat on the bike. Neither of them had heard it run yet! For those familiar with the history of the Harley-Davidson XR 750, you will recognize the significance of this 1972 model. This was the legendary alloy XR when it was brand new! Larry Darr and Bob Frank might as well have unloaded a UFO. Nothing comparable would happen for 47 years until Brandon Price showed up at The Fritchie in 2019 with the first Indian FTR750 to be raced here.

Larry was fast right out of the box. The bike felt great and on a grain farmer's income the winner's share of the purse would sure help justify the $3,200 price tag for a new race bike. In a quirk that eventually became frequent XR strategy, Darr had a problem with his new bike that Day. The brakes *"malfunctioned,"* dragging on the rotor and causing some resistance to the rear wheel, which Larry overcame by twisting the throttle harder! Darr would not only win the race but during qualifying he beat the track record set in 1969 by (the first 50th anniversary winner) Royal Sherbet.

Until 1986 road racing – on pavement - was part of the Grand National Championship series and while Frederick was not a GNC race, Larry Darr was a GNC racer. As such, it was the following March during the Daytona 200 that Larry experienced a mechanical problem causing his bike to slow. Grand National Champion, #1 Mark Brelsford misjudged Larry's speed and in a tight corner at near 100mph, hit Darr's bike broadside.

The fiber glass fuel tank ruptured, the pipes were ripped from the jugs and with raw flames coming from the cylinders, both motorcycles instantly burst into fireballs.

All this happened while centered in the viewfinder of a local news photographer's camera. The photographer, whether on purpose or out of shock, held the shutter button down and his motor winder captured an incredible series of still photos as the two Harleys and their riders, all engulfed in flames, desperately tried to escape. Both men did escape and no, it was not the end of racing for them. Not yet!

Note: the photos referenced above are easily found on the internet for those who wish to see them. I have chosen not to include any crash photos in this book.

George Roeder Sr. #3f and Larry Darr #94

Note very early full-face helmets, (1st yr.) 1970 "iron" XR750's and carboard "armor" duct taped to their legs.

Today, in AFT competition, a rider's number might as well be an amendment to his legal name. It becomes part of his personal branding. Name and number, once united, are synonymous for one's career (except for national champions who temporarily adopt single digit numbers). Yet, George Roeder Sr., appearing in the preceding photograph is recognized by many even today by the number 94. George held that number from 1956 until 1968.

In 1969 Roeder did not follow the circuit and his number was adopted by neighbor Larry Darr. A year later in 1970, George decided to make somewhat of a comeback and used his district number, complete with his Ohio district "*F*" letter.

While both men were technically privateers, both also enjoyed "*support*" from Juneau street in Milwaukee. Paying particular attention to the date, Harley-Davidson fans will note the air cleaners on the right side of both of the bikes in the photo above... in 1970! Larry Darr has confirmed that both were new, first-year, ironhead, XR 750s.

After Larry's retirement at the end of the 73 season the #94 would ride on 16 different bikes until landing on another north Ohio Harley ridden by George Roeder Sr.'s youngest son. When Jess Roeder earned his national number, #94 had just been issued the year before to Steve Champine. Considering the background, Steve did not object to giving Jess the number except that he had already made a considerable investment in leathers, plates, paint, and all the other gear necessary to a national race effort, all sporting his new number - 94.

Jess understood the dilemma and did not push the issue. Ninety-four became available again the next year when Champine gave up racing and Jess grabbed it. Jess Roeder held the number 94 until 2008, just one year less than his dad ran the same number.

Since 2016 the national number 94 has been campaigned by Ryan Wells.

75th race, 1996

Steve Morehead

Flagman Al Wilcox waiting for Steve Morehead to finish his victory lap in 1975

With five expert wins at Frederick, Steve Morehead of Findley Ohio is the second winningest rider in the history of the Barbara Fritchie Classic. Noted as a ½ mile specialist during his career, his success at Frederick is not unusual, at least not for Morehead! His Frederick wins span three decades including 1975, 1987, 1988, 1996 and 1997. Morehead retired from active racing in 1999 to take a job as operations manager for the AMA Grand National Championship series. He currently holds the same position with the AFT series. The Frederick cushion agrees with many Midwesterners. Both the #1 and #2 winningest riders on this eastern track came from Ohio to dominate it.

Steve Morehead inspecting turn one at Frederick in his role as an AMA official.

239

This 75th running of the Fritchie was witnessed by many who had long ago made the event an annual tradition in their lives. Two of them were 82-year-old Carl Hacher mentioned elsewhere and 83-year-old Albert Meisky of nearby York, Pennsylvania. Meisky had been riding his Harley from York to Frederick for the race since 1930, but Al had been coming to this race since he was fourteen years old in 1928. Meisky, citing his extensive experience as a dirt track motorcycle race fan placed the day's winner, Steve Morehead, as his personal pick for #1 rider of all time. Al reluctantly admitted that he had sold his bike the previous year but baring catastrophe and as long as he could wrangle a ride with someone, he vowed that *"I'll be here next year!"*

The milestone - for both the race and the fan - was also witnessed by a man who had grown up immersed in motorcycles, racing and annually, the Barbara Fritchie Classic. R.L. Lyons was the son of Falls Church, Virginia Indian dealer and capable tuner and racer, Robert Lyons. Richard Lyons' many, many contributions to this book have been repeatedly noted throughout. Many of the vintage photos and ephemera, not to mention his memories of people and events, were provided to me for use. He is a walking reference for U.S. motorcycle racing data, particularly pre-1960 information, and scarce (original) Indian history.

Richard had been at the 50th BFC, and because his dad was racing it, he had also been at the 25th.* When he found himself making a connection at a Maryland airport on the day of the 75th anniversary... There was no question that Richard Lyons *had* to reschedule the second leg of his flight to accommodate an afternoon of racing at the Frederick fairgrounds.

The Barbara Fritchie Classic had become the sort of tradition that people planned to attend a year in advance. It is the same sense of tradition that kept this race alive through the lean years. In fact, as 1957 winner and nationally acclaimed race starter Al Wilcox once remarked, ***"Never make any plans for me on the 4th of July. It's the one day every year that I do know where I'll be, Frederick, Maryland!"***

* The 1947 race was actually the 26th but counted as 25 due to being the 1st race after the war.

Barbara Fritchie
classic

75th

July 4, 1997

75th Anniversary

Frederick Fair Grounds
Frederick, Maryland
Free Souvenir Program

George Roeder II

Most Fritchie wins in history

Six-time BFC winner, George Roeder II, of Monroeville Ohio has fond memories of Frederick. When I finally connected with him in the spring of 2020 that familiar racer's memory offered up some surprising details. In fact, I already had a photograph of him at Frederick and other than identifying several riders by their numbers, I knew nothing else about the photo. Not even the exact year. George filled in all those blanks and then some!

The 1992 event described by Geo Roeder in 2020. The second restart.

Far left in this photo is George II. In the foreground being pushed away from the camera is Steve Morehead's #42 Harley. Next is #3 Ricky Graham riding a Honda RS750. #44 is Kris Kiser next to a rider assumed to be #72 Larry Pegram. Next is Roeder's #66 XR750 being held by the legend himself, George Roeder Sr. Last is Rodney Farris (#92). In the background is an R.F. Kline Construction company water truck from this period when Kline's backed the race on behalf of the Lions Club.

1992 was George Roeder II's first win at Frederick. His description might leave you thinking this was an accident. A quirk. Plain old good luck. After five more wins on the same track in twice as many years though, almost half of which he did not race here, and it becomes obvious that Geo had something figured out about Frederick Maryland. Something more than luck. With his dad once holding the lap record here, I think it's safe to assume there was a team effort behind Geo II's domination of the Frederick track. What follows is his own description of that first time as retold by him almost 30-years later.

"I remember going there in the 90's. I showed up and Ricky Graham was there, Steve Morehead and Rodney Farris, too! There were several Hondas that year because the local Honda dealership put up a bonus for if a Honda motorcycle won the main event. So I was running ok and the track started to grove up, which wasn't normal for Frederick, especially in turns 3 and 4. Can't remember if I lined up in the first or second row for the main, but I do remember Georgie Price jumping the start, but they still threw the green flag. Going down the back straight I was running 4 or 5 and when I went into turn 3, everyone was running the grove down low, so I went high and passed everybody into first place, but coming out of turn 4 they threw the red flag for Georgie Price jumping the start and that pissed me off. So, a complete restart happened. After the restart everyone didn't ride the grove on turn 3, they went high like I did and took my line away. So, then I worked my way to 3rd place. Graham and Morehead were in first and second. On the fourth lap or so going into turn 1, Graham and Morehead went down. Trying not to run them over, I went high. When doing this I hit a hay bale. I almost went down because of it, but I knew if I could stay up, I would be first on the restart. I gave it everything I could to keep the bike up and gave it a handful of throttle as soon as I hit the bale. Lucky this worked and I got to restart at the front and then won the race. That is how I remember it anyway.

Another memory of Frederick... I remember one-time Rodney and I tangled in the final with Rodney going down. I thought Rodney would be pissed, but he came over and shook my hand after the race. He and I tangled more than once, but I always had much respect for him and hopefully he felt the same of me. Another time, I won both races, the singles and the twins. I think it was the only time I ever did that! I was riding Eddie Fatzinger's single that day. All good memories!" – George Roeder II

244

That old *"around the outside, highline pass"* especially through turns three & four is always a ballsy move. At Frederick, it is even more so. The Frederick track is known for being narrow. The mid-point between three and four where Geo made his move is *THE* narrowest place on the whole track. I recall another old video interview with Geo Roeder where he remarked, *"I guess sometimes I'm kind of an aggressive rider…"*

Uh huh. Sometimes ya just gotta send it Geo!

George Roeder II running it around the outside of Larry Pegram in turn 2 at Frederick – WFO

In this photo George Roeder is riding an XR750 belonging to Tom Hyser, of Hyser's Cycle Center at Laurel, Maryland. Yup! That's right. The winningest rider in Frederick history rode a Harley provided by one of the Honda dealers behind the efforts for a Honda to win this race. In the ultimate twist of that story, here we see George, on Tom Hyser's Harley, passing Larry Pegram, who got the hole shot *on the Honda!*

Margo King,

First Lady of The Fritchie

In 1976 the big story about The Fritchie was an event that had its true beginning innocently enough seven years earlier.

In 1969 an eighteen-year-old amateur rider from Tacoma Washington applied for an AMA pro racing license. The application was summarily denied by the AMA due to a disqualifier that seems rather odd today. The applicant was a woman. Debi Selden would file a lawsuit to force the issue and two years later in 1971, AMA would finally begin issuing licenses to women riders.

By 1976 there were a handful of women racers around the country. They were still an unusual entrant at any but their hometown races, but it was sort of a hometown racer who would surprise the fans at Frederick during the year of the nation's bicentennial.

Margo King had grown up on a farm about fifteen miles from Frederick. Hardly a "feminist" Margo King was much more comfortable among the chickens, sheep, and cows than at the mall or other chic 70isk hangouts. She was and continues to be a "doer" who makes her own way in the world. As she put it, the first time she went to The Fritchie and got pelted with pea gravel just walking up to the grandstand, she knew she *had* to do that!

After graduating from Damascus high school, she enrolled at U.MD. To help pay for school, she took a part-time job at a Safeway grocery. That is where she discovered motorcycles… sort of.

It is a long story, but Margo became acquainted with motorcycles through a co-worker at Safeway. She bought a Yamaha DT1 and began riding in regional off-road events. The farm and orchard at home provided plenty of room to practice and practice she did. Eventually, through an innocuous date, she was introduced to the TT track 50 miles south at Winchester Virginia.

Margo told me that by 1975/76 she did not encounter any problems obtaining her racing license from AMA. That page had already been turned by someone else. In fact, by 1977, a year after Margo's debut at The Fritchie, Diane Cox had already advanced through the ranks of the GNC from novice to junior and by then, had gotten her expert license. There is a common sentiment among women who race. So much so, the question is hardly asked anymore. From Diane Cox to Shayna Texter and all the woman who have, who do and who will race, Cox's comment from a 1977 interview is timeless; *"We're all out there to win. The guys treat me just like any other racer when we're side-by-side at 110 or so…"*

Just as riding cow trails led to motocross, TT races bridged the gap between motocross and track racing. The TT soon led to ovals and **THE** oval around there has of course always been the ½ mile at the Frederick fairground.

By the time 24-year-old Margo King came to The Fritchie in 1976 she was a lost cause regarding motorcycle racing. She now owned several bikes, which usually rode in a trailer behind her VW beetle. This was all new and curiously unladylike to the folks at Frederick, but Margo was just as serious about *her* racing as anyone there. No doubt, much more so than many! July 4th, 1976 Margo King would be riding a competitive Champion framed Yamaha RT3 she'd bought from former GNC champion, Gary Nixon. It is noteworthy that Margo's first introduction to track racing was on the GNC caliber Winchester (VA) TT track.

Pictured here during a 1965 national are #1 Roger Reiman, #76c Drayton Tylee, #52 Ronnie Rall, #44b Bob Sholly, and #31 Don Twigg. The rest of the field is uncertain but that *is* the ABC Sport's, mobile studio truck in the background. This race was taped for broadcast on the next Saturday afternoon's *"ABC's Wide World of Sports."*

Margo on her Penton. She called it her favorite off-road bike

Earlier in 1976 Margo had graduated from U.MD with an anthropology degree. It seems though that her priorities had changed. Not only did Margo King ride motorcycles. Not only did she race motorcycles, she was totally independent (if necessary). With the help of her dad, she had built a workshop on the farm where she maintained, modified, and repaired her own bikes. Not *just* a pretty face, Margo King was that and so much more. In fact, her skills both mechanical and riding, would put many guys to shame, particularly when one of them felt compelled to mansplain some "*technical issue*" to her. …never underestimate a determined woman boys. Just don't!

After that first Fritchie, Margo bought a proper 70's race van, outfitted it with a mini stove & icebox together with a makeshift bed and room for two bikes, then she went on a serious quest of the eastern dirt tracks. Pennsylvania, New York, Ohio, Maryland, Delaware, Virginia, and occasionally a more distant swing through the mid-west. It was on a trip to Daytona Florida that she discovered another kind of motorcycle racing she had never encountered back home – speedway.

Later that summer in Oswego, New York Margo would get a chance to ride a speedway bike and soon became the new owner of what was very possibly the only speedway bike in Maryland.

A year later she loaded her van for a trip to California to get her Yamaha RT rebuilt. She was expecting to be home in two weeks. Maryland is no place for a speedway racer and Margo's mom knew as she pulled out, her daughter would not be coming back. In the spring of 2020 I asked Margo what ever happened to anthropology? Without hesitation she said that she knew if she was ever going to explore and live her dreams, she had to do it then. If for whatever reason that did not work out, anthropology would still be there waiting for her!

That was 1978. Other than occasional visits, Margo's mom's premonition was correct. She has had an eventful and successful life as a speedway racer, motorcycle shop owner, motorsports announcer, and finally (in "retirement"), once again, a farmer. Through it all she has continued to ride ***and race*** motorcycles!

That skinny girl whom Fritchie fans suspected of pulling some women's lib stunt in 1976, is still riding 44 years later! Today Margo and her husband Lance still live in California. She has ridden thousands of miles on the streets. She has road raced at Daytona. She has raced her XR-750 on ½ miles and miles. She has ridden in trials, Supermoto, MX, short track and the trails back home at the farm. Margo King is no act, no stunt, she has no agenda. She is just a woman who loves motorcycles. If you pick up a dictionary and flip it open to "bad assed women," Margo King's photo will be at the top of the page.

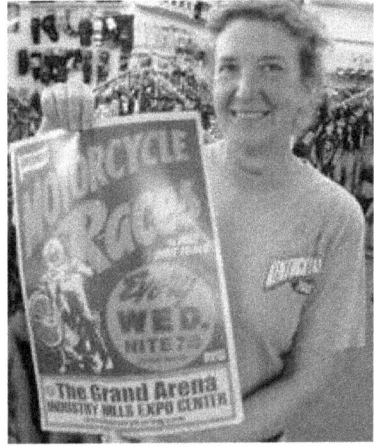

Margo announcing at an event around the early 2000's and more recently, displaying a vintage speedway poster at her Montclair, California *Cycle Rider* store

Margo King with good friend, Howie Zechner and her XR 750

GARY NIXON

22-year-old Gary Nixon in 1963, Bob Myers photo

Gary Nixon is larger than life. Even ten years after the world lost this amazing man, his image, his myth, has only grown. We've all seen him hanging it out, backing into the corner at 90 mph, one foot firmly on the clay and all the while, sticking his tongue out and hamming it up for the photographer. Of all the hundreds, perhaps thousands of racers who've been inspired through the years by Bruce Brown's film, "*On Any Sunday*," many don't realize that the on-track footage was shot with twenty-odd pounds of cameras duct taped to Gary Nixon's helmet in the days before featherweight digital go pro cameras. Gary Nixon did not merely give us incredible racing performances. He gave us an actual rider's vision of the racing during the golden age of the sport.

When *Maryland* and *Nixon* are mentioned in the same breath, a handful of old-timers still think of Spiro T. Agnew. If that doesn't ring a bell, you'll have to Google it. We're talking about that other Nixon though. Not the president, but the crowned prince of Triumph racing. Gary Nixon came out of Oklahoma like a spring tornado. Once he touched down in Maryland, he was eagerly embraced and will forevermore be part of Maryland's racing heritage.

Gary once told an interviewer that as a boy he had been a huge sports nut. Anything competitive, baseball, football, basketball, anything. Then all the other kids kept getting bigger and he didn't. He still had the drive and the competitiveness. He just didn't have the size to get on the team. It was that pivotal point in most guy's lives when they realize they are not going to be a famous sports star. It is that time when most resolve themselves to turn on the TV, sit down with a beer and critique the performance of all those who did make it into the big time.

After winning the 20-mile National at Sacramento California in 1964

Bob Myers collection via David Sites

Gary Nixon though, was not about to feel sorry for himself. He would always be a sports fan but watching was never going to be enough. It was then that he saw a motorcycle race and recognized it as something he did not have to be a giant to excel at. Lucky for us!

Gary Nixon put everything into whatever he did. If there was not someone else to beat, he would try to outdo himself. Flat track fans are familiar with the Nixon boast; "*Which one of you sons of bitches is coming in **second** tonight?*" Confidence though is a racer's greatest ally. If you don't have confidence in yourself, *unwavering confidence*, you may want to look for another line of work. If you undermine your competition's confidence a bit in the process, that cannot hurt either.

On March 20, 1988 Frederick again became part of the Gary Nixon story. That night, a gas tank from Gary Nixon's 1967 and 1968 GNC championship bikes, a set of leathers and a helmet were stolen from the van of Gary's friend, national number 99, Mike Sponseller at the Linganore administration building. Mike Sponseller was asked about the incident during research for this book and explained that the items showed up at his office after the story appeared in the newspaper the next day. It turned out that rather than someone planning to make a fortune selling the stuff to collectors, it was just some mischievous neighborhood kids who did not have a clue what they'd taken. Gary was delighted to get his keepsakes back and Mike was relieved at not being responsible for him losing them.

Various, more recent riders have been credited with originating the physical fitness regimens that are a mantra in today's sport. Gary probably wasn't the first either, but, "*physical fitness,*" carried a rather different expectation in his time. Known for partying into the wee hours the morning before races, it would also seem very odd today to take a break from your workout to relax with a cigarette! Just the same, Gary was one of the first to be known to engage in targeted physical training. Gary Nixon was known for doing one-handed pushups to demonstrate his fitness. Conditions were definitely different. Some vintage videos make it appear that track prep was primarily to control the dust for the spectators' comfort. As well, bikes were a lot heavier. Races were typically 20 to 25 laps. Nixon's physical strength was one of the factors he could control. A factor he could improve on rather than simply accept the consequences of like a bad track or a mechanical problem. It was something he could do better than his competition to gain an edge. Today, that edge is gone. Fitness is now a requirement if you want to be competitive. Next time you are in the gym, pounding out reps and asking yourself why, thank Gary Nixon. Or do as Gary would have... cuss him!

Whether it happened because of him or despite him, Gary's presence – his physical presence *and* his aura – in Maryland is a frequent focus whenever the development of other mid-Atlantic racers is discussed. 2019 AFT Rookie of the Year, Whitehall Maryland's Brandon Price credited Rodney Farris as inspiration in his podium speech when he won the 2019 BFC. Rodney Farris though, was undeniably influenced, mentored, coached, and cheered on by Gary Nixon. After several serious injuries in 69 & 70, Gary concentrated on road racing for the remainder of his career until finally calling it quits completely in 1979.

Like most racers, Gary rode just about every brand of motorcycle at some point in his career. It is Triumph though that is most often associated with Gary Nixon. Nixon's blue on white paint scheme and helmet chevron is probably what most Americans first envision when the word "Triumph" is uttered in racing circles.

Nixon and Triumph. Triumph and Nixon. Neither one *was* from Maryland, but both found a welcoming home in Maryland and both will forever *be* from Maryland.

Gary L. Nixon 1941-2011

Robert "Bob" Myers

Bob Myers was not from Frederick. He did not race at Frederick. He had no real connection to Frederick other than occasional, at least annual, visits to the city. Bob Myers is however indelibly connected to this story. His own story is fittingly placed *here* in this book since the man in the previous chapter would not have the popularity he does in Maryland if it were not for Bob Myers.

Photo courtesy of the AMA Motorcycle Hall of Fame Museum

Bob is perhaps best remembered in the motorcycle community as the owner of Free State Cycles. Infected by the motorcycle bug early in life, Bob began what would become his career working at Blalock Cycles. At that time, Blalock's was down the street from Bob's home in Wheaton, occupying a former gas station.

From that job selling BSA's for Bill Blalock, Bob Myers took a leap of faith into the business he loved. Very uncharacteristically for the period though, instead of some old gas station or obscure back ally location, Bob Myers rented space in… a new shopping center!

Bob Myers, Bill McDowell (adv. mangr. Tricorp), Dan Sallenberger & Jack Mercer (field reps. Tricorp) in front of Free State Cycle, Bladensburg, Maryland

Jack Mercer photo courtesy of the Bob Myers Collection via David Sites

Sponsorship was a bit harder to earn in the pre-social media days. Name dropping on the podium was not going to be enough in those days and nobody was going to see your sponsor's name on your leathers on TV or the fuzzy black & white photos in bike magazines.

There are not many AFT championship contenders earning their keep today by selling motorcycles to high schoolers at the local dealership between races. That was *one* of Gary Nixon's duties (along with being an "as needed" mechanic) back when he first came to Bob Myer's place as a struggling rider. Before this, Gary had a reputation for bumming rides from his competitors just to get to the next race. When he did finally acquire a car to pull his own trailer, that car was also Gary Nixon's home! A few hours shop duty between races was well worth it when compared to the relatively easy life, he was living under Bob Myers' sponsorship. No longer sleeping in his broken-down car, Nixon even had his own room in the Myers home. It was only one of the positive changes brought to Gary Nixon's life by this man few have heard of today.

Gary Nixon demonstrating the new Triumphs to a perspective customer.

Photo courtesy of the AMA Motorcycle Hall of Fame Museum

Bob Myers is one of the first to introduce a new style of motorcycle business. A business model which has become the standard we expect today. That Shopping center location, while expensive, was timely. The "shopping center" was the pre-cursor to the shopping mall that became so popular a decade or two later. While the stores were separated by outdoor space in the 60's that outdoor space was a plus for a motorcycle dealer.

Jack White's 1900 "*steam whirlwind*" could not compare to the excitement of the Laurel high school quarterback and his girlfriend buzzing through the shopping center parking lot on their way to the theater on a 305 Honda Dream on some 1961 Friday evening.

Bob Myers' story is worthy of a book of its own. His support for racing in every form. His backing of many who became notables. His role in revolutionizing the motorcycle business and especially, his unsung role in the Triumph story, both here in The States and especially behind the scenes in the U.K...

It is not any of those remarkable accomplishments I want to recognize Bob Myers for though. No. Bob Myers' contribution which has added invaluably to this project, rather than any of his business ventures is his non-paying hobby!   Bob Myers was an amateur photographer who practiced his hobby while he was at the races. Luckily, because he was an organized businessman, Bob did a fantastic job of organizing and storing his photos. His young friend who would eventually inherit the collection has taken it further by beginning to identify and catalog some of the photos, but the sheer volume is daunting.

As a young man, David Sites worked near Free State Cycle where he became acquainted with the personable Bob Myers. He bought his first motorcycle from Bob, and over the course of their lives, David became a close and trusted friend in addition to a frequent customer. When Bob passed away in 2015. David Sites became the new owner of Bob's cherished house in the country and his collection of vintage race photos. David is still humbled by Bob's children honoring him to be the steward of this unbelievable collection of racing heritage. It is through the incredible generosity of David Sites that these photos are in turn, shared with the world. The quantity, just as it relates to Frederick, is overwhelming. Many appear throughout this book from the Fritchie, as well as other venues. What follows is a sample of the Bob Myers collection from the 1960's into the 1970's. Collected at many tracks, most of which are in the east, but some are not. The one most endearing rule concerning Bob's photography is that he seems to have had no rules!

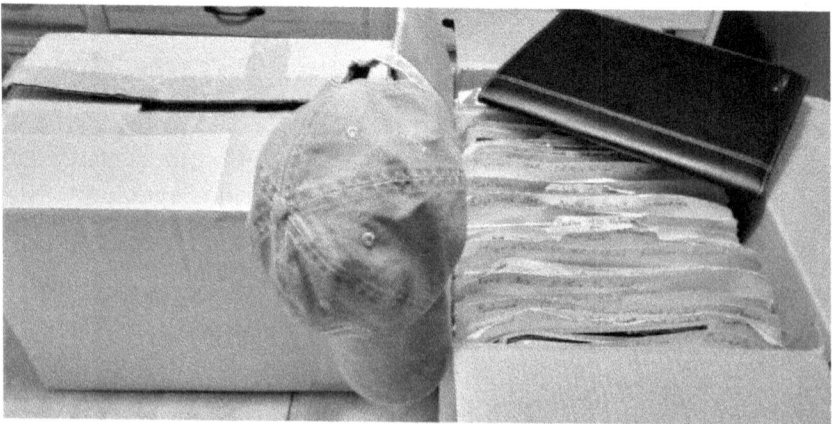

Two boxes of "*The Bob Myers Collection*." There are dozens of photos in each folder!

Shortly after gaining access to the Bob Myers Collection I noticed there were a number of photos in a stack without a file folder. I went through them and was able to recognize where all but a few were taken and was able to sort and reunite the photos with their respective track's folders. One of those loose photos stood out though. It is an image I have seen a thousand times in as many different places. Like many of Bob's photos, there is no identifying information. Who it is of course, is obvious. Where it is appears to be a track Bob Myers has no other photos of... in these boxes. But there are numerous photos in this collection of another west-coast track nobody thought he had photographed.

There are no processer markings that might confirm this as an original print or provide any other reliable information. There is nothing to indicate Bob Myers took this famous photo. There is nothing indicating he did not. It is clearly an original darkroom print, from the correct period. The patina and handling marks on the print are genuine. I have not been successful in locating any information giving credit to anyone else, and the photo has been reproduced so often we may never know. Could this really be *THE* Gary Nixon tongue photo? Bob Myers was certainly the kind of friend Gary would have had this type of fun-loving relationship with.

Bob Myers was a remarkable photographer. In the era of film photography, Bob seems to have shot like a digital photographer. A digital photographer with a mega-giga-big memory card. Examining the negatives that survive however, shows he did not shoot randomly. He shot what caught his eye and he had a good eye for photo content. While there are many posed shots, there are also lots and lots of candid ones. Most of his photos are action shots but many of those, whether at local, regional, or national meets, are often riders we seldom see… or even hear the names of. Riders captured for what they did rather than simply who they were. These musty boxes are also the quiet repository of photos of the famous icons of the sport. Dick Mann, Bart Markel, Mert Lawwill, Don Castro, Dave Aldana, on, and on. And of course, there are dozens of Bob's close friend, Gary Nixon. Come along and flip through a very small sample of *"The Bob Myers Collection."*

Robert "Bob" Myers,

May 10, 1932 – Sept. 7, 2015

Billy Lloyd 1963

Theodore Hall

Jack Mercer about 1960. Race photography was a little bit different back then. Jack was another of the movers and shakers in the TriCorp story. Together with Bob Myers, he gave us a look into the 1960's racing scene that is generally missing from previous generations.

Larry Palmgren and Bart Markel

Ronnie Smith 1969

#4 Bart Markel, #5 Larry Palmgren, #58 Jody Nichols, #98 Bob Sholly

"So close you can throw a blanket over them..."

Number 31b is1968 amateur class winner, Louis Montz but my attention was captured by the rider behind him. The number appears to be 30c.

Amateur class rider #30c, Ron Adkins, would crash into a down bike later in this race and lose his life. A top-level employee of TriCorp in Maryland, he would have been *very* well known by Bob Myers. It would have been traumatic for the photographer.

Greg Edmonds, at Rosecroft (horse) Racetrack, Oxen Hill, MD. 1974

A significant photo, since this was the only motorcycle race held at Rosecroft.

266

Rider's meeting. Hagerstown 12-mile National, 1968

Dick Mann, George Roeder, Tony Murguia, Buddy Elmore

Hagerstown, 12-mile national, 1968

Don "Rainy" Myers, of Honey Brook, Pennsylvania at Frederick in 1968

#76c, had to be the coolest guy in the 1968 paddock! Rocking that 60's kind'a number font, those awesome goggles and the Playboy bunny on his leathers, he looks almost bored as he pours out of turn four onto the front straight.

1967 BFC novices

BFC officials, 1967

L to R, Jack Dunegan, Berkley Bacon, Red Mosser, Bob Rudy, Shorty Dunford, Billy Bell, Al Wilcox, Dave Warren

269

BFC Novices 1968

A dirt prepped Yamaha TD2 on the start at the 1968 Winchester, Virginia TT.
With half his weight on the bars, the front still wants to come up!

I would love to hear Canadian, David Siehl's story behind the carpet padding duct taped around his leg at Cumberland in 1967.The Cumberland Maryland ½ mile, became kind'a famous two years later, in 1969.   Anyone who has seen Bruce Brown's *"On Any Sunday"* will recognize this next shot!

No. This is *not* a still from the movie. This is a Bob Myers photo. One of a couple dozen Kodachrome beauties from that day.

For those three of you who have not seen the movie yet, Mert Lawwill won.

271

The 3, 2, 1 finishers lined up here on May 4, 1969 for what passed for a podium shot. Dick "Bugsy" Mann, Gene Romero and Mert Lawwill.

In 1964 Bob took enough time away from work to accompany Gary to a big race. Here Gary is leading Ronnie Rall. Bob must have brought luck with him because Nixon won the thing!

A couple guys deeper in the field. Mert Lawwill & Bob Bailey.

1964 Sacramento Mile winner, Gary Nixon

...of Wheaton, Maryland!

A Dirt Track Dynasty

Shayna Texter, 2018 BFC Expert Twins winner Cory Texter, Cruise Texter

Shayna and Cory Texter are just the latest generation of the Texter family to be BFC alumni. Their father Randy was a crowd-pleasing rider and Randy's Dad, Ray, who owned Lancaster Harley-Davidson, was a huge racing supporter. Somewhere previously in this book is a photo of Tex doing tech inspections at a race in the 60's with neighboring Harley dealer, Bud Laugerman. Cory's little boy, Cruise, has been in the pits at various tracks, including Frederick, almost since birth and his shy smile has become a crowd pleaser whenever he's spotted – often on his push bike.

Most teams come to the Fritchie in vans and pickups. The Texter's were among the first to bring a motorhome. In this photo are (L to R) Ray, Shayna and Randy, mechanic Rich Meisenbach and Cory Texter. Randy and the kids would show up in the bus, then Tex would roll in on his Harley. A true old-school motorcycle dealer,

Ray Texter *used* his own motorcycle. Grandson Cory has mentioned that Tex rode his bike into his eighties and up until only months before his passing.

You can see Randy visualizing what Shayna is explaining. Cory seems to be waiting to hear what Randy suggests for the issue and it looks like maybe Tex *already* has it figured out.

There are many multi-generational racing families and it's common to see them working together in the pits. Technology has made a huge impact on this sport but the basics - the racing - is a thing of tradition, feel and intuition. A thing that transcends eras. Grandpa may have experienced the same things in 1970 that you will today. What worked for him might just work for you as well. At worst, it's worth trying and if it doesn't work, grandpa will be the first to tell you so and suggest something different.

The Texters are featured here because they are so familiar to Frederick fans. Their longevity and familiar family connection epitomize so much of the Fritchie sprit. Not merely a family, the Texter's are a dynasty spanning more than half of this race's history.

Sadly, the dirt track world has lost both Ray and Randy Texter, but the dynasty, like every dynasty, lives on.

Carl B. Hatcher

In 1993 in addition to the trophies awarded the top three racers in each category, a special plaque was awarded to 78-year-old Carl Hatcher by the Frederick Lions club. Carl had been coming to The Fritchie – every year – since 1922. *"I remember when they were one-cylinder powered and no brakes...the one thing that hasn't changed is the racers giving everything they got."*

Carl, his dad and his uncle Albert came to the race every year and sat in the same seats. Carl did a stint in the navy but after the war, he returned home and to The Fritchie. He made a career as a machinist and was regarded as a carburetor tuning wizard. Carl Sr. passed in 1958 but the tradition continued with Carl's son Wayne accompanying his dad. For many years after moving to Louisiana, Wayne took vacation, flew up to Maryland and drove the elder Hatcher to The Fritchie. Aviation machinists' mate, Carl Hatcher Jr. stopped coming to the races not long after this award was presented. In 2001, he was interred with honors at Arlington National Cemetery.

"I've been to races all over, but there isn't any other race like the one here. No sir, they don't even come close." Carl Bennett Hatcher, July 4th, 1993

A Fritchie Sampler

Not everyone dreams the same dream. For many, like vintage racers #85 Pat Duffy and #68 Freddie Sweigert, the BFC holds a personal meaning running much deeper than winning or losing. Just being here is symbolic. The entry list as important as the winner's list.

For many who compete on the regional circuit, this is the big time. For those truly just in it for fun, the Fritchie might as well be the Springfield Mile. For those who have nothing to prove to anyone except themselves, this can be the place to do it. It is a chance to dream your own dream!

"Riding a bike is like an art, something you do because you feel something inside."- **Valentino Rossi**

Craig Ship photo

National #92, Brandon Price on the starting line, visualizing his entry into turn one. It is the same intense, nothing-else-in-the-world concentration inherent to those who race. It is a look dismissing the bumps, ruts and gremlins and focusing instead only on the future beyond and planning how you are going to get there. ...and accepting, that occasionally despite all your plans and best efforts, the gremlins find you.

The great motorsports announcer Dave Despain once said; *"You see it best in the eyes of the great racers. That look of determination. That certain spark that tells you, this one is something different..."*

Cody Bauer, Billy Worthington and Phil Miller of M&J Racing on Mike Poe's bike at the 2018 BFC

Staging for the vintage class at Frederick may give the appearance that Tricor (Triumph Corporation) is still distributing motorcycles from Baltimore. During the golden age, Triumphs were king for a few years and all of them east of the Rockies came from Baltimore. Tricor was a huge presence in mid-Atlantic racing. In Maryland, especially around Baltimore, that heritage and tradition, *that pride*, lives on even today, more than 40-years after the call came from Meridan reporting that Tony Benn's experiment with socialist "workers co-ops" had failed miserably, and suffocated a giant.

A GENUINE
MERIDEN BUILT
TRIUMPH

BEWARE OF IMITATIONS BUILT ELSEWHERE,
THEY ARE NOT OF THE THOROUGHBRED STRAIN

We love to see the faces and hear the names of celebrities. We feel some connection, some underlying sharing of their greatness by having met or even just seen them in person. The next level, one that many young people have attempted to succeed at throughout time, is to become one of them.

In the 1970's during the last big dirt track racing bubble, someone, somewhere coined the phrase "*young matadors*." It became cliché when there were so many who aspired to be racers. As with greatness at anything, very few make it to the top. Sport has an uncanny way of being assigned lesser priority as young men's lives go forward. Especially for those who never quite break through to the true big time. At this level of this sport though, the *formerly young* matadors often still challenge.

Frequently yesterday's racers face today's in the vintage class and in this sport where experience and technique play such a huge role, that old adage regarding the exuberance of youth vs. the experience of age is not to be ignored. The effective reach of those *old* matadors is momentarily extended …if the race stays under ten laps that is.

"The older I get, the faster I was." — Evel Knievel

#39c Billy Roberts, took third place in the novice main in 1968. He was sponsored by Roy Byers' shop in Hagerstown, Maryland, and riding a 250 Harley-Davidson Sprint. The folder for this 1968 race had about 100 photos. Only three of them were of novices. All three of those novice photos were Billy Roberts!

Apparently, he made an impression on Bob Myers who had a good eye for rider potential. Billy had bounced between orphanages and foster homes (farms) until he was about 14 years old. That's when he ran away (the *last* time) and was taken in by Roy who allowed him to do odd jobs around the shop for his keep. Roy taught him to ride and along with Mr. Kitchen & Myers, the local Honda dealers, sponsored Billy's racing.

Billy still lives in Hagerstown, here kicking back in the pits with Curtis Fisk in 2017.

283

Fritchie regular, #18 Josee Stedding knows how to ride. The professional horsewoman recognizes that bikes and horses have a lot in common despite the differences between hunter/jumpers and 450's. At the track everyone is equal. Gender, complexion, religion, or any other trait that divides people elsewhere, is dismissed here. We just want to race.

Craig Ship photo

The one thing that does separate motorcycle racers is age. The late Kyle McGrane, Colton Smith, and Kolby Carlile (in 2013) emphasize the need for plenty of sparkling cider on the podium along with the traditional champagne for "adult" winners.

While the Lion's club has not sponsored the race for decades, they are still welcomed back annually to sell their 50/50 raffle tickets to raise funds for the organization's programs. Here Richard Riley is announcing the winning number of some lucky supporter.

As clutches are dumped, throttles twisted wide open and tires spin in search of traction, things can get hectic on the starting line. Wheelies are common. Races sometimes start in what appears to the uninitiated as a mass near-crash. Sometimes, it is a crash.

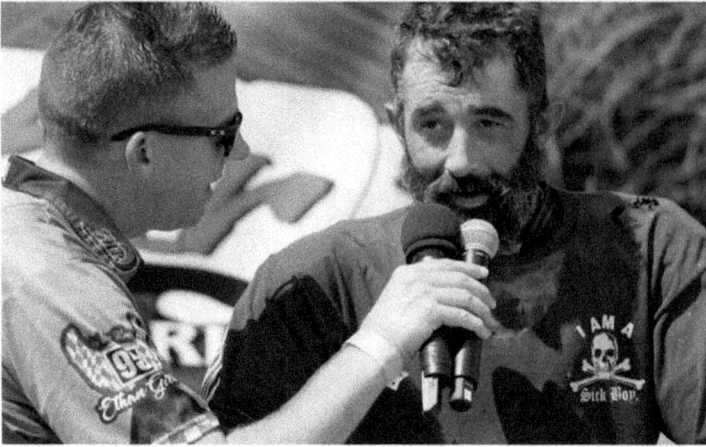

Craig Ship photo 2019

"*Sick Boys, he rides a big motorbike…*" Rick Winsett's choice of shirts may have been an accident. Maybe it is his lucky racing shirt, but he certainly lives up to Social Distortion's lyrics. Rick epitomizes the persistence of dirt track racers. I once saw him high side. His visor parted company from his helmet as he slid face-first across the track. He got up, brushed himself off, restarted the race from the back row and within two laps was in 3rd place. Rick Winsett has been racing at the Barbara Fritchie Classic for decades and regularly being interviewed in the winner's circle. He has won or been a contender in GNC nationals, regionals and district races all over the map for longer than some of his competition have been alive.

Yeah, he's a sick boy.

Randy Neal and his Yamaha XS750 about 1978

It was *about* 1976 that Randy Neal got into racing. A late bloomer (he was 30 years old) He jumped into the deep end of the pool. "Pappy" Twigg of Twigg's Cycles in Hagerstown made him a great deal on the Eddie Adkins tuned XS750 Yamaha raced by Willie Crabb. Randy traveled around the mid-Atlantic region but was a regular at nearby Trailways Speedway where he became friends with another regular, Randy Texter. Neal had a bad crash at Dorsey Speedway in 1984 and stopped racing until learning of the planned Randy Texter Memorial race in 2014 at the York, Pennsylvania fairgrounds. At 68, after a 30-year absence, Randy prepared a bike and renewed his racing license so he could honor his old friend.

Randy Neal, 2014 Randy Texter Memorial York, PA.

Randy rode a 350 Harley-Davidson Sprint in that race. The Sprint had some issues though and after a couple years, (at 71 years) Randy traded up to a Hooligan-type 1000 Sportster. Since ending his 30-year hiatus from racing Randy Neal has always made The Fritchie as well as a few other nearby races. The cancellation of the 2019 BFC was a major disappointment for him.

He's slower than he used to be. Age and previous injury has made him more cautious, but he still has the heart of a racer. Fritchie regulars recognize Randy annually where he typically receives more cheering from the Grandstand than even the pros. He is an inspiration to all, young and old alike.

At 75, his plans to ride the 100th Fritchie are threatened by an old knee injury causing him some concern about that heavy Sportster. Give up? Not Randy! He has a backup plan to ride a friend's Harley-Davidson SX250. About the only thing that can stop him now is if he suffers another injury this winter during his other hobby – snowboarding!

Randy Neal and his Sportster at Frederick, 2017

2018 450-Pro winner, Cameron Smith.

One of a new generation of *"Young matadors."* Today, just being the best rider is no longer all that is necessary to make a success of racing. The struggle to secure the sponsorship and support necessary to a season-long national campaign is perhaps even tougher than being the best rider. We look forward to seeing Cam more frequently in AFT races, but whatever he decides, we look forward to at least seeing him at Frederick for years to come.

R.J. Hart in 2013. Craig Shipp photo

We first met R.J. Hart when he won the minibike race as a ten-year-old in 1999 and next when the fourteen-year-old entered the vintage class and beat his own father. As his dad Rick Hart said that day, *"he almost lapped me!"* The 100th anniversary will be R.J.'s 22nd

Legends, Ricky Graham with Rod Farris in the background, 1992 BFC

Jethro Halbert, Richard Riley and Sammy Halbert, in an early morning discussion in the infield at the Barbara Fritchie Classic. Do we even *want* to know what they were talking about? The stars, from Joe Petrali and Lester Hillbish to Sammy Halbert, Jared Mees and Cory Texter, and all the big names in between are easily remembered. The less famous are harder to recall for most fans, but every one of them, the famous as well as the obscure, rode anyplace that was having a race at some point during their careers. This is not a trade. People do not enter into this sport unless they already love doing it. Some may make money at it, but for each one who does, there are a hundred who pour every spare nickel into their race efforts.

"I didn't start racing motorcycles because I thought I could make a bunch of money from it. It was just a way to have fun riding motorcycles. If you could make some money... well, that was just something extra." - Eddie Fisher, former national number 42

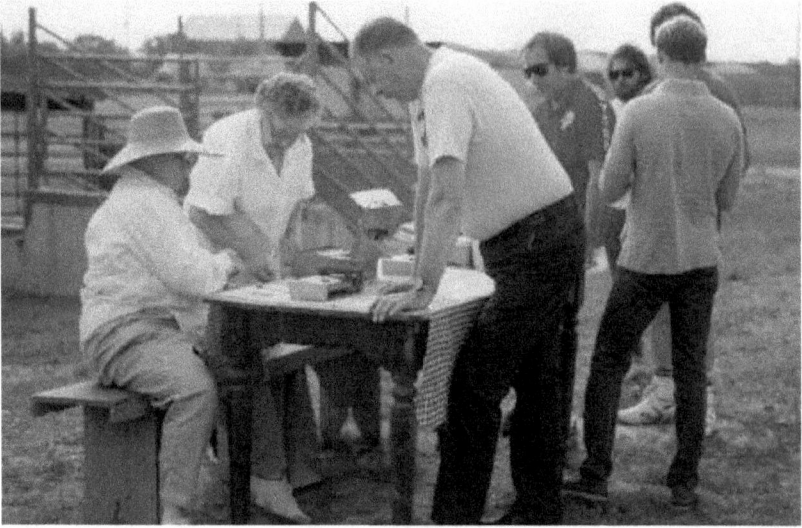

Unique is a recurring word when describing the Fritchie. The antique farmhouse table and bench are a bit different, but where else does registration use a proper tablecloth? Can the potato salad and sweet tea be far away?

From Ray Weishaar and his pig, to Bill Minnick and his racoon, to… Jamie Richards and his goose??? When it comes to flat track mascots, anything is possible.

Eddie Boomhower, Frederick, Maryland, 2015

Eddie Boomhower of Chesapeake Virginia was the 2015 Grand Marshal. He was formerly of Richmond, where he ran Richmond Harley-Davidson for decades. To most, Richmond Virginia and Frederick Maryland don't seem very near, but in the dirt track racing world, one is practically in the other's backyard and both were "home track" races for riders from both ends.

Eddie has contributed tremendously to preserving the history of dirt track motorcycle racing. Mr. Boomhower's memories are noted throughout this book. He is once again, as we've encountered before, one of those bridges between eras of this sport. Together with fellow racing historian George Ireland, they produced an online book / website called "*The Racer's Reunion.*" It was graciously provided free to the public to spread awareness of this endangered history and held a wealth of data. Unfortunately, it no longer exists online.

Did I mention already that *"unique"* is a recurring theme when describing the Frederick crowd? When viewed by the general population that may be the case. Compared to county fair infields on race day anywhere else in the country though, this one is not all that terribly unusual.

Lap one, turn one. This is the reason so many have proclaimed getting a good start as the key to winning this race. The track tightens up, squeezing an already chaotic field of racers as each fights to get ahead of all the rest. Most of the riders in this photo are Fritchie veterans. Each one knows where he *wants* to be in that turn. Few are lucky enough to be where they would prefer.

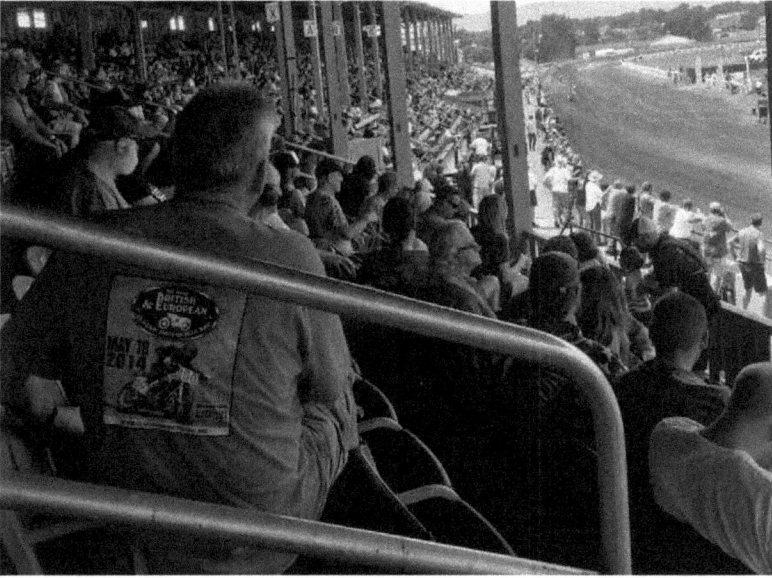

Many photos showing the Fritchie grandstands in the background are early in the day during practice and qualifying. As such, they tend to give a false sense of the attendance at Frederick. This one provides a better indication of the modern BFC crowd *during* the races. And that is only the grandstand.

"I don't remember the first time I was here, but I don't remember a time that I've ever not been here on the fourth of July," Curtis Fisk to Frederick News-Post correspondent John Cannon.

Curtis Fisk is another Frederick area native who as a young boy would pester his dad to take him to see the races. Eventually, his dad would be coming to see Curtis race. Curtis and those like him epitomize the people who poised dirt track motorcycle racing for the unlikely comeback it has made in recent years. Like Henry Nusbaum, the civil war veteran who lived across the street from the fairground and watched the earliest motorcycle races here, Curtis Fisk is a bridge between eras. A craftsman, who mastered the hands-on skills of the mechanical-industrial era and meshed them with the emerging technology his generation grew up with in the technology age. Curtis' thrill at racing on a shifting bed of dirt, elbow to elbow with a dozen other guys, is the same thrill Frederick native, Bill Gosnell, got on this *same track* in 1909.

Despite the advances in technology, the story of this race is a living, breathing, *continuing* history. These men and women pass this experience from one to another like a metaphorical relay baton reverently handed from generation to generation.

Everyone loves to see the famous riders. The up and comers are equally exciting. Fans wondering who is going to be the next to become famous. Those they can tell everyone, "*I saw him race.*"

Cam Smith, smoothly gliding through a rough and rutted turn one.

Cameron Smith, Dalton Gauthier, Brandon Price, and many more are part of the Fritchie family. We have watched them grow in the sport. All have carried their share of trophies away from Frederick. We are anxious to see them accomplish even more on the national circuit and equally anxious to cheer for the next crop of future stars.

Dalton Gauthier checking out Brandon Price's bike in staging.

A wide-eyed Ryan Varnes backing it into turn two.

As we've seen before, growing up racing pea gravel tracks has prepared Ohioan Jarod Vanderkooi for the BFC. Throughout the years, he has won his share of trophies in Frederick, Maryland.

The vintage and veteran classes have their own following in Frederick. In this sport, which is so dependent on nostalgia, it is a treat for many simply to see some of these bikes displayed. To see them being raced the way they were built to be raced forty or fifty years ago is genuinely exciting. Adding to that excitement is seeing the guys who've been riding them just as long... still riding them.

Jay Maher

Randy Neal

Daryl Jakubowski

Generations of racing results in generations of racing friends.

Bill Blackwood, Richard Riley, Donnie Smith, Curtis Fisk, R.J. Hart

The "*Coke Building*," refers to the huge Coca Cola sign covering the windows, of this art deco structure that has been a backdrop in photographs since it was constructed in 1929 as the "*Ladies and Household*" exhibition building... just in time for the beginning of The Great Depression. Little else has changed except that sign. Certainly not the racing!

Between the building and turn two has always been a popular spot to view the races. Riders come into turn one at or near their highest speed of the entire track and this is the only spot other than the grandstands that is higher than the track, thus, giving a great perspective. The turn one crowd are a hardy bunch though. The prevailing wind is across the fairgrounds from turn three & four to turn one & two. Add to that, the bikes throwing roost through and over the fence all the way around both turns even when there is no wind. The result is those watching from the fence at turn one have a great vantage point, but they also wear a lot of the Frederick track home with them.

The roost can be hard on both bike and rider. Pea gravel cushion tracks such as Frederick Maryland will take the paint off your bike and the skin off of you! With the motorcycles traveling at 50-90 miles per hour, the stone dust coming off the tires has been compared to a shotgun blast when you suddenly find yourself in the cone of debris spit from the wheels of someone ahead. It can be hard on camera lens to!

Many bikes running cushion tracks will be seen with tape covering vulnerable parts such as the gas tank and the front of the rider's helmet as seen in this photo of #28A Rick Winsett.

#135 Dalton Winkler demonstrates just what all that tape is protecting. There *is* a number on that front plate and his leathers were black and white when he arrived that morning, instead of varying shades of grey. You can usually tell who is having a good or bad day by the amount of the track stuck to the bikes. Dalton was *actually* having a pretty good day, this was just near the end of it. Dalton had just yanked a pull-off from his visor to give him clear vision as seen here despite the dust covering everything else.

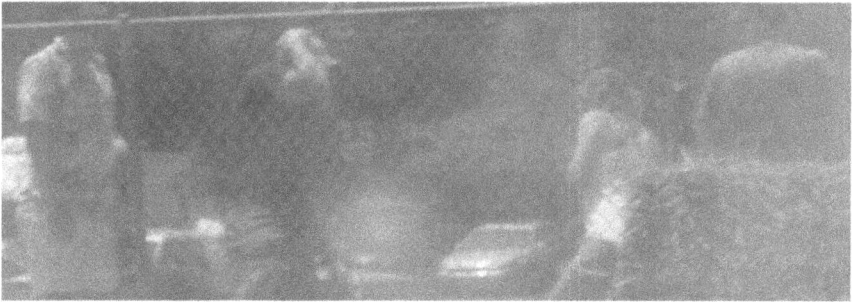

The roost can be brutal on those who choose the wrong place to stand along the fence. The roost and the dust though, is part of the experience. Veteran fans choose their seats accordingly, hoping for a steady breeze to carry the dust away. Spectators realize there is much, much more to this dirt track stuff than it first appears. A cushion gives a visual sense of speed. It is a feeling that must be experienced in person. Blue groove tracks are fast, but there is something about a cushion. Maybe it is the connection to the horse racing origins of the sport. Who knows? ...But there is just something special about a cushion.

Nichole Mees (former national #15) may have never raced *The Fritchie*, on the 4th of July, but she is well acquainted with the iconic event thanks to regular visits by her husband Jared.

A small sample of the motorcycle racing memorabilia in just one Frederick area shop. As the years go by, you meet a lot of folks who attain some degree of fame, but we'll never know what keepsakes have been lost by fans before the rider reached his peak.

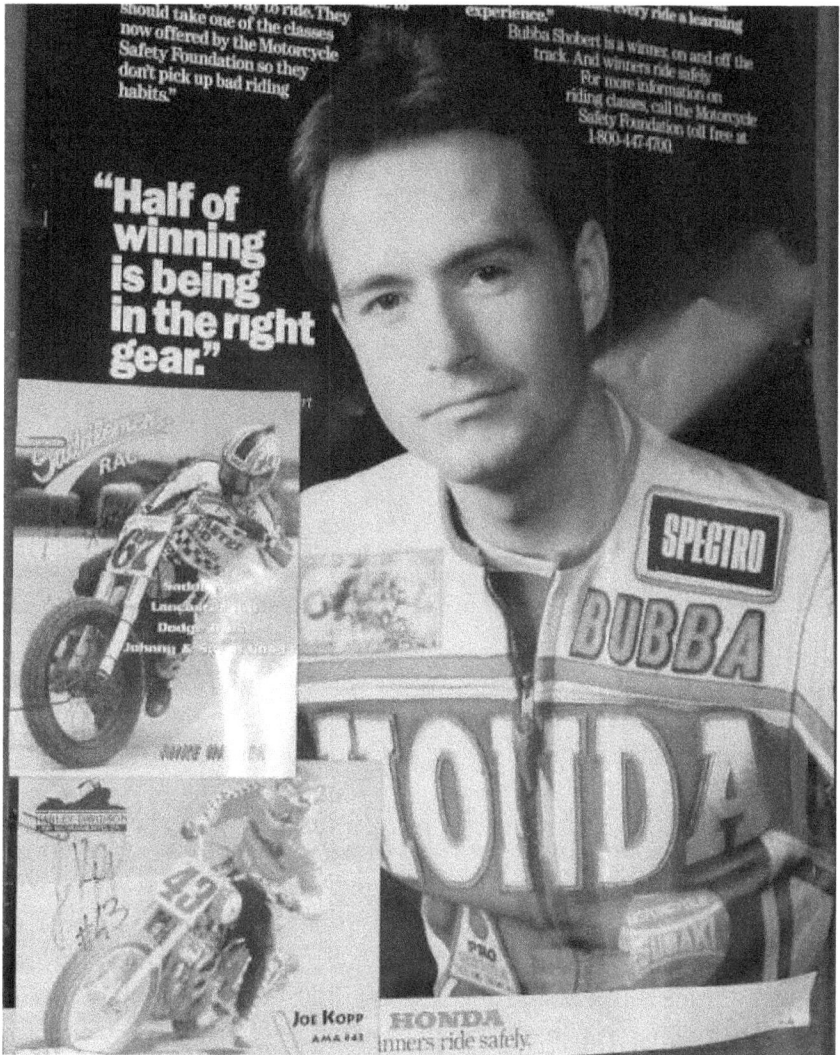

Bubba Shobert, Mike Hacker and Joe Kopp watch over Texanna Detrow from the office wall. Fond reminders of past visits.

Joshua Shear and Brandon Price between heats.

There is a lot of waiting in dirt track racing. A lot of time to think about your next ride. A lot of time to think about everything that you are not doing at home or work today.

Thinking too much about the wrong things can ruin your day. Not thinking enough about the right things can have the same effect. Watching the bikes screaming around the track can present a deceptive impression of what it is like to be a motorcycle racer. Dirt track racing is a contest of strategy and will. The uncertain and changing track surface and the moving bikes you are mingled with mandates a constantly evolving plan, whether you are trying to stay ahead or get ahead, nothing is assured. It requires constant thought and awareness. Nothing is absolute until you hit the kill switch at the end of the race. ...and then it is time to start thinking about the next one.

"Racing is life. Anything before or after is just waiting."- Steve McQueen

The grandstands at the Frederick fairgrounds have sheltered and shaded generations of motorcycle race fans. They have sat in these seats to watch Jared Mees, Kenny Coolbeth, Larry Pegram, George Roeder, I & II, Ricky Graham, Bart Markel, Gary Nixon, Bob Lyons, Larry Palmgren, Lester Hillbish, Joe Patrelli, Fred Toscani, Billy Huber, Tom Cannon, Gene Walker and hundreds of lesser known racers such as Frederick native Bill Gosnell, who first won *on this track* on July 4th, 1910. Men – and women – who have striven to get the hole shot from the same starting line. Riders who gave it their all to be the first to cross the same finish line, …for 112 years on this track and 120-years in this town. Most of those years have been like that very first time, on Independence Day. This is not just another race. Not just a day at the track. This is living history and tradition, continuing as it does nowhere else in the world. This is Frederick Maryland on the fourth of July!

There have been races elsewhere of course. There have been earlier races elsewhere. The Barbara Fritchie Classic though has continued for more than 100 years. It has continued on the exact same track. I have searched for likely candidates and believe that Frederick Maryland is the oldest still running motorcycle racing venue. Earlier races have not continued. The Isle of Mann, the only one which has, has not been on the same course. Motorcycles have been documented running regularly on the same ½ mile oval at Frederick since *at least*, 1909.

This loud, dusty, gritty, guttural sport is not so easily embraced. From its origins, side-by-side with motordrome racing, dirt track has always been the "blue collar" motorcycle races. Running on fairground tracks for the entertainment of farmers and factory workers, this is racing for the love of racing. Yet, even after 120 years, Frederick remains relevant. It has given us and continues to give us heroes of the oval. It is a precariously surviving reminder of how this sport originated and how it got here in the 21st century from a frail dusty seedling a century ago. The Fritchie is both past and future. A unique place where opposites not only attract, they mesh like the gears of a fresh transmission. A relic where the stars of the future continue to emerge from the dust of the past. The Fritchie is a gleaming silver chain stretching from horizon to horizon of flat track motorcycle racing as it does nowhere else.

This sport of motorcycle racing has seen tremendous evolution since its birth at the turn of the 20th century. It has progressed through jerking, lurching starts, restarts and questionable results. The sport's history is not unlike one of its own races when viewed from the perspective of its whole. Sanctioning organizations have come… and gone. FAM, M&ATA, AMA, AMA/GNC and today we have the Steve Nace All Stars and AFT. Racing though, is not an organization. Racing is not a title or record. Titles are only relevant to the organization bestowing them. Records, as every racer knows, are made to be broken. Every race is a contest. Every race is both important and irrelevant.

The local events, most of which are unknown to fans more than 100 miles away are contested and enjoyed by as many, sometimes many more than a national. These events are the stuff that drives racing. It is no accident there are clusters of nationally ranked racers around certain cities or regions. *Those places have a track!*

Without the local 1/10th, 1/4 or 3/8's mile short tracks cut into some race fanatic's back yard or farm field. Without the ½ mile fairground tracks that continue to be lost, there would not be national racing. Without these incubators, these local tracks and local races, there would be no racing. Most racer interviews touch on how they got started. Many recall their first race at 10, 8, 5 or even four-years-old. Those were not nationals' folks! A 5-year-old on a 50 makes worse lap times on a 1/10th mile than a pro on a 750 does on a ½, but it is no less important to the rider and their family. The term "grassroots" is overused today but local racing, is one place it applies.

Support your local race. Support your local racers, even if they *never* win! The drive and commitment it takes just to go out there deserves your appreciation.

I hope The BFC survives for another one-hundred years but as the sport evolves, as with everything in life, the future is never certain. For that reason, I hope every flat track fan, and every flat track racer, at least once in their life gets to experience…*The Barbara Fritchie Classic*.

"THERE'S NOWHERE ELSE TO BE!"

The Motorcycle Business

through the years in Frederick

In 1880 George Conklin opened a popular store near the Frederick town square that sold all manner of articles from jewelry to housewares. Ten years later in 1890 the Brish brothers, Henry, and Murray, bought the business and expanded it even more. One of the things they added was motorcycles.

Brish Brother's former location at 10 W. Patrick Street.

A 1904 article in "*The Frederick Citizen*" newspaper, the store was noted as having "a first-class workshop" in the rear of the business for "all kinds of automobile and bicycle work." Also, in this 1904 article, only two years after public sales had begun, Brish's is noted as *"selling agents for the Indian motor cycle*." The Brish brothers are thought to be the first motorcycle dealership in Frederick.

Henry Brish was born just eleven months after Barbara Fritchie died in 1862. It was his little brother J. Murray Brish, four years younger than Henry, who was the primary motorcycle guy though. A brief article in the September 15, 1917 *"Frederick Evening News"* mentions that J. Murray Brish, Walter Lipps, Robert Burrall and Austin Mantz had recently returned from a motorcycle trip to Springfield Massachusetts to visit the Indian factory.

On a side note, emphasizing how much things have in fact, *not changed*, despite our impressions. Three-years earlier on September 4, 1914, Bob Burrall who rode to Springfield with Murray Brish, was involved in an accident near Shipley's store on N. Market street. In a scenario all too familiar today, a driver approaching from the opposite direction made a left turn in front of him and Bob T-boned the guy. Bob's headlight was broken, and a footrest bent. The horse, the buggy and the distracted driver were unhurt. Yes, the horse and buggy. While we can be sure the driver was not "texting," it is almost certain he told the police that he *"didn't see Bob coming."*

CLASS, STRENGTH AND SPEED
Are all Conspicuous in the 1910 EMBLEM

Our New Model, the 7 H. Twin

Completes a Trio of the Best Machines for the Prices on the Market.

Fitted for both V and flat belts; 55 in. wheel base; battery and coil tank occupying the entire space between the seat mast and the rear wheel guard; the front lower main tube is slightly curved to conform with the curve of the front wheel guard; magneto if desired.

Write for our catalogue and our Agency proposition

EMBLEM MANUFACTURING COMPANY, - ANGOLA, N. Y.

Harry Franklin Shipley sold Harley-Davidson, Reading-Standard and Emblem motorcycles at his store on the corner of Market and Church streets. The Emblem brand disappears from local advertising in 1916 and it is assumed to then cease being sold by Shipley.

Harry was the first Harley-Davidson dealer in Frederick, beginning sometime between 1909 when Harley first began to accept dealers, and 1911 when the first advertisement for Shipley *selling* motorcycles emerges. That 1911 advertisement, however, suggests

Harry Shipley was already established in the motorcycle, if not the Harley-Davidson motorcycle business.

It is uncertain exactly when the Delphey brothers entered the trade. Oral history has suggested the brothers began buying, repairing, and re-selling *used* motorcycles in 1914, but there is no documentation of that beyond Delphey family stories.

H.F. Shipley's store at the corner of N. Market and W. Church Streets.

There is a news story from July 9, 1914 reporting that Clarence and Paul Delphey, along with their friend Isaac Shipley had recently returned from an 800-mile motorcycle trip. The young men, all in their twenties, had made the trip in one-week and all three of them on the same motorcycle! According to the story in the "*Frederick Evening News*" one operated the machine while one rode in the sidecar and one "*on the luggage rack*." Of interest to our purposes is the mention that the motorcycle had recently been bought by Chester Delphey from Harry F. Shipley, a cousin of Isaac Shipley who accompanied the Delphey boys. Presumedly, this was the first

Delphey Harley-Davidson. It is the first I have found documentation of. It definitely would not be the last!

Additionally, Harry Shipley's brother "Fred" (Joshua Frederick) Shipley worked with Paul and Chester in the machine shop at the Ox Fiber Brush Company. Fred was also married to their sister Naomi with whom he would live next door to the Delphey store on W. Patrick Street for much of his life.

While the how, why and when of the Harley-Davidson business transitioning from Harry F. Shipley to J. Paul Delphey remains unknown, it is certain that these men were well known to each other and almost certainly, good friends in what was then a rather small town and particularly in the close, North Market Street neighborhood where they all then lived.

The Harley-Davidson company archives have the Delphey franchise originating on April 4th, 1919 in the (sole) name of J. Paul Delphey. This coincides with newspaper ads that begin showing up for Delphey selling Harley-Davidsons beginning in the spring of 1919. Since it was in 1919 that Harry Shipley began construction of his new "modern" store at 105 N. Market Street, we can assume he dropped the motorcycle dealership at that time, or perhaps he sold the franchise to Delphey for additional capital for the new store project. This was also the end of the war and new motorcycles would once again be available for the first time in several years, assumedly giving Delphey a welcomed boost in his first year of business.

There is a 1916 article regarding a run by the Baltimore motorcycle club including 35 Reading Standards to pass through

Frederick on May 17. That article mentions the Frederick R-S dealer as William H. Solt, indicating Shipley had disposed of that line as well. Reading-Standard went bankrupt in 1922.

There are still a few people around Frederick who remember the Delphey store on W. Patrick street. That store however was itself a later addition. The original shop, the 1880 era Ebert's Carriage and Wagon factory warehouse was back off the street closer to Carroll creek.

NOTE - Shipley appears to have dealt in *used* motorcycles for several more years.

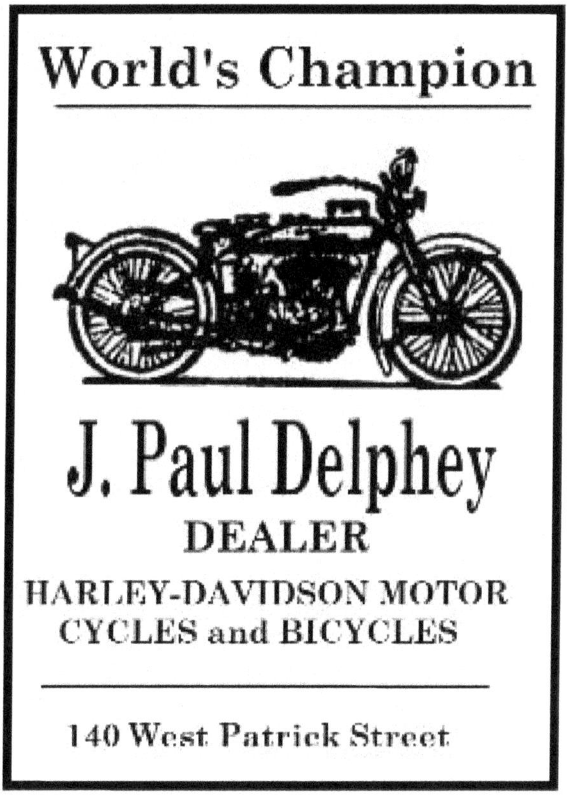

World's Champion

J. Paul Delphey

DEALER

HARLEY-DAVIDSON MOTOR CYCLES and BICYCLES

140 West Patrick Street

The entrance to the former site of Blickenstaff's ("Blick's") Indian Motorcycle shop in the rear of 9 East Third Street.

By mid-century motor vehicle sales had become a business genre of its own. No longer a sideline of department or hardware stores as it had originally been. Also, unlike the earliest days of motorized machinery, motorcycles were well on the way to becoming purely pleasure vehicles. Motorcycles were no longer, or at worst, were *rarely* considered as daily, year-round transportation in a world that had become totally dependent upon motorized transport. Motorcycling had become recreation, and as such, motorcycles did occasionally still find a place in… sporting goods stores.

In Frederick, it was actually a motorcycle shop, Delphey's motorcycle shop, that had evolved into a full-line sporting goods store, but the other motorcycle shops that remained, or the new ones that emerged, would be mostly stand-alone businesses.

320

Dutrow's Sales & Service, 1965 & 2020

Most of these mid-century motorcycle shops are gone but one, Dutrow's Honda, remains for now. The building looks different today, but it is still right where it has been on Baltimore National Pike ever since it opened in 1965. That day, Julian Delphey, disappointed to be losing a good man in Ted Dutrow, warned his former employee that he would never be able to make a living in this tough business. Dutrow's as it turns out, is only a tad over three years younger than Delphey's shop was when Julian sold his own motorcycle dealership. Julian Delphey was right about the motorcycle business being tough though. A tough business in which Ted Durtrow's Honda Shop has lasted fifty-five years. Not a bad run!

Dutrow's was described in advertising as *"three miles west of Frederick,"* in those days when a visiting, barely teenaged, Rodney Farris rode a dirt bike out the showroom door to rip up the field where U.S. Rt.40 is today. Dutrow's location at the foot of Braddock mountain has today been caught, and passed, by the city of Frederick.

321

While officially named *"Dutrow's Sales and Service"* everyone around Frederick knows it simply as ***"Dutrow's Honda."*** Ted Dutrow was a huge flat track fan. He introduced his wife Texanna to the sport in 1958 and ever since, she too has been indelibly hooked right up to the present. When I first interviewed Texanna, she told me about spending over five hours the night before watching the AFT races, which had aired live on the internet from Texas.

The Fritchie was special to the Dutrow family. July 4th was Ted Dutrow's birthday and the family always celebrated at the fairgrounds. They only missed one year due to a death in the family. Dutrow's Sales and Service have sold Honda motorcycles and power equipment since the shop opened in 1965. While Ted and Texanna dabbled in boats, outboard motors, bicycles and snowmobiles, the only motorcycles they have ever sold, and the backbone of their long-standing, successful business, has always been Honda. Over 50 years of Honda sales and service in the same location. The same building.

For many years Dutrow's was the premiere Honda dealer in the region. Throughout the 1980's when the Honda factory racing team was a major force in GNC competition, the riders always spent a day doing a "meet & greet" at Dutrow's whenever the circuit swung them through the area (typically at *Hagerstown Speedway*). During those meet & greets, the Dutrow family became good friends with several factory riders and the Dutrow shop is littered with one-of-a-kind memorabilia. It would however be the legendary Ricky Graham who made a particular hit with the Dutrow's despite his celebrity, rather than because of it.

Once, while admiring the equipment at the shop, Ricky mentioned to Ted Dutrow that he (Graham) had recently bought "a farm" in California and he needed a rototiller. If a rototiller seems like an odd selection for farm equipment, it was explained that Ricky Graham's *"farm"* turned out to be a mere three-acres! None the less, when the GNC stopped in Mineral Wells, West Virginia later that summer Ted Dutrow was there with a brand new Honda rototiller that was transferred to Johnny Goad's van for the cross-country ride back to Ricky's California *"farm."*

An autographed poster of Ricky Graham on a Harley, (in 1982) hanging in a Honda dealership for over three decades. This is more than just decoration!

I had not been in the Dutrow shop for decades. When I visited to gather information for this project, I was taken back by the racing memorabilia displayed everywhere. Every wall of the shop seems to hold some gem of flat track history, or several. Posters, advertising materials, photos… Not just riders from the golden era, but what today is a legend of its own, *the Honda era.* Ted and Texanna Dutrow and *"Dutrow's Sales and Service"* lived that era. They were part of it and while we unfortunately lost Ted in 2012, Texanna, her family and the business itself, are still here doing what they have always done at the same place in Frederick.

HOT NEWCOMER FROM HONDA

HONDA
SPORT 65

New power, new styling, new perform-ance, new engineering perfection. The Honda S-65. Low initial price; easy terms. It's ready for you today, at

DUTROW'S SALES & SERVICE
2 Mi. West Of Frederick On Rt. 40
Open: Mon.-Sat., Tues., Thurs., Fri. 'til 9

WAS $330 **NOW $315**
"YOU MEET THE NICEST PEOPLE ON A HONDA"

Dutrow Honda newspaper ad from opening year of 1965 and Texanna Dutrow and her son Jason in Oct. 2020 with Bubba Shobert looking on from the office wall.

Texanna and Ted a year or three ago

More 1 of a kind Ricky Graham items.

Bottom right is Ricky accepting his new rototiller from his friend Ted Dutrow.

For several years Frederick was a 500cc race. Honda had 500's and more than one Dutrow Honda was used by local racers. Texanna recalled once giving Johnny Goad a CR450 for his stable, but Dutrow's did not *"sponsor"* riders as that relationship is typically understood. The Dutrow's considered Johnny Goad a friend... like Ricky Graham. It was racers like Ricky Graham, Bubba Shobert and Larry Pegram riding RS750's that fueled Honda Fever in the 80's and 90's. Honda dealers were proud whether they were involved or not.

55 years is a lifetime for many people. When Robert Pirsig was riding his C77 Super Hawk and contemplating what would be one of the most successful books of all time – *"**Zen and the Art of Motorcycle Maintenance**"* - Ted Dutrow stocked the parts Bob needed to fix his bike. Those bits may still be lying in that parts bin!

* During my last interview with Texanna and Jason, I learned they had sold their property and the dealership was expected to be taken on by another Frederick motorcycle shop. The details of which were not yet finalized at the time of writing.

Anyone knowledgeable about The BFC knows about Fredericktown Yamaha. Few, however, know there was a Yamaha dealer before Richard Riley. In fact, there were two!

C.E. Bierley and Son operated a motorcycle and scooter shop in the alley behind west 5th Street for many years. The discreet concrete block building looks like what it is today, someone's personal garage. One conspicuous remnant of its days as a motorcycle and boat shop remains though. The horizontal sign mast projecting from the gable end of the roof. A mast that once held *"a swinging sign"* advertising the *"swinging world of Yamaha."*

Except for a few advertisements, little evidence remains to the specifics of Bierley's business. Clearly it existed for quite some time though as Charles E. Bierley died in 1948. Yamaha didn't exist until 1955 – in Japan! The marque did not arrive in America until 1960. Despite this, the business was named *"C.E. Bierley & Son"* even after Mehrl E. Bierley sold the Yamaha franchise in 1969. In 1970 a new business, **Yamaha of Frederick** opened in a nondescript brick building at the once forked intersection once known as *"Evergreen Point."* For approximately five years Al Shaw and Robert Diaz would operate the shop. After several years they moved to a new building just down the street on the corner of Rt. 355 & Grove road.

The last known souvenirs of the short lived "*Yamaha of Frederick.*"

The industrial park building once housing "Yamaha of Frederick."

Yamaha of Frederick would be a short-lived business and as many Fritchie fans have heard the story, September 7th, 1975 was the day *Fredericktown Yamaha* opened its doors for the first time. The Riley's also sold Triumph and Moto Guzzi in the 1970's.

Fredericktown Yamaha & Triumph at Rt. 355 & Grove Rd.

When the Triumph marque was revived in the 21st century, Fredericktown Yamaha, renewed their relationship with Triumph and picked up where they left off almost fifty years ago.

Another shop selling European bikes was "*Frederick Service Center,*" which relocated around the city several times during the lifetime of the dealership.

A former mail man, Warren High, who had never owned a bicycle himself, somehow ended up in the bicycle business in 1960 on East Patrick street in Frederick. Three years later as his son James became a young man, "*High's Cycles*" relocated to North Market street and branched out into motorcycle sales with the addition of the

329

Bridgestone brand. They later became the first Suzuki dealer in Frederick until passing that marque on to *"Two Wheels of Frederick"* in the mid-70's.

BRIDGESTONE 90 Sport

Track Bred
...Road Proven!

Sweepstakes

Win one of 36 new Bridgestone 90 Sports to be given away during Bridgestone's Giant Motorcycle Sweepstakes.

nothing to buy
nothing to write

To be eligible, simply stop in and register or write for registration blank. Sweepstakes ends July 15, 1966.

Register today at

High's Cycle Center

NEW LOCATIONS
311 North Market St. &
2-C West Fourth St.
PHONE 662-6633

An X-6 Rustler at heart—

with the most spirited styling a scrambler ever had!

SUZUKI X-6 SCRAMBLER

• 29 hp, 250cc Dual Stroke engine
• 6-speed racing shift pattern
• heavy-duty skid plate, reinforced bars
• built in tach, folding pegs
• Posi-Force automatic lubing
• Suzuki 12 month/12,000 mile Warranty

$749.00

HIGH'S CYCLE CENTER

Corner of 4th & Market Sts.

330

Delphey's Sport Store, 140 W. Patrick Street Frederick, Maryland not long
before the store was razed.

331

Of course, as we have become familiar, Delphey's Sport Store was the Harley-Davidson dealer from 1919 until 1978. On March 21, 1978 Michael Vantucci became the official owner of Harley-Davidson dealership #1813. He named the business "*Harley-Davidson of Frederick*" and located it next door to the original location of *Yamaha of Frederick*, at Evergreen Point. Also like that business, Vantucci would later relocate to the (opposite) corner of Grove road and Rt. 355.

Many of the motorcycle shops in the Washington and Baltimore metro areas had close connections to the Fritchie and the motorcycle community in Frederick. Tom Hyser's "*Hyser's Cycle Center*," and Bob Myers' "*Free State Cycles*" immediately come to mind. Blalock Cycles, Boutwell's, White's, all the Harley shops, and the dealers in nearby Hagerstown, Leesburg and Winchester, Virginia, and north into central Pennsylvania have all contributed to the local motorcycle scene. There have been other motorcycle businesses in and around Frederick through the years and there *are* other shops here today! What are highlighted above though are an historical sampling. To those whom I have neglected, I sincerely apologize. It is a subject I'd like to spend more time on one day.

THRILLS – SPILLS – EXCITEMENT
PROFESSIONAL
MOTORCYCLE RACES

MONDAY, JULY 5
FREDERICK FAIR GROUNDS
Time Trials 1 P.M.—Races start 2:30 P.M.

If tickets are purchased previous to July 4th you
SAVE $1.00. Tickets are now on sale at Blue Ridge
News Agency, Delphey's Sport Store, Cappello's,
Food Mkt., Dutrow's Sales & Service, High's Cycle
Center, Chas. E. Bierley & Son, Yamaha of Fred-
erick or any member of the Lions Club for $2.00.
Admission to the Fair Grounds $2.00 — To the Grand-
stand $1.00.

Advance Sale of tickets will go off July 3rd
No Alcoholic Beverages Permitted
Sponsored by The

LIONS CLUB OF FREDERICK
Proceeds Will Be Used For the Blind and Other Charities

1971 BFC advertisement listing various Frederick motorcycle dealers.

333

In Memorial

While everyone involved in this sport does everything within their power to make each race as safe as possible, motorcycle racing, by its very nature, is a dangerous activity.

Today's helmets, leathers and other gear combined with space-age synthetic armor and futuristic padding in strategic, medically identified locations, have helped tremendously. The most recent advance being computer monitored "air suits" which are instantly inflated in the event of an incident. Technology has taken a quantum leap in every piece of race equipment, yet the races are still held on tracks which are little changed in over 100-years. Only partly due to that factor, despite all the precautions and all the developments, the unforeseen can and does still happen. The unthinkable is still an ever-present possibility in every race.

It should be no surprise that in 100 years, Frederick has seen its share of incidents and a few tragedies. Other favorites of the Frederick oval have met untimely ends at distant venues. It is a dark side of the sport we never get used to. A side we never want to see again but reluctantly, we accept it as an ever-present possibility because danger and this sport are one.

+ + + +

While this chapter was planned from the very beginning, as this project progressed, I became increasingly undecided on including it. Then, one night while watching a long-ago race on the internet I decided that this chapter _must_ stay in the book due to a comment a racer made to Larry Maiers during one of those time filling paddock interviews contained in that old video. That rider was Fritchie regular, Rodney Farris. The interview was not long before his death.

Hauntingly, Rodney mentioned not wanting to be forgotten by the fans.

You're not Rod. Not today. Not ever!

Note – Oral history has long maintained that a death occurred at the Fritchie prior to 1950. I have searched every source available without discovering evidence to substantiate this claim.

#30c Ron Adkins

On July 4, 1968, Ronald F. Adkins, was involved in a crash during the 1st junior class heat when Bennie Johnson of Cary NC went down in turn two in front of Adkins. Ron could not avoid hitting the disabled bike and was thrown over the trackside fence by the impact. It was there that Adkins struck a telephone pole and received most of his injuries. Born in Peoria, Illinois, July 15, 1938, 29-year-old Ron Adkins was the creative manager of the sales promotion department at Triumph Corporation, Baltimore, Maryland during the height of Triumph's prominence in America.

Incredibly, despite many who consider the Frederick track as overly dangerous, Ron Adkins is the only <u>documented</u> fatality at a *Barbara Fritchie Classic* in over 100 years of racing.

Ron Adkins at Richmond, Virginia, 46 days before his death at Frederick

#22u Mike Bird

On August 5, 1973 during time trials in a ***Cycle Racing Corp., Gold Cup*** race held at the Frederick track, Bellefonte Pennsylvania's Mike Bird encountered unknown problems exiting turn two. His bike struck the fence and Bird was thrown over the barrier. Hauntingly, like Ron Adkins five years earlier, Mike Bird then hit a 12-foot-tall sign pole outside the track. He landed outside the back straightaway, not far from where the ambulance was staged. Paramedics were on the scene immediately. A Maryland State Police helicopter landed in the infield and Bird, who had sustained severe head injuries was Medevac'd straight from the scene to the University of Maryland, Shock-Trauma center in Baltimore. Despite the trauma center only being minutes away by helo and the absolute best efforts by first responders and the team at Shock Trauma, Mike Bird's injuries proved fatal.

#92 Rodney Farris

    National number 92, Rodney "Hot Rod" Farris, a native of nearby Cockeysville Maryland, lost his life in a racing incident at the Du Quoin mile on July 2, 1995. Rod was a protégé of Gary Nixon and a perennial favorite at Frederick. Nixon ran his race workshop next to the motorcycle shop of Rod's dad. Rodney grew up racing the two-time GNC champion on minibikes out back of the shop. Nixon once said himself, *"I didn't cut him any breaks because he was a kid either…"* Rod learned early what makes a GNC champion! Rodney won the main at Frederick in 1984, 1986, and 1989, but he had been coming to Frederick with his dad since he was six years old. Norm Farris was then a Yamaha Factory rep who sometimes helped out at the race. Rod's death just two days before the 1995 race cast a pall over the 74th BFC. The event had previously been expected to have more pros than usual due to scheduling of the various nationals, but after Rodney's death several riders made it known that out of respect they were staying away from what was considered to be Rodney's "home track." Rod Farris, in addition to countless regional and club races throughout the country, racked up 15 podium finishes in Grand National Championship competition. He finished in the top ten 109 times and the top five, forty times. He finished the season among the top ten riders in the country during half of the 13-years of his pro career, and that is only his GNC stats! Rodney was 32 years old.

RODNEY "HOT ROD" FARRIS
Professional Dirt Track Racing

NATIONAL
92

#99 Kyle McGrane

Kyle McGrane of Gap, Pennsylvania, just 85 miles from Frederick, was an incredibly talented young man. He left us much too soon, the result of a racing incident in California in 2016. In his second year of GNC2 (today's AFT Singles class) competition, Kyle qualified for the main event in 11 out of 14 AFT races that year and he finished in the top ten in <u>every one</u> of those races. His best AFT showing was the Arizona mile on May 14, 2016 where he finished 2nd. Kyle first raced at Frederick in 2005 when the (then) six-year-old won the minibike class. He was a regular here ever since.

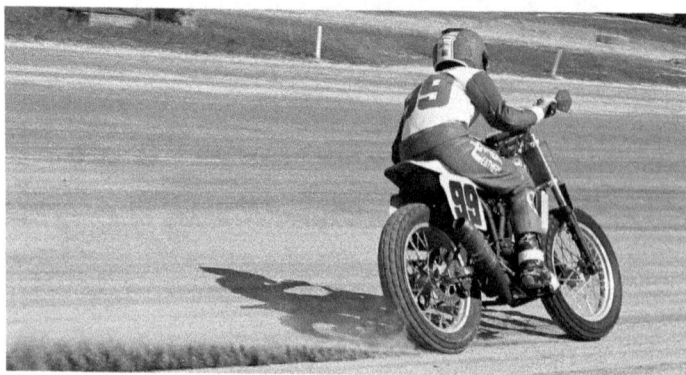

Ride on Kyle. We'll catch up to you at the finish line...

340

This is perhaps a fitting place to acknowledge the 99th BFC. ***"The race that should have been."*** As fans already know, the 2020 BFC was cancelled three weeks before race day due to the government restrictions then in place due to the covid virus which swept the globe beginning in January 2020. This was not an unprecedented decision. It is one that J. Paul Delphey had to make several times. The decision was out of the promoter's hands and as J. Paul stated in 1942, *"I don't need money badly enough to act contrary to the requests of the governor of Maryland"*

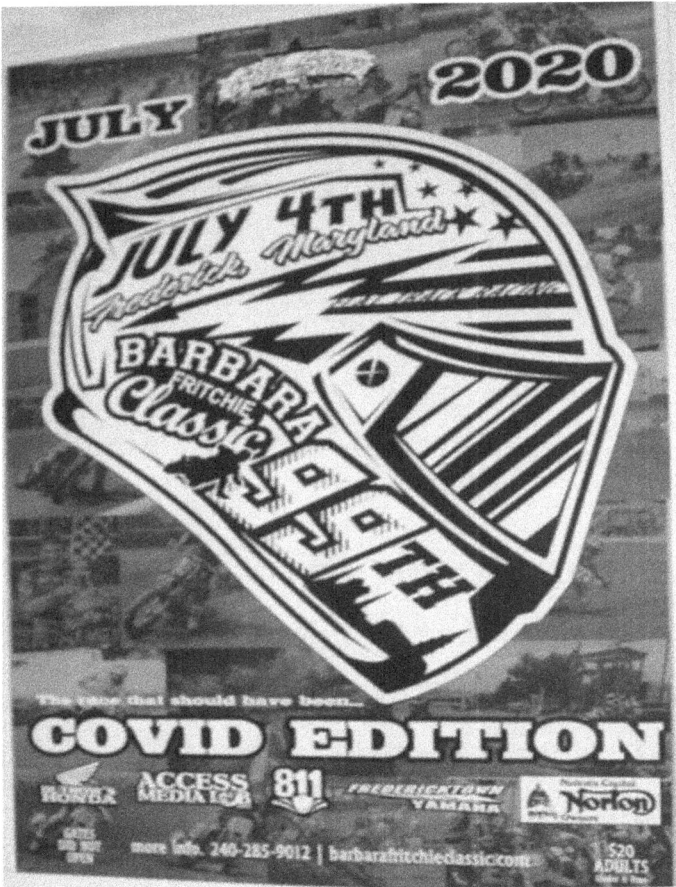

A lot of fans were upset. We lost the chance to have a race but many around the world, to include some honored members of the extended Barbara Fritchie Classic family, lost much, much more than a motorcycle race. Our hearts go out to their families. We can race another day, but to do so, we must first be here to race.

The place to improve the world is first in one's own heart and head and hands, and then work outward from there. Other people can talk about how to expand the destiny of mankind. I just want to talk about how to fix a motorcycle. — Robert Pirsig

"Everytime I start thinkin' the world is all bad, then I start seeing some people out having a good time on motorcycles and it makes me take another look." — *Steve McQueen*

The End...

of the first 100-years!

The Rooks County Fair

The Rooks County Free Fair is held annually at Stockton, in north-central Kansas. What makes this relevant is the claim that the Stockton race is the oldest ½ mile dirt track race. My job researching the Barbara Fritchie Classic and its similar claim required that I investigate this obvious conflict. The last thing I wanted to do was change any of that narrative. Both are events for their respective communities to be incredibly proud of. As every racer grudgingly accepts though, there can only be one first. One winner!

Just as my initial searching discovered at Frederick, documented history for the Stockton race, when it does exist, is well hidden. What there is, is a lot of handed down memories and oral history. Again, as has been demonstrated previously, such stories often prove to be correct. I reached out to the fair board at Stockton without success. I contacted the Rooks county historical society and the representative said she would try to find something but at that time she was buried in existing projects without an end in sight. The story is that motorcycle racing began at Stockton in 1906. I located an online article about the 100th anniversary celebration held in 2006 but attempts to contact the writer were fruitless.

William "Bultaco Bill" Snyder of Manhattan Kansas has been a dirt track racer through seven decades. When perusing that 100th anniversary article, I discovered that Bill Snyder had written two racing history articles for the 2006 Stockton anniversary race program. It was the evidence I hoped would finally provide some documentation or at least some solid clues. I asked around and I got contact info for Bultaco Bill.

Bill is a really, nice guy. When I called him I asked if I might get a copy of what he'd written for that 2006 program. I thought that perhaps he'd saved a digital copy of some form that he could print, or even email to me. When I asked, he paused, then said *"you must be the luckiest man in the world."* Bill went on to explain that just the day before he had found a copy of that 2006 race program in the bottom of a dresser drawer. *"Text me your address and I'll mail it to you."* I was speechless.

Bill did send me his 2006 Rooks County Free Fair race program. I gratefully photocopied it and sent the original back. While it is an amazing piece of flat track memorabilia, it did not provide the *documentation* I was hoping for.

Stockton Kansas is a town of just over 1,200 people. The Kansas State Data Center notes that Rooks county's year of all-time highest population was 1910. The population has been gradually declining ever since. I discovered there was a newspaper in Stockton Kansas from around 1885 until approximately 1924 and I began searching the archives of *"The Stockton Review"* for any mention of motorcycle races. While providing considerable data on the fair, the business meetings of the fair board, the activities and events at the fair, even the winners of the exhibits and events, not to mention all the other news of Rooks and surrounding counties, it did not provide any insight into motorcycle racing during the period I was searching for.

I searched backward from 1906 to 1899 for any possibility that racing was *older* than remembered. I searched the other fifty-one weeks of the year 1906 in case the elusive first race was not part of the annual fair. I searched other Kansas newspapers for the same period then I searched nationwide for any mention of motorcycle racing *in Kansas* between 1900 and 1910. Motorcycle racing in Stockton was not mentioned until 1909. That 1909 fair advertisement announces, **"*Motorcycle Races!*"** as one of the scheduled attractions. Unfortunately, there is no post-fair mention of the races taking place. There was no mention of winners or any other report on what may have transpired during the announced races as there was in the various articles on *every other* fair activity from the horse races, to the baseball games and poultry show. There is no mention in any other publication anywhere in Kansas or elsewhere in the nation. The only reasonable conclusion is that the 1909 race was canceled for unknown reasons.

Pre-fair ads once again promised motorcycle races in 1910 and this time, unlike the previous year, follow-up articles in the Stockton Review do describe the races and the race results *in detail*.

I am not about to dispute tradition or oral history from a thousand miles away! Regarding documentation though, in absence of evidence confirming an earlier date and until and unless such documentation can be found, I must place the first *documented* race at Stockton Kansas as between September 6 & 9, 1910.

The Stockton Review appears to have gone out of business in 1924, ending the most reliable source of data. It is almost certain the early races there were not M&ATA or FAM sanctioned (AMA was not formed until 1924). There is no indication the earliest races at Stockton were intended for anyone but local riders. Neither does it appear that the Stockton race was annual/continual even from 1910 to 1924. At the very least, there are not consistent records of it in the Stockton Review. Judging by the other events that are mentioned those years such as ballgames and horse races, the absence of motorcycle racing cannot be attributed to rainouts.

While "The Stockton Review" appears to have gone out of business in 1924, there is another paper still operating in Stockton Kansas today. *"The Stockton Sentinel."*

The Sentinel has been published since 1989. The lady answering the phone there was very helpful. She provided several leads for people she thought may know more about the history of the race. One of those who has proven *very* helpful is Stockton native, Ryan Stewart. Ryan is one of those who has *personally* witnessed racing at Stockton for almost half its total history there.

Ryan Stewart also bears the distinction of personally holding one end of the thin silver thread connecting both ends of the Rooks County Free Fair motorcycle race story. At the other end of that thread is Ira W. Stewart, the brother of Ryan's great grandfather! Ira Stewart was one of the five entries in that first documented Stockton race.

Motor Cycle Race.

One of the interesting races at the fair was the motorcycle race. There were five entries, Keene of Alton, and Ira Stewart, Clyde Maris, Ralph Keilholtz and Wilber Ba'ker, all of this place. There were four five mile heats and contrary to expectation, the race was won by Ralph Keilholtz. Ralph was not an experienced rider, and was in the race largely for the practice it would afford in riding. The first heat was won by Keene, but afterwards it seemed that Keene couldn't get his m...

Sept. 15, 1910 page 2, Stockton Review.

This detailed story, one column wide and about half a page in length (pictured example has been cropped) covering one single event at the fair was *very* unusual in fair coverage for the Stockton Review. The extent of the story and the verbiage; "*One of the interesting races...*" is like articles identified as "first race" reports elsewhere.

Interestingly, there was also a road race in Rooks county in 1910. In absence of more definitive evidence, I again looked to the verbiage used in reaching for *any* clues to the origins of motorcycle racing in the county. None of this is proof of anything other than that a race did happen on May 23, 1910. We still cannot say if it was the first one or the twenty first! It is however, along with the 1909 fair advertisement, among the earliest documentations of motorcycles of any description in Rooks county Kansas that I have been able to find.

August 1910 was less than a year since the first national motorcycle race was staged at Indianapolis Indiana by the F.A.M. Motor vehicles were new. They were a popular curiosity and a huge draw. Both motorcycle and auto racing held great expectations for many cities and towns hoping to capitalize on the new sport of motor racing.

Woodston is half-way between Stockton and the town of Alton Kansas. Interestingly, while it is described as "on open road," Alton or Stockton are both about nine miles in different directions from Woodston. The race is described as a *"three-mile race,"* indicating it was not a town-to-town event as early road races frequently were. Instead it clearly used some long-lost circuit at or around Woodston Kansas.

> There will be a free for all motorcycle race against time on open road, at Woodston, Monday, May 23, at 2 o'clock, to be a matched race. Motor cycles from Stockton and Alton besides the Woodston motor cycles will take part in the race. Everyone come out and see our first motor races. This will be a three mile race.

19 May 1910, The Woodson Argus, Page 3

Lawrence "Ray" Weishaar, that iconic pig toting member of the Harley-Davidson wrecking crew grew up in Wichita and cut his racing teeth on the Kansas and Oklahoma fair grounds tracks beginning in 1908. By 1914 Ray had won the Kansas state championship twice (once with one handlebar after crashing) and he had moved on to national "class A" competition. He became part of the Harley-Davidson team in 1916. It was 1920 as mentioned in a previous chapter that Weishaar won the Marion Indiana road race by an incredible 18-minute lead and became immortalized in photos featuring his Harley Jersey while sharing a Coke with his pet pig. In 1923 Weishaar accepted a lucrative job at the Ascot Speedway in Los Angeles California. The following April while contesting for the lead on the fast, banked Ascot track, Indian rider Johnny Seymore drafted past Ray which brought on a tank slapper that put Weishaar through the (wooden) Ascot fence. Initially thought to only have minor injuries, Weishaar's wife who had seen him injured many times, casually drove him to the hospital in her own car. The hospital where Ray died several hours later of internal injuries.

"The Kansas Cyclone" Lawrence "Ray" Weishaar of Wichita KS. On a big H-D single about 1922.

Since the demise of the FAM in 1919, racing had become sketchier for those who made their living on the board and dirt tracks around the country. The high-profile deaths of stars such as Weishaar and Indian's Gene Walker just several weeks later, together with the formation of the AMA that same year, resulted in several rules designed to gain some control over the dangers of racing. One of which was to restrict ½ mile tracks to 21 cubic inch (350cc) engines.

Kansas in general and Stockton Kansas specifically, continue a tradition of motorcycle racing to be proud of whether you are from Kansas or anywhere else. I wish I could say I found evidence to confirm the oral traditions of Rooks County. Records though are for scholars.

Just like at Frederick, Maryland, when you roll up to the starting line and gaze into turn one at Stockton, when you envision your line into turn one as countless generations of racers have done before. You don't need documentation to tell you this track is special.

From Ray Weishaar before anyone outside Kansas knew his name, all the way down to the present. From Ira Stewart to Ryan Stewart, the Stockton motorcycle races, like the Frederick races 1,2000 miles away, are the history of dirt track motorcycle racing.

Interestingly, while motorcycles racing the clock is documented as early as 1900 at Frederick Maryland. While multiple motorcycles racing each other are documented at Frederick as early as 1901. Motorcycle racing has not been proven to have taken place on the ½ mile Frederick fairground track that is still in use, until 1909. Only *ONE* year before the one that I have been forced to recognize as the earliest <u>documented</u> race at Stockton. If someone can produce proof the advertised 1909 Stockton race did happen, the balance would shift again – by a mere month! In racing, there always must be a winner. Often, the margin is close. Difficult as it is for everyone else, someone has to be *"first."* But a month or even a year is cutting it close for something that happened more than 100 years ago.

I certainly didn't plan it this way. Never expected it to happen. But there it is. The possibility remains that someone may one day stumble upon evidence that either race ran earlier. I have found pieces of the puzzle in weird and unexpected places. Who knows what may still be out there in a shoebox, the wrong file folder… or the bottom of some old racer's sock and underwear drawer?

Despite my job of documenting the *Frederick* race, failing to prove Stockton's 1906 story remains a disappointment. On July 14, 2020, the Rooks County fair board made the difficult decision to cancel events and attractions for the 2020 fair due to the covid virus.

Photo from the 1916 Rooks County Free Fair race provided by Ryan Stewart

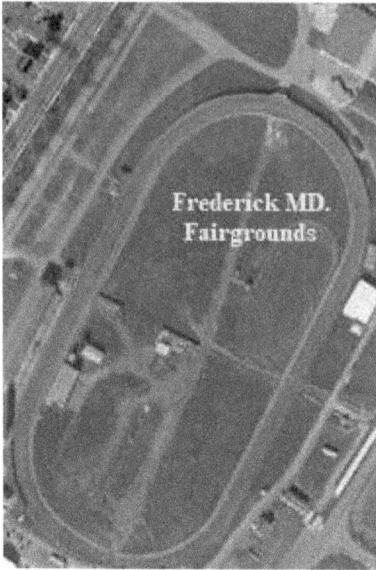

Frederick and Stockton, the oldest operating motorcycle racing tracks anywhere, bear some striking similarities.

Glossary

This section is included for the benefit of those unfamiliar with dirt track motorcycle racing. Particularly those who may be using this book for its relevance to Frederick history rather than racing history.

Air Suit – A leather suit with an air bladder incorporated as a lining. Using proprietary computer equipment, the suits are programed to "sense" when a rider is in an unusual situation and instantly inflate the suit, thus creating a cushioning layer to lessen or prevent serious injury in a crash.

Board Track – A type of racetrack popular for a brief period in the early 20th century whose surface was constructed out of wood. Also called motordromes or speedways, the tracks were usually 3/8 to one mile in length (circumference) and banked, often steeply, which allowed much greater speed. The tracks allowed racers to attain speeds greater than the equipment of the day was capable of handling. The result was numerous crashes from blown tires, bent forks or rims and other mechanical or structural failures. Riders wore no meaningful safety equipment. As well, there was typically no barrier between track and spectators. Out of control bikes too often careened air-borne at up to 100mph into the crowds. The result was that as deadly as the racing was, it resulted in as many or more spectator deaths. Despite rivaling baseball as the largest spectator sport during its heyday, the numerous gruesome crashes resulting from board track racing soon brought discredit to the sport by an appalled public and by the mid-1920's board track racing began fading into oblivion.

Class – rider categories – Every race is broken down into various classes or rider classifications. Generally, riders of similar proven ability only race against riders of like ability to avoid dangerous situations. Depending on the race, there may be classes for youngsters under 12 or under 16. There are as well classes for riders over 40, 50 and 60! There are classes for vintage bikes and various power ratings (engine size). A recent class is the so-called Hooligans, basically street bikes (often barely) adapted for racing, harkening back to the original intent of Class C racing. In the national championship AFT series, riders are separated by Premier – 750cc special race-only motorcycles (formerly GNC expert class), Production Twins – 750cc twin cylinder motorcycles based on consumer available production engines (*somewhat* akin to the old class C), AFT Singles – 450cc motorcycles based on production motocross bikes. Women have competed equally with men in flat track racing since 1971.

Cushion – The tracks used for flat track racing are either clay, with a hard, smooth, packed surface* or what is known as "cushion." Cushion tracks are typically those which are designed for horse racing, especially harness racing. The surface is most frequently covered in a thick layer of very fine gravel known as "pea gravel" or "stone dust" which provides somewhat of a cushioning effect for the horse's hooves. It provides a very unpredictable surface for motorcycle tires. The techniques for riding cushion and clay tracks can very considerably.

*While clay tracks appear smooth from a distance, the actual surface is typically quite rough by comparison to a paved road.

Dash for Cash – A short – typically five laps – race among a small group of riders, usually the top five qualifiers, for a specified cash prize. Some races may award 2nd and 3rd place prizes, but traditionally it is an all or nothing race with the 1st place rider winning the entire prize.

DIS – Disqualified. Riders can be disqualified from competition by race officials for various reasons, before, during or after a race is completed.

DNF – Did not finish. Signifies a rider who started but did not complete a race.

DNS – Did not start. Signifies a rider who was entered but did not report to the starting grid at the beginning of a race.

Draft – Known otherwise as "slipstream." A phenomenon whereby a rapidly moving object overcoming the resistance of the stationary air in front of it, creates a small pocket of air behind it moving at the same speed as the object. In terms of racing, if one rider can enter this pocket behind the rider in front of him, he can theoretically go faster with the same effort due to not having to overcome the air resistance. "Drafting" racers are often seen pulling out and passing the leader in a sudden burst of speed at an opportune time. The draft is however very small, necessitating following VERY close. It is a dangerous practice, but one that can provide huge benefits.

Flag – The race was traditionally controlled by a flagman / starter. Stationed at the start/finish line, the flagman signals riders with a variety of hand-held flags. Green = Go / race in progress. Checkered (black & white) = finish / race is over. White =1 lap remaining. Yellow = Caution, hazard on the track. Red = immediate danger / *stop*. Blue = You're in the way / allow others to pass. Black = Disqualified / leave the track immediately. So called "corner workers" are stationed around the track to provide timely warning in the event of a yellow or red flag situation and assist riders as applicable. Today, traditional flagger's duties have been largely replaced by automatic signal lights at larger races where even the flagman/starter is largely symbolic. Timing is by electronic devices attached to each motorcycle (see "transponder") and the starting line is monitored by laser sensors. Yet many smaller and / or traditional races continue to employ a starter and corner flaggers.

GNC / Grand National Championship - The name adopted for the national racing series created by the AMA in 1954 to crown a national champion based on the accumulation of points awarded depending on finishing position at each race of the season-long series. When the GNC was sold to Daytona Motorsports Group in 2007, the GNC name continued to be used until 2017. The name was then changed to American Flat Track (AFT).

Grid / starting grid – The order in which individual riders are positioned to start a race. "The pole" position (left frontline) is typically regarded as the choicest starting position and the remaining slots in the grid are filled by descending order of qualifying times. See re-start

Groove / Blue Groove – The groove is the preferred portion of the track used by the majority of riders in a race. Typically, the fastest way around, it may be concentric to the outline of the track or very non-concentric depending on various factors. A Blue Groove is the term for this portion of a track, which after practice and qualifying, begins accumulating a layer of rubber worn off the tires. On an otherwise brown clay track, this layer of deposited rubber often takes on a blue appearance, hence, "blue groove."

Hack – Side car

Half-mile - One of the four types of tracks used in American dirt track racing today. A half-mile is a track measuring at least one half-mile in length when measured eighteen inches from the inside edge of the racing surface.

Hay Bale – The common name for the bales of straw placed at strategic places around many tracks to lessen the impact of a crash. In pro competition hay bales have been largely replaced by "air fence" which is a sort of inflated bag lining the track in hazardous locations. The air fence deflates in a controlled manner on impact to envelope and cushion a rider rather than deflecting him back onto the track. Some tracks have begun using other re-usable replacements for hay bales to include synthetic foam blocks ("tough blocks") and large bags filled with cushioning material.

High Line / Low Line – The rider's chosen path around the track nearer the outside (high) or inside (low) edge of the track.

High side – A crash involving the rider being thrown from the top of the motorcycle. Frequently forward over the handlebars. Usually the most violent and injury producing of non-collision type crashes.

Hole shot – A term used to describe the fastest rider leaving the starting line. That rider typically has the advantage of choosing his line entering the first turn rather than having to contend with the crowded pack behind him. The first rider into turn 1 can often extend that lead as those behind grapple for a fast line. Six-time national champion and three-time Fritchie winner, Jared Mees once described getting the hole shot at Frederick as *"75% of winning this race."*

Infield – The area encircled by the racetrack. Frequently where the pit area is located to segregate it from the spectator area.

Jumped / jumped the start – A term used to describe a rider who crossed the starting line before the official starting signal. The penalty for jumping the start is losing your starting position and moving to the last position in the grid.

Lap – A single circuit around the track. Races are measured in laps (10-lap, 5 lap, etc.).

Lap-time – the elapsed time it takes a rider to complete a single lap around the track. Lap time is used in qualifying but not necessarily in the main event. A rider who has fallen behind can log slightly faster (individual) single lap times than the winner without catching up to him before the end of the race.

Leathers – The full coverage – ankle to neck - leather suits worn by racers. A huge improvement over the wool sweaters and cotton jerseys worn by early racers. Traditionally, leathers primarily provide abrasion protection in a crash, but tight leathers can support limb alignment and reduce air resistance. Advances through the years have added padding and "armor" at strategic locations such as elbows and knees and more recently, chest and spine plates have been incorporated. In the second decade of the 21st century, the "air suit" has become the latest innovation. (see air suit)

Light / Christmas tree – The starting light is a reliably unbiased electronic replacement of the flagman for starting races. The light has red, yellow and green lights like a traffic signal. The race light however, uses two yellows. The red light is followed by the first yellow light for five seconds. Then the second yellow replaces the first for a random and un-anticipatable length of time from 0.01 to a maximum of 3 seconds before changing to green. Nobody knows when the light will change from yellow to green and everyone wants to be the first off the line. The light is sometimes called a Christmas tree for its multiple colored lights.

Line – The line is the chosen path a rider uses around the track. Riders will use individual strategies riding "high" or "low" and frequently crossing the track through a corner. A slow rider being approached from behind by a faster one is expected to "*maintain his line*" (as observed and anticipated by the approaching rider) to allow the faster rider to safely pass.

Low side - A crash involving the rider and motorcycle falling onto the side of the bike and ideally, sliding to a stop in a *somewhat* controlled crash.

Main / main event – The main event is the final race (in each class) of the meet. The winner of the main is named the overall winner of the event.

Mile - One of the four types of tracks used in American dirt track racing today. A mile is a track measuring at least one mile in length when measured eighteen inches from the inside edge of the racing surface.

Motordrome – SEE BOARD TRACK

National number – From the beginning of class C racing in 1933 until 2018, professional racers were annually awarded a two digit* number that was good in any AMA race in the country. Hence, the name, *"national number."* To qualify for a national number after 1954, a rider had to qualify for a main event in at least one Grand National Championship race the previous year. This qualifying process was originally modified and then in 2018 dispensed with entirely by AFT.

* Number 1 was and is still reserved for the previous year's champion. Numbers 2-9 are previous champions (*not* in order).

P1,2,3 etc. – Official results of a race *"P4 = placed 4th."*

Paddock – Generally a reference to the pit area but occasionally used to describe all the riders collectively. see Pits.

Pee Dub – Yamaha model *PW50* specifically. Or in general, any very small, child-sized, typically 50cc minibike.

Pit – The pits are the area at the racetrack reserved for the racers their teammates and their equipment. Frequently located on the infield of the track, the pits are separated from the general spectator area for both privacy of the racers and the safety of fans.

Points / season points – In addition to individual prizes awarded at and by specific races, regional clubs and organizations as well as the AMA and at the pro level, AFT, award "points" based on a rider's finish in each race in a particular series, or circuit. These points are calculated at the end of the season to determine how an individual rider placed season-long against the others in the series or circuit. The points are maintained in a running tally, event by event, often resulting in intense competition.

Privateer – A race team that is not funded or primarily supported by a manufacturer or major supplier. The privateer is the ultimate grassroots racer. Frequently a family effort or owner/operator.

Purse – The total amount of prize money at stake in a race meet. The total is typically distributed between classes and an individual's winnings is based on his finish placement according to a predetermined disbursement schedule.

Qualifying – The process of elimination by which the fastest entries advance to the next race. Each rider's lap time is individually measured during qualifying laps, the fastest times are used both to advance to the next race and often to determine the rider's position in the starting grid.

Re-Start – The act of starting over a race that has been stopped due to some incident and re-started to complete the remaining laps. The re-start grid, rather than straight lines, typically forms a diagonal line with each bike offset one position to the side and one back so none are immediately behind another. The re-start positions, front to back, are the same as each rider held in the race when the race was interrupted.

Rev limiter – The limiter is a safety device that interrupts motor function when the engine reaches a pre-set speed or "rev" (revolutions per minute). Its purpose is to prevent damage to the engine.

Roost – The debris that is sprayed from the wheels of motorcycles. Originating from the phrase "rooster tail," to describe the arching plume of dirt and dust coming primarily off the rear wheel.

Safety wire – A thin, soft, pliable metal wire used to securely attach parts that could theoretically come lose and become a hazard on the track. In practice, safety wire is used for the intended purpose as well as every conceivable expedient repair that can be imagined – and many that can't be imagined.

Scratch race / handicapped race – An obsolete starting line-up where the faster riders were placed in the rear of the pack to provide slower qualifying riders somewhat of a head start. The slowest qualifier sometimes having a full ¼ mile "handicap." In some races, if a leading rider was passed by a faster rider coming from behind him, the passed rider was automatically disqualified, or "scratched" from the race.

Short track – One of the four types of tracks used in American dirt track racing today. A short track is defined as any oval track less than 1,750 feet in length as measured eighteen inches from the inside edge of the track.

Slide – (power slide) A practice unique to dirt track racing where the rider intentionally causes the rear wheel to slide out to the right-side of the motorcycle in a turn. There are various reasons for using this practice but what appears to the uninitiated as a near loss of control, is in fact the complete opposite. Use of sliding is much more pronounced on loose surface cushion tracks.

Speedway – Typically a reference to a specialized type of racing resembling flat track racing but differing in some very specific ways. The bikes have no (shifting) transmission, no brakes and all use the same basic engines. The track is more compact, usually about ¼ mile and races are typically between only four riders at a time. See also "Board Track" some pre-1930 board tracks were called "speedways." Similarly, it has become a popular though largely generic term for any motorsport racetrack in recent years.

Start/Finish Line – The point on the track marked by a white stripe across the track where the (1st row) bikes line up to begin a race. This line also marks the finish line. When multiple starting lines are used for multiple rows of bikes, the line nearest turn #1 will be the start/finish line.

Steel shoe / Hot shoe – The "hot shoe" is a steel device that covers the entire bottom of a rider's left boot to allow sliding the foot along the surface of the track without snagging or sticking.

Sulky – A lightweight two-wheel cart used for harness (horse) racing, where the jockey rides in the sulky, which in turn is pulled by the racehorse.

Tank Slapper – Also called a speed wobble. It is an uncontrollable rapid movement of the handlebars back and forth due to some sudden irregularity. Causes and results are varied but always frightening.

Tape – (duct tape or painter's tape) Tape can be an event saving expedient repair tool. Sometimes used to seal openings in leathers or helmet visors, a protective covering for painted surfaces, or even improvised number plates… Tape is also frequently encountered in the pits teamed with a shred of paper towel as an impromptu bandage. Tape rival's safety wire for importance in the racetrack toolbox.

Tear-off – A very thin sheet of optical quality plastic covering the helmet visor or goggles. Each one has an individual tab the rider pulls to remove the tear-offs, one at a time, as hampered vison requires. On very dusty or dirty tracks, as many as a dozen tear offs may be stacked and frequently, all of them are used before the race is finished.

Transponder – A transponder is a small electronic device that emits a signature radio wave unique to each unit. By sensing exactly when the transponder passes the stationary receiver at the finish line, timing and recognition of winners has reached an all-time level of accuracy without the chance for human error.

Tri-Corp – Triumph Corporation. U.S. Distributor for Triumph motorcycles east of the Rocky Mountains. Ceased operations in 1978.

TT – (TT track/race) The term TT entered AMA regulations in 1933 in company to the new (1932) Class "C" rules adopted to promote "normal" consumer-style motorcycles. Originally named for the European tourist trophy road races, the most famous being the Isle of Mann. The idea of the TT was essentially a small easily viewed (dirt) road course. The concept was described in the new rules as; "…*should embrace, to the closest possible extent, all the conditions that would be met with in driving on the open road*." It was further required that the course have; "*both right and left hand turns…*" as well as; "*if possible, a hill that will necessitate gear changing…*"As the sport and the tastes of spectators have evolved, today's TT track has morphed into a dirt track with at least one righthand turn and the hill has become a jump so that today, a TT race seems to share more in common with motocross than road racing.

Tuner – A common term for the mechanic who prepares, adjusts and "tunes" a race bike. There are many, many more factors and adjustments that go into the ideal set up for any particular track or conditions than simply being fast. Experienced tuners who have been around the various tracks with various riders, possess a knowledge that rivals the ability of the rider in importance. A good rider and a good tuner are a winning combination. The best tuners are frequently (but not always!) former racers.

Wheel spin – Occasionally, the bike applies such power that the rear wheel spins uselessly on the surface of the track instead of pushing the bike forward. The tuner's goal is to build a bike with the greatest power *and* the ability to transfer every bit of it to the ground to produce forward movement.

Works bike – A term used to describe a special built race only bike that is not available to anyone to the public. Typically using unique one-of-a-kind custom-made performance parts and traditionally, a "factory bike" from a sponsoring manufacturer, but occasionally from a custom builder.

Timeline of Motorcycle Racing at Frederick Maryland

Except for the 1911 road race, all races after 1909 were held on the current fairground track still used today. It is suspected there were other races for which there are no records.

The various dates from 1900 – 1923 were promoted, often several per year, by the bicycle club, the horse racing club, the motorcycle dealers and the county fair. Motorcycle racing essentially eclipsed (track) bicycle racing before 1910 and horse racing by the late 1920's.

Motorcycle racing was sporadic at the fair until dropped completely in 1938.

The harness racing club originally held the July 4th date, which was adopted by Delphey in 1931.

There continued to occasionally be multiple races per year into the 1970's.

The sidecar world record set by Bill Minnick on Decoration Day (May 30) 1927 remains standing today.

Some dates for reference.

1st M/C race at Stockton Kansas ½ mile – (Depending on source) 1906 or 1910

1st Isle of Mann Tourist Trophy race - 1907

Brook Lands (UK) racecourse opened – 1908 (closed, 1939)

Indianapolis speedway opened 1909 (1st event was a motorcycle race)

Daytona 200 racecourse (beach course) opened – 1937

First race at Illinois State Fairgrounds (Springfield mile) - 1937

1st Black Hills Classic, Sturgis South Dakota – 1938

July 4, 1900 – Exhibition laps, no results underline documented – Henry Smith & T.E. Goode

July 5, 1900 – 2-mile underline timed event on *"The Devil Catcher"* - Henry Smith & T.E. Goode - 4:13 (min:sec.)

Aug. 3, 1900 – Timed event Steam motorcycle "Whirlwind" - Charles Callahan & Jack White – 1-Mile 2:07 (min: sec.)

July 5, 1901 – 1st multi-bike race – winner, Clark (4-laps / 4 min. 15 sec.)

Oct. 23, 1909 Fair Race

5-mile Race (six bikes, all Indians) - "Chick" Thomas – 5:50

July 4, 1910 Harness Racing Meet

10-lap open motorcycle race - Wm. Gosnell 1st , Howard Smith 2nd , August Zimmerman 3rd

Oct. 22, 1910 Fair Race

5-mile Race

Chick Thomas - 6:21

3-mile Novice Race

John Blakeny 4:15, John Johnson 2nd C.S. French 3rd Floorkenny 4th.

(announced that the crowd for the M/C racing surpassed the harness racing crowd)

May 30, 1911

Road Race – Washington to Frederick

W.M. Sweet – 1 hr. 58min.

May 7, 1912

Plane vs Motorcycle race

DNS - William Gosnell riding a Harley-Davidson motorcycle was to race a Curtis aero plane, the first plane ever to visit Frederick. The race was canceled due to heavy rain.

July 4, 1912 Harness Racing meet

DNF – race called after crash in turn 3 due to fork failure (folded!). No serious injuries.

Oct. 24, 1912 Fair Race

DNS – Race called due to rain.

July 4, 1913 Harness Racing Meet

Leslie Brandenburg won in 9 laps (1-mile / 1:40 avg. speed)

Novice race

William Gosnell 23 laps in 18:54, Robert Reifsnider 2nd

Sept. 2, 1913

Robert Reifsnider 4:2

William Gosnell 2nd

These were the only two contestants and Reifsnider was married immediately after winning. Was it a re-match from July 4th? Did Gosnell throw the race in honor of Reifsniders wedding? Was it how the young lady decided between them? We'll never know.

July 4, 1919 Harness Racing Meet

Two-mile Sidecar Race - Charles Eyler – H-D - 2:58, Chester Delphey – H-D - 3:12

(The track had been covered in a deep layer of sand and was deemed too dangerous for solo motorcycle racing. Races were part of the official "Welcome Home" celebration for WW-I veterans)

Oct. 20, 1920 Fair Race (total purse $120)

Five-mile solo - Bruce Shafer, Chick Gosnell 2nd

Ten-mile Sidecar Race - Paul Delphey & Oscar Laddie 13:21, Chester Delphey & Robert Wright 2nd, Clarence Little & Frank Smith 3rd (DNF)

All winners were H-D's

Nov. 11, 1920 Indian vs. Harley-Davidson race - co-promoted by Delphey's / 1st motorcycle race held at fairgrounds not held in conjunction with other types of racing.

10-mile solo

John H. Fisher – Ind.

Bruce Shafer – H-D

10-mile sidecar

Paul Delphey – H-D

Bruce Shafer – H-D

5-mile solo

John H. Fisher – Ind.

Bruce Shafer – H-D

5-mile Sidecar

John Conner – Ind.

Nov. 11, 1921 – Race officially announced but no results located. However, there is a news report of injury due to a crash during the Armistice Day race, thus confirming it was held. First race solely promoted by Delphey's making it the first race of the series that became the Barbara Fritchie Classic

July 22, 1922 – William Minnick

No detailed results located

July 14, 1923 (rain date / Nat'l)

National Championship

5-mile solo

Gene Walker – HD – 11min. 52 2/5 sec. New Record

Bill Minnick – IN

Tom Cannon - HD

10-mile solo

Gene Walker – HD –

Bill Minnick – IN

Gilmore Oaks - HD

5-mile sidecar

Tom Cannon – HD

Charley Pattrell(?) – HD

Dynamite Scott - IN

10-mile sidecar

Tom Cannon – HD – 11min. 2sec. - World Record

May 30, 1924 (Nat'l)

National Championship

William "Wild Bill" Minnick – HD – Wilmington DE,

Five-miles in 5min. 34sec. - World Record for ½-mile track

Expert main

Paul Anderson 1st – Milwaukie WI

"Dynamite" Scott 2nd – Springfield MA

W.B. Wooten 3rd – Roanoke VA

May 30, 1925 - Dynamite Scott (Nat'l)

May 30, 1926 - William Minnick (Nat'l)

May 30, 1927 (Nat'l)

10-mile solo (class A)

Art Pechar – Ind. – 11:21

William Minnick – H-D - DNF

5-mail solo Class B

John Bodnar – H-D

Rudy Adams – H-D

Walter Stoddard – H-D

5-mile solo class A

Art Pechar – Ind. 5:25

Walter Stoddard – H-D

William Minnick – H-D

Ten-mile solo class B

John Bornar – H-D – 11:42.5

Rudy Adams – H-D

Walter Stoddard – H-D

10-mile solo class A

Art Pechar – Ind. 11:21

Walter Stoddard – H-D

William Minnick – H-D

Timed Trial for ½ mile record / 350cc(21ci)

William Minnick – H-D 90sec. (new world record / still standing)

Art Pechar – Ind. 63.2sec.

Walter Stoddard – H-D – 65.5sec.

Other riders entered;

Arthur Lots – H-D, J.H. Fisher – Ind.,

(article notes 3,000 spectators)

1928 RAIN OUT

1929 NO RACE

1930 NO RACE

1931 NO RACE

July 9, 1932 - Rural Murray (Nat'l)

July 4, 1933 - Louis Balinski (Nat'l)

July 4, 1934 - Louis Balinski (Nat'l)

July 4, 1935 - Joe Petrali (Nat'l)

July 4, 1936 - Joe Petrali (Nat'l)

July 4, 1937 - Fred Toscani (Nat'l)

July 4, 1938 - Fred Toscani (last Nat'l at Frederick)

All 1921-1938 Delphey races were Class A (professional) events.

Oct. 14, 1938 (Fair race)

1st use of *"electric eye"* timing. Race marred by 3 crashes – one requiring hospitalization - ending motorcycle racing at the fair.

Lester Hillbish winner*

Other entries: Bill Huber, Vernon "Red" House (injured), Richard Fox, Bob Beatty

*(John) Lester Hillbish, having won the Springfield mile in 1937 was reigning national champion until Aug. 21, 1938. He was inducted into the AMA hall of fame in 1998

July 4, 1939 - Lester Hillbish

July 4, 1940 - Billy Huber

(Billy Huber of Reading PA would lose his life in a crash at Dodge City KS in 1953)

July 4, 1941 - RAIN OUT

June 5, 1942 Races cancelled

Paul Delphey contacts AMA requesting all sanctions be suspended until the war ends.

July 4, 1947 Racing resumes

45 entries for a $900 purse adjusted for 2020 dollars = $10,369. Over 7,500 spectators

<u>Expert 16 lap main</u> John Butterfield – HD – Newport News VA

<u>Novice 10 lap main</u>   Joe Burroughs – Ind. – Alexandria VA, Al Moran – Ind. – Parkland MD

Lloyd "Bud" Laugherman – HD – Hanover PA

<u>Amateur 10-lap main</u>

George Sabine – HD – Gaithersburg MD

Gibby Stern – Ind. – Washington DC

Bill Keane – HD – Bethesda MD

Other entries: Armin Hosetter – Matchless – Hanover PA, John Droneburg – HD – Frederick MD, George Becraft – BSA – Washington DC, Robert Cartwright – IN – Back Bay VA, Bob Lyons – IN – Vienna VA,

July 10, 1950 – rain date from July 4th

Chet Dykgarf – Grand Rapids MI

July 4, 1951 – RAIN OUT

July 4, 1952 – Bob Boutwell

July 4, 1953 – Tommy McDermott

July 4, 1954 – Bob Boutwell

July 4, 1955 – No Race

Cancelled (June 23) 12 days before race date due to controversy with other race scheduling.

July 4, 1956 – 1ˢᵗ race promoted by the Frederick Lions Club / winner, Tommy McDermott

July 4, 1957 – Al Wilcox

July 4, 1958 – Tommy Morris

July 4, 1959 – Bart Markel

July 4, 1960 – Richard Croach

July 4, 1961 – Tony Murgia

July 4, 1962 – RAIN OUT

July 4, 1963 – RAIN OUT

July 4, 1964 – RAIN OUT -the last of this 3-year period of violent storms included a tornado in Frederick.

July 5, 1965 (Monday) Expert main Larry Palmgren – Freehold NJ, ?, Don Twigg – Hagerstown MD

Amateur main Chuck Palmgren, George Longabaugh, Charles Hildebrand

July 5, 1966 - Gary Nixon

July 4, 1967 – RAIN OUT

July 4, 1968 – Chuck Palmgren

July 4, 1969 – Larry Palmgren

July 4, 1970 – Jack Warren

July 4, 1971 – Royal Sherbet

July 3, 1972 – Larry Darr

July 4, 1973 – Billy Eves

July 4, 1974 – Billy Schaeffer

July 4, 1975 – Steve Morehead

July 5, 1976 (Monday) – Brent Lowe

July 4, 1977 - <u>Expert main</u> - William Eves 1st, Wm. Schaeffer 2nd., Wm. Crabbe 3rd, Steve Freeman 4th, Jay Livingston 5th, Brent Lowe 6th, Davey Singelton 7th

<u>Junior (amateur) main</u> - Lance Jones 1st, Wm. Donaghy 2nd, Joseph Purdue 3rd, Mark Cox 4th, Stephen Powell 5th, Delbert Busche 6th, Robert Griffin 7th, James Williams 8th

<u>Novice main</u> - Peter Brethauer 1st, Leroy Myer 2nd, Thomas Duma 3rd, Robert Crabbe 4th, Larry Sweeten

July 4, 1978 – Joseph Purdue

July 4, 1979 – RAIN OUT

July 4, 1980 – Stephen Hall

July 4, 1981 – RAIN OUT

July 4, 1982 – Darrin Erichsen

July 4, 1983 – Fran Brown

July 4, 1984 – Rodney Farris

July 4, 1985 – Doug Davis

July 4, 1986 – Rodney Farris

July 4, 1987 – Steve Morehead

July 4, 1988 – Steve Morehead

July 4, 1989 – Rodney Farris

July 4, 1990 – Rusty Rogers

July 4, 1991 – Larry Pegram

July 4, 1992 - George Roeder II

July 4, 1993 – Rusty Rogers

July 4, 1994 – George Roeder II

July 4, 1995 – RAIN OUT

July 4, 1996 – Steve Morehead

July 4, 1997 – Steve Morehead / American Hot Shoe Series begins

July 4th, 1998 - John Nickens

July 4th, 1999 - Kevin Varnes

July 4th 2000 - George Roeder II

July 4th 2001 - George Roeder II

July 4, 2002 – George Roeder II / AMA bans use of bikes larger than 600cc at Frederick.

July 4, 2003 – Dominic Beaulac

July 4, 2004– George Roeder II / Cushion restored / 750s re-allowed

July 4, 2005 – Jared Mees

July 4, 2006 – Ricky Marshall / Promotion of the race assumed by The Kline family. / Hot Shoe ends.

July 4, 2007 – Dan Gedeon / 1st year of Steve Nace's All Star Flat Track series.

July 4, 2008 – Jared Mees

July 4, 2009 – Dan Gedeon

July 4, 2010 – Sammy Halbert

July 4, 2011 – Sammy Halbert

July 4, 2012 – Brad Baker

July 4, 2013 – Sammy Halbert

July 4, 2014 – Jared Mees / Promotion assumed by the Riley family.

July 4, 2015 – Jeremy Higgins

July 4, 2016 – RAIN OUT

July 4, 2017 – Sammy Halbert

July 4, 2018 – Cory Texter

July 4, 2019 – Brandon Price

July 4, 2020 – CANCILED due to state emergency regulations.

Multiyear winners

Six Times – George Roeder II (1992,1994,2000,2001,2002,2004)

Five Times – Steve Morehead (1975,1987,1988,1996,1997)

Four Times – Sammy Halbert (2010,2011,2013,2017)

Three Times –Rodney Farris (1984,1986,1989)

Jared Mees (2005,2008,2014)

It must be noted that years noted as rain outs typically reflect the running of the main event – the actual *"Barbara Fritchie Classic"* - the last race of the day. To that end, in many of those cases, the event was staged. Practice and qualifying took place and perhaps other classes. It was only mid-way through the event that it was rained out, thus, preventing the actual BFC race.

Similarly, some of those noted as "winning" have been award the win of such races for their place in the field when the race was called, or their scoring during qualifying where the main was canceled completely.

Postscript

Early In the month of December 2019 I visited Fredericktown Yamaha & Triumph in Frederick, Maryland specifically to speak to the business owner, Richard Riley about a plan I had to sponsor a motorcycle race near my home. It was something I had never done myself and something Richard had been part of on a rather large scale for years. I gave Richard one of my previous books and explained that I do a little historical research and Richard jokingly suggested I write the history of the Barbara Fritchie Classic.

My race idea was running into more headaches and roadblocks daily it seemed. With increasing doubts on the possibility of the race working out, and in part, to escape the race issues, I sat down at my desk after supper that evening and began digging around concerning motorcycle history in Frederick. My idea was that maybe I would turn up enough to produce an article for the program, or a pamphlet or brochure for the 100th anniversary. It would be a way to kill some time and energy, and, as always, address my own curiosity. At four o'clock the next morning, when I forced myself to get up and go to bed, I knew this was going to be more than I expected. At 7:00 when my wife left for work, since I could not sleep anyway, I went back to work too. By that second afternoon, when I realized there was not enough time to cook even a late dinner, I knew I had gone down the rabbit hole. Like Alice, I was feeling rather small standing among all this data that continued oozing out from everywhere I looked. My next project had found me.

There was so much more to this story than I had imagined. There were some twists and turns along the way that nobody realized. The reach turned out to be much farther than was previously known. From morning until late-night or more typical, early morning, I dug and dug non-stop for a week. It became a full-time job with unlimited overtime. Then, I called Fredericktown Yamaha and told Ian and Richard, "*I have to write this book!*"

From the beginning in mid-December 2019, I established several guidelines for this project. Rule #1 was that it had to be affordable. There are some excellent "motorcycle history" books out there. The vast majority though are rather expensive. That said, I will be the first to say they are ***not*** overpriced! Many of those works contain stunning illustrations. All are the result of daunting research. If the writer (assuming only one person was involved!) was compensated at $10/hour, most would still be waiting for the rest of their money for the effort they invested. Writing is not always the lucrative, leisure profession most envision it as! ...at least not for most who try it.

My second "rule" was that this book had to be available for purchase by Christmas 2020. The reason for this goal, rather than having to do with selling books, was to provide the necessary time for planning the 2021 racing season for all parties involved. The purpose of this book, from the initial conception, has always been to spread awareness of this race. *"Christmas"* was merely my way of marking time. *"Finish it by Thanksgiving and have it available by Christmas."*

Several issues would complicate that goal, but the biggest I would encounter was my own underestimation of the scope of the research ahead of me. My third criteria was to recognize those racers who had been lost at The Fritchie. At the time, the number was rumored to be much higher than the research would ultimately bear out. As time went on, I would have second thoughts about this subject nobody ever wants to think about. I would worry about how survivors may feel about their loved one's tragedy being brought up *again*. I worried perhaps too much, but this is a sensitive issue – particularly for me. As is explained in that chapter, I ultimately kept it in and am glad I did.

Finally, this *"history book"* would target people who do not normally read history books! That seems like a sure-fire way to fail from a business perspective. Attracting that audience though, was one reason for keeping the book affordable. Affordability (even *disposability!*) was an incentive for people to buy this impulsively interesting book. People who would appreciate that someone had done it, but who would not ordinarily buy their own copy. I am not interested in selling books. I just want to spread awareness, to encourage ***appreciation*** for this race. This is a *"history"* I wanted people to know, *a history I wanted to share*, or else I might as well leave it buried. But they would have to read it to appreciate it and they would have to buy it to read it. In the end, overhead costs would require bumping the planned MSRP a couple dollars, but I hope you agree that it is *still* "affordable."

When I passed two-hundred pages in what had originally been anticipated as an article for the race day program, it was exciting. When I passed 300, I realized it was serious. When I approached 400 pages, I began to fear defeating the original purpose of a book that non-book people would read. This story could easily be a two-volume set and still not touch every aspect of this subject. To be fair, half of this book is illustrations, but 200 pages is still a lot of text.

From December into February I worked on research an average of twelve hours a day, seven days-a-week. The first week of March I had a trip to Florida scheduled to visit a friend and interview two key sources who happened to live nearby this convenient home base where I would be staying. Then, the week before I was to leave it became apparent the covid virus was going to become much worse than previously anticipated. By the time I arrived in Florida, I was having second thoughts about meeting these people I had come over 1,000 miles to talk to and possibly endanger them, or they, I. I did meet with one and due to non-virus-related circumstances, failed to make the connection with the other before I had to head north. The threat of the virus though, would prevent a return visit or any in-person interviews for most of this research. Anyone who has ever worked on a similar project will recognize the serious complications this presented. Museums, archives, and libraries were closed for months. The simple uncertainty surrounding everything, made some people reluctant to talk to this stranger who called or sent them emails or instant messages. A further complication was the crippling of the internet. With hundreds of millions of locked-down people sitting around twiddling their thumbs, things *were* affected. I am no techie but even I noticed speed and connectivity issues.

...did I mention I had a deadline? No pressure!

By early autumn 2020, with the nuts & bolts of the history of the race completed, I was trying to fill out the personal side of it. The individual stories. Photos, memories, and memorabilia. The previously mentioned complications, but especially the cancellation of the 99th BFC in July 2020 due to the covid pandemic, was crippling to efforts to connect with those who held these gems. As the virus restrictions began to loosen, I finished up a few interviews that had been on my list and as a last ditch effort, set up a table for a "*covid-safe meeting place*" outdoors in the parking lot of Fredericktown Yamaha. The Frederick News-Post graciously gave me a mention in their "community bulletin board" section of that Saturday's paper. It would prove critical to the day's success! Only a few contacts were made, but they turned out to be totally priceless. There were two or three people I had wanted to interview since the very beginning of this journey who were still M.I.A. and there were some rumored items I still wanted to see and photograph.

In late October as I read over (*another!*) a draft copy of the manuscript, I realized **the story** was all there. Could it be better? Maybe. Was there more out there hiding in dresser drawers, dusty closets, and the lonely memories of un-interviewed witnesses? *Absolutely*, but there always will be. You never find everything.

But that deadline was coming fast. There was post-production work to be done and complicating it was that printing and shipping can take longer than usual this time of year and I had committed to having the books available locally at the time of release. I went back to work full-time on the book for two weeks then ordered one last "proof copy" to review before pulling the trigger. It has been a long, bumpy, dusty ride. There were even a couple flags. By the end, I was totally exhausted.

Yet hitting that kill switch and putting a period at the end of this story, has been the hardest part of this race. I do not want it to end. It is that kind of exhaustion that fulfills you rather than making you tired. I often mention that rather than me searching for this story, this story found me. I do not particularly believe in ghosts, but I have often felt like J. Paul was looking over my shoulder, making sure I got it right. Time and time again, I would just be in the right place or talking with the right person at the right time and something was casually mentioned, or shared as an afterthought, and that insignificant item ended up becoming a key element of the story. I could go on forever. The drive is still there but as **ex-*racers*** may relate to, that ominous day finally came. The day I simply *knew* it was time. It was just time to stop.

The official launch would be in November 2020, right where this journey began as a joke in the showroom of Fredericktown Yamaha and Triumph. It was exactly 100-years after the very first Indian versus Harley-Davidson motorcycle race Joseph Paul Delphey was involved with promoting. It was 99-years since J. Paul held the very first race that he promoted all by himself. The first race at Frederick Maryland that was officially sanctioned by the M&ATA. The first *professional* motorcycle race in Frederick.

99-years since he first race of the continuing series that we know as,

The Barbara Fritchie Classic!

Safe racing!

Ted Ellis

NOTES

NOTES

NOTES

NOTES

NOTES

www.ingramcontent.com/pod-product-compliance
Lightning Source LLC
Chambersburg PA
CBHW062146080426
42734CB00010B/1579